Archaeology, Bible, Politics, and the Media

Duke Judaic Studies Series
Volume 4

Series Editor
ERIC M. MEYERS

Editorial Board
KALMAN P. BLAND, MALACHI HACOHEN,
and LAURA LIEBER

Previously Published

1. *Galilee through the Centuries: Confluence of Cultures*, edited by Eric M. Meyers
2. *Liturgy in the Life of the Synagogue: Studies in the History of Jewish Prayer*, edited by Ruth Langer and Steven Fine
3. *Aramaic in Postbiblical Judaism and Early Christianity*, edited by Eric M. Meyers and Paul V. M. Flesher

Archaeology, Bible, Politics, and the Media

Proceedings of the Duke University Conference, April 23–24, 2009

Edited by

Eric M. Meyers and Carol Meyers

Winona Lake, Indiana
Eisenbrauns
2012

Library of Congress Cataloging-in-Publication Data

Archaeology, bible, politics, and the media : proceedings of the Duke
    University conference, April 23–24, 2009 / edited by Eric M. Meyers and
    Carol Meyers.
        pages ;   cm. — (Duke Judaic studies series ; volume 4)
    Includes bibliographical references and index.
    ISBN 978-1-57506-237-2 (hardback : alk. paper)
    1. Archaeology in mass media—Congresses. 2. Archaeology—Political
aspects—Congresses. 3. Archaeology and history—Mediterranean
Region—Congresses. 4. Archaeology and state—Congresses. 5. Cultural
property—Protection—Congresses. I. Meyers, Eric M., editor. II. Meyers,
Carol L., editor.
    CC135.A7322   2012
    930.1—dc23
                                                              2012036477

The paper used in this publication meets the minimum requirements of the American National Standard for Information Sciences—Permanence of Paper for Printed
Library Materials, ANSI Z39.48-1984. ⊗™

Contents

Part 4
Voices of the Media

Part 5
The Media:
A View from Jerusalem

List of Contributors

A. K. M. ADAM has taught New Testament at Eckerd College, Princeton Theological Seminary, Seabury-Western, Duke, and now at the University of Glasgow. He has been involved in the theory and practice of on-line technology for more than ten years.

ETHAN BRONNER, the national legal affairs correspondent for *The New York Times*, was the *Times*'s Jerusalem bureau chief from early 2008 until mid-2012.

RAY BRUCE is the Head of Programmes and Executive Producer of London-based television production company CTVC.

MOIRA BUCCIARELLI is Managing Editor of the Bible Odyssey Web site for the Society of Biblical Literature.

NINA BURLEIGH is an adjunct professor at Columbia University Graduate School of Journalism.

TONY W. CARTLEDGE is Professor of Old Testament at Campbell University Divinity School and Contributing Editor for *Baptists Today*.

ERIC H. CLINE is Professor of Classics, Anthropology, and History as well as Director of the Capitol Archaeology Institute at The George Washington University.

THOMAS W. DAVIS is Professor of Archaeology and Biblical Backgrounds at Tandy Institute for Archaeology, Southwestern Baptist Theological Seminary. He was the Director of the Cyprus American Archaeological Research Institute in Nicosia, Cyprus from 2003 to 2011.

BERT DE VRIES is Professor of History and Archaeology at Calvin College in Grand Rapids, Michigan, and is the director of the Umm el-Jimal Project in Jordan.

PATTY GERSTENBLITH is Distinguished Research Professor and Director of the Center for Art, Museum, and Cultural Heritage Law at DePaul University College of Law.

MARK GOODACRE is Associate Professor of New Testament and Christian Origins in the Department of Religion at Duke University.

DONALD HAGGIS is Professor of Classical Archaeology in the Department of Classics and the Curriculum in Archaeology (Research Laboratories of Archaeology) at the University of North Carolina at Chapel Hill.

MORAG M. KERSEL is Assistant Professor in the Department of Anthropology at DePaul University.

JODI MAGNESS is the Kenan Distinguished Professor for Teaching Excellence in Early Judaism at the University of North Carolina at Chapel Hill.

BYRON R. MCCANE is the Albert C. Outler Professor of Religion at Wofford College. He is a biblical scholar who has excavated in Israel, Jordan, and Italy.

MILTON MORELAND is Chair of Archaeology and Associate Professor of Religious Studies at Rhodes College. He has participated in excavations in Israel since 1993 and currently directs the excavations at the Ames Plantation in Tennessee.

CAROL MEYERS is the Mary Grace Wilson Professor in the Department of Religion at Duke University.

ERIC M. MEYERS is the Bernice and Morton Lerner Professor in the Department of Religion at Duke University.

S. THOMAS PARKER is a professor of history at North Carolina State University and has directed several archaeological projects in Jordan. His major publications include *Romans and Saracens: A History of the Arabian Frontier* (1986) and, as editor, *The Roman Frontier in Central Jordan: Final Report on the Limes Arabicus Project, 1980-1989* (2006).

MARK I. PINSKY, longtime religion writer for *The Los Angeles Times* and the *Orlando Sentinel*, is author of *A Jew Among the Evangelicals: A Guide for the Perplexed* (Louisville: Westminster John Knox, 2006).

CHRISTOPHER A. ROLLSTON has published widely within the field of Northwest Semitic epigraphy and is the editor of the scholarly journal *Maarav*. He currently holds the Toyozo Nakarai Professorship of Old Testament and Semitic Studies at Emmanuel School of Religion.

CHAD SPIGEL is Assistant Professor of Religion at Trinity University in San Antonio, Texas, and is the author of *Ancient Synagogue Seating Capacities: Methodology, Analysis and Limits* (Tübingen: Mohr Siebeck, 2012).

REBECCA L. STEIN is an associate professor of Cultural Anthropology and Women's Studies at Duke University and the author of *Itineraries in Conflict: Israelis, Palestinians, and the Political Lives of Tourism* (Durham, NC: Duke University Press, 2008).

ANNABEL WHARTON, William B. Hamilton Professor of Art History at Duke University, works on late ancient and modern architecture and urbanism. She is currently finishing a project tentatively titled *Building Pathologies: Jerusalem to Las Vegas.*

JOSEPH ZIAS is the former curator of anthropology and archaeology with the Israel Antiquities Authority.

Introduction

ERIC M. MEYERS AND CAROL MEYERS

The idea to hold the conference "Archaeology, Politics, and the Media" had been brewing for a long time. Archaeological discoveries relating to the Bible are always making headlines; even scholarly debates relating to biblical narratives have been covered in newspaper and magazine articles, on-line reports and forums, radio broadcasts, and television news and documentaries. Yet the academic world, it seems, is not well prepared to respond to public discussions in their field that draw so much attention.

As a result of this situation, a number of individuals in the media, especially television documentarians and some journalists, have been able to take advantage of the public's seemingly insatiable appetite for this sort of material and regularly put forward information and materials that are neither reliable nor responsible. Moreover, a small number of scholars often participate in this sort of ill-informed public discussion perhaps because they find it flattering to appear as an expert in the eyes of the public, or because they are naive about how their views may be misrepresented, or because there is some personal gain. Even though some of the television productions are highly entertaining and present their subjects in interesting ways, the public in general has not been well served in recent years because of the egregious distortions and oversimplifications that characterize so many media productions; and there seems to be little hope that the situation will improve. That said, there are exceptions to this bleak state of affairs, an excellent example being the Providence Pictures recent NOVA special, *The Bible's Buried Secrets*.

The way archaeology, especially discoveries relating to the Bible, is presented to the public is also an issue in the arena of national and international politics, where national interests—notably but hardly exclusively in relation to the holy city of Jerusalem—are served by archaeological data. The intersection of archaeology and politics itself has become newsworthy in recent years, as reporters strive to inform the public about how archaeology affects issues of contested space in Jerusalem. In addition, most countries in the Middle East draw on archaeology to present their stories of national origins to the public in the

1

form of national parks, signage at excavation sites, tourist attractions, Web sites, and posters. But the results are often riddled with contradictions and fraught with biased information. That is, nation states rightly embrace archaeological discoveries as part of their cultural heritage but are not always evenhanded in the way they present that heritage to the tourists who visit and to the world in general.

This problem is especially acute in divided cities, such as Nicosia and Jerusalem, which have different cultures and different national and religious traditions claiming ownership of the archaeological heritage. So in addition to the archaeological facts on the ground, the public has to deal with the political realities that inevitably affect the interpretation of what they see when they visit archaeological sites. Indeed, the political implications of a particular site or discovery are what often draw the attention of the media and all too often compromise the possibility that it will receive fair and balanced treatment.

Do the concerned parties—the media and the scholars—have a communication problem? It is our belief that, at present, and with respect to the Middle East as a highly important geopolitical region, the public is not being well served by the media or by scholarship as it relates to the public. Thus, the conference was organized in the hope that an open and frank discussion about the problematic status quo might promote a better awareness of the problems of communicating the results of scholarship to a wide public. A related aim was foregrounding how archaeological discoveries relate to the numerous local communities in the region and the interested public. In bringing together a group of scholars with people who work in the media—both with vested interests in disseminating information about archaeological discoveries—to talk to each other, we hoped to make both groups more aware of the problems and issues that affect their interactions and the quality of what is presented to the public. The papers presented at the conference held at Duke University in April 2009 and now in this volume represent one small step forward in opening an informed dialogue between the media and the academy.

It should be noted that the title of this book is slightly different from the title of the conference ("Archaeology, Politics, and the Media"). When the conference ended, we realized that the majority of the papers dealt in some way with the portrayal of the Bible in various media or with archaeological discoveries that had a "biblical connection." And many of the papers, it turned out, reference the same few discoveries— such as the Talpiyot Tomb claimed to be that of Jesus and his family, or the structures in the City of David—that have been problematically sensationalized in recent years. In so doing, they draw attention to the media dynamics, sometimes with political implications, created by discoveries with a real or putative link to the Bible. Thus, we altered the conference title slightly, adding *Bible* to it in order to make the book's title—*Archaeology, Bible, Politics, and the Media*—more indicative of its contents. However, the reader should be aware that not all contributions engage all four of the terms mentioned in the title.

The conference comprised five sessions and two major presentations: one by Patty Gerstenblith, who spoke about legal and ethical aspects of cultural heritage, and the other by journalist Ethan Bronner, who shared his perspective as a newspaper reporter based in Jerusalem. The order of essays in the table of contents is not the same as the order in which they were presented at Duke; we decided to regroup the essays once it became clear how they related to each other. For this reason, although papers grouped together at several conference sessions were followed by responses, not all of the essays now in a section of this book have responses.

Gerstenblith's essay, "The Media and Archaeological Preservation in Iraq: A Tale of Politics, Media, and the Law," draws attention to the looting of the National Museum of Iraq in Baghdad in April 2003. A leading legal expert on the looting of antiquities and cultural property, Gerstenblith uses the Iraq situation as a case study of how the media brought attention to the legal and moral obligations of the U.S. military in dealing with a foreign country's cultural heritage in a time of war. She notes the vulnerability of the Baghdad museum as well as the fate of some of its archaeological sites, which are among the most important in the world. The U.S. military, with few experts on cultural heritage to advise it, focused in the narrowest way on its obligations under international law in a time of war. The media's extensive coverage of the looting of the museum drew enormous attention to the situation; but in emphasizing the looting of the museum, the media missed the opportunity to report the looting at hundreds of important archaeological sites all over the country. Gerstenblith also examines the history of looting problems with a lengthy excursus on the colonial legacy of the great powers in the Middle East and a critique of those who think that creating a market for antiquities will alleviate the problem. She follows this with an extensive discussion of international law, including an explanation of the role of the Hague Convention of 1954, and the marketplace for looted antiquities. She concludes by describing the current situation in the U.S. with respect to cultural heritage and also by noting how the Iraq war and the media's coverage of it resulted in a much-improved policy in the military.

The first essay in the section "Archaeology and the Media" is Eric Cline's powerful piece—"Fabulous Finds or Fantastic Forgeries? The Distortion of Archaeology by the Media and Pseudoarchaeologists, and What We Can Do About It"—criticizing the media for its participation in the dissemination of false or misleading information. The fact that reputable outlets continue to follow reports about the discovery of "biblical artifacts," such as Noah's ark or the ark of the covenant, or "biblical sites," such as Sodom and Gomorrah or the Garden of Eden, shows how ill-informed the media is about current scholarship on the Bible and archaeology. In offering numerous examples of this sort of reporting, he chides both the press and the academy for its lack of courage in addressing the sort of misrepresentation of what is otherwise presented responsibly in hundreds of colleges, universities, and seminaries worldwide. He even engages with the popular magazine *Biblical Archaeology Review* and its role in the claims that an inscribed ossuary bears the name of James, brother of the Jesus of the New Testament. Cline concludes by offering a helpful strategy that scholars might use in the difficult terrain of working with the media. Picking up on that last point, Joe Zias, who has had extensive experience working with the media and whose Web site is known for his aggressive stance vis-à-vis the media and its coverage of odd stories relating to the Bible, responds by offering his perspective on media distortions and selective reporting. He also warns scholars to check out the media people with whom they work and urges them to insist they be compensated for participating in documentaries. His comments provide a fitting supplement to Cline's robust piece.

Another infamous archaeological discovery, the Talpiyot Tomb claimed by some to be the burial site of Jesus and his family, appears in several essays. Mark Goodacre examines the Talpiyot Tomb case, which is featured in a book and in several documentary films shown on television, from the point of view of the huge response by internet bloggers. As author of the important Web site *New Testament Gateway*, Goodacre is well positioned to participate in the extensive coverage the films and book have received. His meticulous examination of the details of the debate about the reliability of statistics on name usage in the 1st century and of archaeological reporting and its relation to the New Testament demonstrates clearly that one ignores academic blogs and Web sites at one's peril. The timeliness of the reporting and its engagement with a diversity of opinions in the scholarly world and blogosphere illustrate how successful internet discussions can be. Goodacre also offers some apt cautionary advice about blogging. In responding to Goodacre's essay, A. K. M. Adam praises Goodacre's Web site, noting that when this sort of site engages in debates about issues such as the Talpiyot Tomb and James ossuary, and as more and more scholars take part in the discussion, the site becomes increasingly important, even in the early stages of a discussion. However, Adam is quick to point out that in the digital age more sources should be consulted, some reliable and some not, and that scholars must exert due caution as they proceed.

Morag Kersel's essay, "The Power of the Press: The Effects of Press Releases and Popular Magazines on the Antiquities Trade," echoes aspects of Gerstenblith's essay but is concerned specifically with the impact of the media on antiquities sales. As one might imagine, some items have brought enormous profits to individuals; and a growing number of people, given the uncertainties in the economy, consider the acquisition of antiquities to be a safe means of investment. However, in considering that a lively antiquities market means illicit looting and illegal trafficking in antiquities, another picture emerges. To make her point, Kersel examinees the problematic Sotheby's sale for 57.2 million dollars of the Guennol Lioness, a small (3.25 inches high) limestone sculpture dating to the third millennium B.C.E. and reportedly from a site near Baghdad. Using data from her own research to illustrate the sharp divide in the community that values artifacts, Kersel reports the varying perspectives of collectors, museum directors, and "cosmopolitans" on the sale of antiquities. She also offers sobering words of caution in arguing that any sale of antiquities promotes looting. As an archaeologist, she asserts that an artifact loses its value if its true context is unknown. In response, Annabel Wharton cites Aristotle's argument that "the financial market, as a mechanism for producing profit, is ethically problematic." At the same time, she is realistic enough to recognize that most academics are helpless in stopping illicit traffic in antiquities. However, academics should not be helpless in combating the kind of faux history that collectors hope will add value to an object. She notes several examples and urges scholars to be engaged in the digital world in order to spot and contest archaeological fictions.

The James ossuary appears again in Jodi Magness's engaging piece, "Confessions of an Archaeologist: Lessons I Learned from the Talpiyot Tomb Fiasco and Other Media Encounters." Magness notes that even in the best of circumstances scholars are misquoted or have little effect on the outcome of a documentary. As an example, she details her experience with the press after the premier of the 2007 Discovery Channel movie on the Talpiyot Tomb and James ossuary. Because the media often reduces a scholar's comments to sound bites, what a scholar says can fail to correct false information. Faced with this situation, Magness decided to post her fuller remarks on the Web sites of several academic societies. Her actual views on the subject, rather than those presented by the press, were thus made available, albeit in a more limited venue. Like many others, Magness calls on academic societies to help prevent serious mistakes in media reports, especially in productions relating to Jesus and early Christianity. Chad Spigel's response stresses that scholars appearing in documentaries are providing their interpretations of data but that the viewer takes scholarly opinions to be established fact. He urges academics to fight misrepresentations not only in the media but also in the classroom, a venue that in the long run can change public perceptions of media reports.

Byron McCane tackles the Talpiyot Tomb issue head on in his essay "Scholars Behaving Badly: Sensationalism and Archaeology in the Media." He begins by pointing out that the discovery in 1945 of an ossuary inscribed with x-shaped marks created a media frenzy that was success-fully handled. Sensationalism, when it comes to discoveries related to Jesus, is clearly not exclusive to the 21st century. But now more than ever, given the global reach of cyber reporting, it is to be avoided at all costs; reporting discoveries must proceed with the utmost caution. This was not the case in the James ossuary fiasco, in which sensationalism ran rampant. McCane argues that sensationalism and the resulting con-troversy corrode public confidence and detract from the ability of the public to understand properly the importance of discoveries relating to the Jewish and Christian past.

Milton Moreland deals specifically with the documentary film genre in his fascinating and informative essay "The Future of the Historical Documentary: Scholarly Responses to 'History Channel Meets *CSI.*'" He recounts how several guidelines for the genre have been used to es-tablish key points in the argument or story. Among them are "accuracy, truthfulness, impartiality, fairness to all participants," and covering "is-sues related to funding, conflicts of interest, and editing techniques." These factors are taken from the benchmark for all documentaries, Frontline and Ken Burns. Unfortunately, recent documentaries relat-ing to archaeology and the Bible, such as the Talpiyot Tomb case, do not meet Burns's high standards. Moreland critiques a number of recent sensationalist attempts but also offers high praise for several documen-taries: "Gary Glassman's NOVA production, *The Bible's Buried Secrets: Beyond Fact or Fiction*, and Isy Moregenztern and Thierry Ragobert's Icarus Films production, *The Bible Unearthed.* Even the Discovery Channel attempted to redeem itself with a three-part series entitled *Who Was Jesus?*"

Christopher Rollston's "An Ancient Medium in the Modern Media: Sagas of Semitic Inscriptions" first exposes the flawed presentation of the names inscribed on the James ossuary in the film and book about this artifact. Turning to other inscribed objects, he reveals how the de-sire to find "biblical" connections can influence the interpretation of inscriptions such as a seal claimed to be that of Queen Jezebel, an ostra-con purportedly bearing the name Goliath, and another ostracon sup-posedly with the name of a family mentioned in Nehemiah. He illus-trates what can happen when a scholar, believing that a discovery has a biblical connection, goes to the media too soon, only to realize later that the initial decipherment or interpretation of an inscription cannot with-stand critical assessment. In this context, he discusses the controversy surrounding the reading and interpretation of the 10th-century B.C.E. ostracon from Qeiyafa about which numerous and probably excessive claims have appeared in the press. He concludes by warning archaeolo-gists who discover inscribed materials not to rush to the media before conducting proper research on their discoveries.

The first essay in the section "Archaeology, Politics, and Local Communities" focuses on the intersection of archaeological sites with American communities, specifically, Protestants eager to visit the Holy Land. Tony Cartledge's intriguing article—"Walk about Jerusalem: Protestant Pilgrims and the Holy Land"—presents the unique way in which Protestants view the Holy Land: He first examines Protestant pilgrimage in relation to other forms of Christian interest in the land of the Bible and to the State of Israel in particular. Do Protestants have the same appreciation of the archaeology of the land of Israel as do other Christian groups? Cartledge convincingly answers this question, characterizing Protestant tourists as a special kind of pilgrim—one who values the landscape itself more than the holy sites that dot it, who worships in outdoor settings rather than sacred shrines, and who takes home souvenirs that evoke memories of the land rather than serve as relics of the past. Protestants prefer the simple and bucolic Garden Tomb to the dark and somewhat chaotic Church of the Holy Sepulcher favored by Catholic and Orthodox pilgrims. Cartledge also explores the strong attachment of evangelicals to the State of Israel, a country they believe represents their biblical roots. In presenting the diverse ways Christians of all stripes view the Holy Land, he opens a window into the religious background of many of the issues contributing to the interest of the media in archaeology.

Bert de Vries examines the relationship of local communities to archaeological sites by comparing the situations at Umm el-Jimal in Jordan (where he has worked since the 1970s) and Silwan Village in Jerusalem. In his detailed and eye-opening essay—"Community and Antiquities at Umm el-Jimal and Silwan: A Comparison"—he points to Umm el-Jimal as an example of historic preservation involving the current inhabitants of the site. Connecting the present with the past has meant that excavators, historians, preservationists, and tourist promoters work together, making the story of the site a shared story. Whether touring the site or entering the virtual reality of a well-designed Web site, tourists and scholars from Jordan and abroad as well as the present-day villagers benefit from the careful excavation and presentation of the site. In contrast, de Vries takes a highly critical view of Silwan and the way its City of David Visitors Center features the biblical period of occupation and pays little attention to the rest of the area's long history. Moreover, as de Vries emphasizes, the excavations and the development of the site have adversely affected the present Palestinian residents and have shown politics and archaeology to be a volatile mix at Silwan. In commenting on the Umm el-Jimal Cultural Heritage Project, Thomas Parker commends its educational and Web aspects, which serve to encourage historical awareness and appreciation of cultural heritage among the Jordanian people.

The intersection of cultural and political factors with archaeology on the island of Cyprus is the subject of Thomas Davis's contribution, "Archaeology, Identity, and the Media in Cyprus." The location of Cyprus, the third largest island in the east Mediterranean, makes it a major bridge between Europe and the Middle East and thus witness to some of the most important developments in Middle Eastern history. Many different peoples have crossed the island or conquered it, leading to its current status as an island divided into two sectors: a largely Christian Greek sector, and a mainly Muslim Turkish sector. This fraught division requires great sensitivity on the part of the media as well as those who investigate and preserve the island's rich cultural heritage. Archaeology has sometimes suffered from the ethnic and political strife, and the Cyprus American Archaeological Research Institute (CAARI) in Nicosia is one of the few places where interest in the legacy of this important island transcends ethnic or political agendas. The issues of a divided island are explored in Donald Haggis's response. He urges the press to highlight the shared identity of all Cypriots and recognize that the island's archaeological heritage can provide a basis for commonality. He offers a rather fresh perspective on the important role of archaeology as providing a way for people to connect to their past.

Silwan is again an issue in Eric Meyers's essay—"The Quest for the Temple Mount: The Settler Movement and National Parks in Israel"— on the group that sponsors the excavations in the City of David, an area of great historic importance and national interest. While commending the archaeologists excavating in the City of David, he also challenges the wisdom of the Israel Antiquities Authority for having given the responsibility for administering the Visitors Center at the site to the settler organization, Elad. This organization has fostered a presentation of the site for the public that is infused with political overtones and fundamentalist ideology. Moreover, Elad's dealings with the local population make it is hard to escape the conclusion that archaeology in the hands of the settler movement has become a device to prevent the local villagers of Silwan from having a voice in planning the future of their village. Like the Visitors Center, the City of David Web site is a platform for the particularistic and exclusionary views of a right-wing movement that has no intention of ever compromising on the status of Jerusalem. Rebecca Stein follows Meyers's lead in her response, "On Tourism and Politics in Israel." She views tourism as a major way in which Israelis experienced the occupation of the West Bank after the 1967 war. The extensive Israeli tourism of the occupied areas in turn laid the groundwork, psychologically and economically, for the Israeli commitment to establishing an extensive presence in the Palestinian territories. Moreover, Stein sees the Israeli media as being complicit in this enterprise.

The rest of this volume brings in the perspectives of representatives of the media, first in the section on Voices of the Media and then in the essay by Ethan Bronner. The contributors to the Voices of the Media section represent various kinds of media, beginning with television. Ray Bruce, the author of "Responses from a Television Producer," has produced numerous British documentaries dealing with biblical topics and has often filmed in Israel. His experience offers a perspective different from that of academics on the relationship between producer and on-screen scholar or off-screen advisor. Academics, he suggests, need to know about the television industry and about how competitive it is. In his view, a healthy relationship between producer and scholar can exist only within a realistic assessment of the industry. An adversarial relationship between the industry and academics, he argues, will only adversely affect biblical scholarship, for it will negatively affect the way the public sector views academia. Calls to "take back the field" are thus, in his opinion, misguided.

Representing the Society for Biblical Literature, Moira Bucciarelli suggests that the academic world needs to be much more proactive when it comes to extending its reach to the public at large. To this end, and with development and implementation grants from the National Endowment for the Humanities, she is overseeing the development of a pioneering interactive Web site called *Bible Odyssey* that will introduce visitors to the Bible and its context, hoping to bridge the gap between biblical scholarship and the public. Unlike other media, which often distort what scholars provide, scholars will have the final say in the content and even, to a certain extent, the design of the site. Academics, she avers, must find a way to tell the public what they are doing and why when it comes to the exciting fields of biblical studies and archaeology.

Once again, the James ossuary case, as well as another problematic artifact known as the Jehoash inscription, is a central feature of a contribution to this volume. "Scholars at the Limits of Science and the Borders of Belief: Finding Proof for Faith. A Journalist's Perspective on the Oded Golan Case" is an excerpt from freelance journalist Nina Burleigh's 2008 book on the shady dealings behind several prominent but perhaps forged artifacts that were widely reported in the media. Relying on her in-person interviews with several of the principals in these cases, she describes in detail the events surrounding the way these artifacts were identified and brought to the public. Golan, the Israelite antiquities dealer involved in the James ossuary case, was brought to trial in 2005 for allegedly forging the ossuary inscription; and, as of this writing, his trial is still underway. Burleigh's inside view of the dynamics of the case provides an exciting window into its byzantine twists and turns.

Another freelance journalist and for many years the religion reporter for the Orlando Sentinel, Mark Pinsky reports on a Bible theme park, the Holy Land Experience, to illustrate another medium in which biblical materials are presented to the public. His engrossing piece, "Not

Another Roadside Attraction: The Holy Land Experience in America," introduces us to the Orlando, Florida park that opened in 2001 and was designed by evangelicals to take the visitor on a journey back in time (mainly to the time of Jesus) and across thousands of miles to the world of the Bible—a journey that would be historical and educational as well as inspirational. With the discerning eye of a reporter, he reveals the motives and dynamics behind this enterprise, which provides a very different kind of Holy Land experience than the one described in Cartledge's article. For example, the overtly Jewish nature of the park, its reenactments, and many of the items in its gift shop were initially meant to attract Jews and win them as converts; this approach earned widespread criticism, even though it did not lead to a decline in attendance. The park was expanded in 2002 when a museum component with many original artifacts was added. Today, it is part of a large Christian broadcasting empire whose reach is far greater than the original founder imagined, and its future seems secure.

Ethan Bronner, whose piece concludes this volume, is well positioned, as the *New York Times* Jerusalem bureau chief, to be informed about media reporting of archaeology. He offers his reflections on reporting three stories dealing with archaeology and the Bible in his essay "How It Looks from the Other Side." He begins with an account of how he came to write a story about the inscription known as "Gabriel's Vision," purportedly from the 1st century B.C.E. and believed to have been found on the east side of the Dead Sea. The inscription mentions a suffering messiah, thus predating an idea thought to have originated in early Christianity. Bronner's piece had an enormous impact, becoming the *Times*'s most read piece for days. People chimed in with blogs and letters with their interpretation of the significance of the inscription in relation to Christian doctrine. Bronner then relates his reporting of the excavation at Khirbet Qeiyafa and the inscription mentioned in Rollston's article. Qeiyafa's importance as a site dating to the period of the early monarchy cannot be overemphasized, but the degree to which it may be related to the United Monarchy of the Bible, as the excavators are wont to do, is another matter. The existence of that monarchy is a hotly debated issue in biblical scholarship, one that pits scholars from the Hebrew University against their counterparts at Tel Aviv University. It is no surprise, then, that Bronner's story about this site provoked a burst of interest similar to that aroused by his story of Gabriel's Vision. Finally, he relates his coverage of the political overtones of the Silwan and Temple Mount excavations. He notes the opposition of several Israeli archaeologists, who call attention to the problematic nature of the sponsorship and presentation of the excavations, as do the essays of de Vries and Meyers. Bronner recognizes better than most the political agendas swirling around archaeology and the Bible.

The editors hope that this collection of essays and responses will provide valuable insights to scholars who seek a better relation with and understating of the media and who hope to avoid the pitfalls of sharing their expertise with the general public. We also hope that journalists, reporters, and documentarians might come across this book and become sensitive to the concerns of those whose expertise is essential to them when they deal with biblical and archaeological subjects. Finally, we hope that all readers will be made aware, if they aren't already, that the discoveries of both biblical studies and archaeology are all too easily distorted and misrepresented by the religious or political agendas of others.

The participants in the conference in which earlier forms of these essays were presented found the conversations prompted by the papers to be very informative, helpful, and often exhilarating. The often-spirited discussions highlighted the continuing need for dialogue between academics working on biblical and archaeological topics and those who present those topics to the public via various media. At the same time, it demonstrated that when it comes to the Bible and archaeology, although there is much to divide these two groups with their different goals, there is much more to unite them in their quests to disseminate information responsibly.

June 28, 2011

Eric M. Meyers
Carol Meyers
Durham, North Carolina

PART 1

Cultural Heritage

The Media and Archaeological Preservation in Iraq
A Tale of Politics, Media, and the Law

PATTY GERSTENBLITH

While the media often present distorted images of archaeology and the methods by which archaeologists piece together their discoveries, the media also play a crucial role in educating the public about the processes by which we come to reconstruct and understand the past. In particular, public opinion is important in the formulation of public policy, including legislative initiatives, in influencing decisions concerning resources that are devoted to protecting archaeological sites and interdicting looted and smuggled antiquities, and in bringing pressure to bear on collectors, particularly public museums, in their acquisition of antiquities that may be the products of recent site looting. In one example, we can see the role that the media played in bringing about both harmful and beneficial results—and the core of that example is the looting of the Iraq Museum in Baghdad in April 2003 during the 2003 Gulf War. This essay will explore some of the events concerning the looting of the museum, the role that the media played in bringing public attention to bear, and the detrimental consequences of not only the looting of the museum but the large-scale looting and destruction of archaeological sites in southern Iraq, the home of some of the world's earliest and most important civilizations. At the same time, unintended beneficial consequences, which can be attributed, at least in part, to the role of the media in raising public awareness of the moral and legal obligations of the United States military during wartime, must be acknowledged.

Pleas by archaeologists and archaeological organizations, such as the Archaeological Institute of America, in late 2002 and early 2003, to both government officials and members of the media intended to bring attention to the possible adverse consequences of war on Iraq's rich archaeological heritage fell largely on deaf ears (Rothfield 2009: 47–48). The only successful effort was the publication of an op-ed piece in the *Washington Post* by Dr. Maxwell Anderson, at that time the president of the

15

Association of Art Museum Directors, and Ashton Hawkins, former legal counsel to the Metropolitan Museum of Art in New York (Hawkins and Anderson 2002). This op-ed brought attention to the possible harm that could be caused to Iraq's cultural heritage and led to a meeting in January 2003 of leaders of the American cultural heritage community, including the Mesopotamian archaeologist Professor McGuire Gibson of the University of Chicago's Oriental Institute, and Defense Department officials (Rothfield 2009: 56–60). But even this meeting failed in its desired effect and may have caused more problems than it ameliorated as it led Professor Gibson to believe that he had a promise from the Defense Department that the Iraq Museum and other cultural sites would be guarded, while Joseph Collins, a Deputy Assistant Secretary of Defense for humanitarian and peacekeeping operations, insisted that no such promise had been made (Jehl and Becker 2003).

In hindsight, we can conclude that the United States military was largely unaware of the extreme sensitivity, fragility, and significance of Iraq's archaeological heritage, including its museum collections. The military was focused on fulfilling only a narrow interpretation of its obligations under international law to avoid directly attacking cultural sites unless such an attack was excused under military necessity. It had been many years since the American academic community had cooperated with the United States military in an open and serious effort, in large part because of the bitterness that followed the Vietnam War. The Monuments, Fine Arts, and Archives teams that had worked so valiantly during World War II to save much of Europe's cultural heritage were a thing of the past, as were also the close ties between the academic and cultural heritage communities, on the one hand, and the Washington political and military elites, on the other. For example, the President of the Archaeological Institute of America during World War II, William Dinsmoor, was able to contact the Chief Justice of the Supreme Court, who, in turn, had direct access to the White House, to discuss establishment of a military unit to protect cultural sites in Europe (Nicholas 1994: 209–10). At the same time, archaeologists, classicists, art historians and museum professionals populated the American and particularly British militaries, including Sir Leonard Woolley, Lieutenant Colonel Mortimer Wheeler, Major J. B. Ward-Perkins, and Captain Mason Hammond (Nicholas 1994: 215–21).

In contrast, at the start of the Iraq War, there was only one museum professional in the entire United States military (Corine Wegener of the Minneapolis Institute of Art and an Army Reserve Civil Affairs major) and barely a handful of others who had any training in fields related to cultural heritage, such as archaeology and anthropology (Wegener 2008: 164–66). This lack of cooperation meant that the archaeological community did not have the contacts within the military to alert it in an effective manner, and the military had not incorporated cultural heritage concerns into its war planning years earlier, when it might have made a difference. On the other hand, the determination of the political leadership of the Department of Defense, the Secretary of Defense Donald Rumsfeld in particular, to go to war with as few boots on the ground as possible may have meant that no amount of warnings, preparation, or cooperation would have produced a different approach to preserving Iraq's heritage.

Adverse Consequences of Media Reporting

When the story of the museum looting initially broke, it fit into a litany of other stories of looting, such as of hospitals, schools, banks, and government buildings, as it seemed to be an accepted policy of the invading coalition forces to stand by and allow looting to occur. Secretary of Defense Donald Rumsfeld reacted to the looting of the museum by saying that democracy is not tidy and that media depictions of the looting of the museum were "the same picture of some person walking out of some building with a vase, and you see it 20 times, and you think, 'My goodness, were there that many vases? Is it possible that there were that many vases in the whole country?'" (Rothfield 2009: 111). Exactly why this policy to permit looting of institutions was promoted is unclear, but the coalition allies may have thought the images of looting of institutions, government buildings, and hospitals would graphically depict the Iraqi people's rage against the Saddam Hussein government or that the Iraqi people were themselves not easy to govern and therefore would need the guiding hand of the American-led Coalition Provisional Authority for some time to come.

Nonetheless, even amid these stories of looting, the story of the looting of the Iraq Museum had much longer "legs" than anyone had anticipated as it did not disappear within the usual 24-hour news cycle. This is somewhat ironic because my personal attempts before the invasion to interest reporters of National Public Radio and ABC National News in stories concerning the potential harm to Iraq's archaeological heritage fell on deaf ears. But after the museum was looted, the story remained prominent in media reports for several days and was further prolonged by the highly visible press conferences and interviews given later by Marine Colonel Matthew Bogdanos, who led the investigation—largely carried out by Immigration and Customs Enforcement investigators— into the details of the museum looting (Bogdanos 2008: 116–21; Bogdanos 2004).

The episode of the looting of the Iraq Museum is well known and need not be rehearsed here (Farchakh 2003; George 2008; Gerstenblith 2006: 288–91). Once the news of the looting was broadcast, the media latched onto the story but did not acquit itself well in presenting factual information. Of significant adverse consequences was the reporting that 170,000 objects had been looted from the museum. The media, and possibly others, should have taken greater efforts to ascertain the truth, and it is still unclear how such a significant error was made. Once corrected, this misreporting led to the conclusion that "only" 15,000 artifacts had been stolen, thus trivializing what was, by any account, still a significant calamity for the museum. As Bogdanos commented,

> [T]he real victim of such inaccuracies was the museum itself: once it came clear that the number of 170,000 was wrong by a factor of at least 10, the world breathed a collective sigh of relief that "only" 15,000 objects were stolen. The word "only" should never be used in such a context and never would have been but for the original reporting. The further tragedy was that once the lower numbers became known, many governmental and private organizations quickly moved on to other crises, thereby depriving the international investigation of essential resources and funding. (Bogdanos 2004: 494)

Another adverse consequence of this misreporting was the delegitimization of those who had attempted to warn the military in advance and were devoted to repairing the damage in the immediate aftermath of the active conflict. Because these were, for the most part, academics, archaeologists, and museum professionals, they were quickly accused of liberal bias and of using the story of the looting for political purposes— as a way of opposing the war itself (Krauthammer 2003; Aaronovitch 2003). On the other hand, those who supported the war touted the fact that so few objects had been looted, with some reducing the number to 45 or even 33 artifacts in all. For example, conservative *Washington Post* columnist Charles Krauthammer wrote, "[The story of the museum looting] played on front pages everywhere and allowed for some deeply satisfying antiwar preening. . . . For Upper West Side liberalism, [the toppling of Saddam Hussein] matters less than the destruction of a museum. Which didn't even happen!" (Krauthammer 2003). This politicization of the story did not help to advance the cause of repairing the damage and attempting to prevent more damage from being done.

Another problem that soon became apparent to the archaeological community was the far more significant damage caused by the looting of archaeological objects directly from sites, rather than the looting of artifacts already in museums. When an object is stolen from a museum, at least its existence is known and its original context (where it was found and in association with what other objects, physical remains, and architectural features) recorded for future study and reconstruction. The looting of sites is far more detrimental to our ability to understand the past because neither the objects themselves nor their original contexts will ever be known. In addition, looters routinely discard those objects that are considered less saleable on the international market, such as fragments of cuneiform tablets, even though these fragments may contain significant historical and cultural information.

In contrast, it is much easier for journalists and the public at large to understand and deplore the theft of objects from a known collection than to understand the full scope of the destruction to our knowledge caused by the looting of an archaeological site. It should have been the role of the media to emphasize and explain this difference to the public and some tried. But the massive looting of archaeological sites, particularly in southern Iraq, did not receive nearly the same level of media attention, with a few exceptions (Banerjee and Garen 2004; Farchakh 2003; Farchakh-Bajjaly 2008: 49–52; Garen 2004; Lawler 2003). This is explainable, in part, because of the danger inherent in attempting to cover this story, as evidenced by the kidnapping of journalist Micah Garen while he was documenting the looting of sites in southern Iraq (Liu and Dickey 2004). It may also be explained by the greater difficulty in presenting the story of site looting to a particular readership that is unfamiliar with its complexity. It ultimately took study of the satellite images of the sites in southern Iraq, carried out by Professor Elizabeth Stone, for this full story to be understood and appreciated (Stone 2008a, 2008b).

While this is more a fault of omission than of commission, it nonetheless was a major shortcoming of the media coverage of the 2003 Gulf War, which had such a negative impact on Iraq's heritage. One also needs to find some fault with the archaeological community in not having established sufficient relationships with the reporters who cover archaeology (particularly the science reporters, rather than the arts reporters) and in failing to educate them over the years as to what archaeology does and why in situ preservation and site protection are so crucial to the work of recovery and reconstruction of the past.

Revival of the Rescue Myth

Throughout the 18th, 19th, and early 20th centuries, private collectors and museums, located primarily in Western Europe and later in the United States, sought to build collections of antiquities, at first of the Classical Greek and Roman worlds and later from throughout much of the world. The motivations of these collectors were many. The founders of the British Museum in 1753, the first museum to style itself as a universal or encyclopedic museum, desired to obtain representative examples of both natural history and human culture from throughout the world so that these could be displayed in one location. Other national museums, including the Louvre, and later American museums, such as the Metropolitan Museum of Art in New York, sought to emulate this example. Private collectors typically wanted to display their erudition, their culture and their wealth by amassing impressive collections of art works, including examples of ancient art works.

Regardless of the motivations of these different collectors, in the 20th century, the construction of these collections often came to be justified under the umbrella of a "rescue myth." The most prominent example of this narrative pertains to the Parthenon sculptures taken by Lord Elgin at the turn of the 19th century and eventually purchased by

Parliament for the British Museum. These sculptures are the preeminent examples of the pinnacle of the Classical Greek period of the 5th century B.C.E., the product of the master sculptor Phidias. In addition, these sculptures, unlike so many others that come down to us from antiquity, are absolutely known to be authentic, as is also their original function and location.

Lord Elgin was given some form of permission from the Ottoman authorities, whose empire included what soon after became the modern nation of Greece; however, because the original firman is not preserved, it is not clear exactly what Elgin was given permission to do. The tale of the sculptures' removal from the Parthenon, damage that was done to the structure in the process of removal, and the temporary loss of a shipload of sculptures that spent 18 months under the Aegean Sea is often forgotten (St. Clair 1998: 98–118). William St. Clair has chronicled the more recent damage done to the sculptures, apparently at the behest of Lord Duveen, who in the 1930s funded the new galleries in which the sculptures were displayed (St. Clair 1999). St. Clair's research formed the basis of a debate between St. Clair and the British Museum's Assistant Keeper of Greek Sculptures, Ian Jenkins (Jenkins 2001). These incidents of damage belie to some extent the persistent belief that the sculptures taken to London were better off than those that were left behind in Athens and that Elgin, despite his personal motivations of self-aggrandizement, had done the world a significant service by rescuing the sculptures and taking them to where they could be better appreciated—in London.

Those who favor international movement of cultural objects see in Elgin's actions a historic act of rescue by which the sculptures were saved from ruin at the hands of unappreciative local populations, war, and the polluted Athenian atmosphere (Merryman 1985: 1903–10). Others see in Elgin's conduct an act of expropriation, theft, and the destruction of what had been an integral monument of architecture and sculpture, an authentic voice of Athenian classical achievement—all masked within the narrative of rescue and stewardship (St. Clair 2006: 80–82). Lord Elgin's acts may also be viewed as irreparably diminishing the sculptures themselves by virtue of their removal from their original context of the Parthenon, the Acropolis, and Athens (Webb 2002: 63, 66–75; Neils 2001: 244–48). To still others, apart from their symbolism (which is admittedly powerful), the fate of the sculptures is less significant than the contemporary protection of archaeological sites and cultural monuments from looting, dismemberment, and destruction.

The notion that cultural appropriation is carried out for the benefit of others rather than for the benefit of the appropriator finds parallels in other historical episodes. The use of ancient historic and artistic objects as symbols of modern national identity and political legitimacy received a new incarnation in the Napoleonic dream of re-creating Paris as the "new Rome." In pursuit of that dream, Napoleon removed Italian and Roman art works en masse to Paris, including the Apollo Belvedere, the Laocoön, and the Discobolus from the Vatican and Capitoline museums. He also included Renaissance paintings, mineral and natural history collections, and valuable Vatican manuscripts. During his Egyptian campaign, Napoleon's armies took many antiquities that were added to what later became the Louvre's impressive Egyptology collection, while some, such as the Rosetta Stone, ended up in the British Museum. The justification for these actions was presented to Napoleon in a petition in 1796, signed by many of the great French artists of the day. The petition stated:

> The Romans, once an uncultivated people, became civilized by transplanting to Rome the works of conquered Greece. . . . Thus . . . the French people . . . naturally endowed with exquisite sensitivity will . . . by seeing the models from antiquity, train its feeling and its critical sense. The French Republic, by its strength and superiority of its enlightenment and its artists, is the only country in the world which can give a safe home to these masterpieces. All other Nations must come to borrow from our art, as they once imitated our frivolity. (Merryman and Elsen 1998: 5)

We see in this statement the modern justifications for the looting of cultural objects. First, the justification focuses exclusively on the benefits that will accrue to the individual or nation by taking possession of another nation's cultural objects; second, at the same time, it asserts a right to the object based on a moral or intellectual superiority. The third element of this justification is an expression of altruism—because the possessor has a greater ability to care for the object, the possessor is, in fact, not acting primarily for its own benefit but rather for the benefit of everyone else (all humanity), including the original owner. Hence, the act of appropriation is done for the benefit of others, not just the taker.

Napoleon's attempt to re-create Rome in Paris was answered by the British desire to re-create Athens in London. Thus, Lord Elgin's taking of the Parthenon sculptures to London and their later acquisition by Parliament for the British Museum fit into the contemporary political reality of the military rivalry between France and Britain in the early 19th century. The presence of the Parthenon sculptures in the British Museum has endured even until today, to some, as the symbol of cultural heritage dispossession and, to others, as an act of rescue.

The looting of the Iraq Museum seemed to give market proponents an impetus for decrying the fact that so many of Mesopotamia's ancient artifacts were located in one place, even though many had been dispersed in the 19th and first half of the 20th centuries to London, Berlin, New York, Philadelphia, and Chicago through the system of partage (the sharing of finds from an excavation among those institutions that participated in the excavation). Market proponents then shifted to the argument that a legalized antiquities market in which finders would be paid the market value of the object or allowed to keep it for sale on the international market should be established in countries that are subject to chaos, military conflict, and poverty as a way to prevent looting. New York columnist John Tierney presented a prime example of this thinking when he wrote, "There is, however, another way to pay for the preservation of antiquities—you might call it the Lord Elgin approach, although no one today would advocate his precise methods" (Tierney 2003). Others who had long advocated creation of a legal market in antiquities, such as Herschel Shanks, quickly took up the mantra that such a market would solve the problems of archaeological site looting (Shanks 2003). Editorialists and commentators thus took advantage of the looting of the Iraq Museum to push forward a previously established agenda to promote the placement of as many archaeological objects on the market as possible. Yet these writers did not stop to explain just how an expanded market would have prevented the looting of the museum.

While I have explained in detail elsewhere why creating a legal market in newly discovered antiquities would not be likely to solve the problem of site looting and would make the task of law enforcement considerably more difficult (Gerstenblith 2007), in this context it is worth noting that the arguments concerning creation of a legal market had nothing to do with the looting of the Iraq Museum. Everyone on all sides of the debate concerning archaeological looting seems to agree that known collections, such as those at the Iraq Museum, are not fair game for the international market and that particularly "valuable" or "significant" pieces would not be part of such a market. Therefore, the attempts to turn the looting of the museum into a rationale for creation of an expanded market in antiquities taken directly from the ground seem to have been particularly transparent ruses to argue for what market proponents have always wanted.[1] The commentators' arguments

---

1. Whether by design or by coincidence, these arguments for expanding the market seemed to echo the goals of market proponents before the beginning of the 2003 Gulf War. Leaders of the American Council on Cultural Policy (ACCP), a now-defunct organization composed primarily of wealthy and politically connected collectors and their lawyers, seemed to suggest that when Iraq's legal system was reformulated after the war, this would present an opportunity for introducing a more open market in Iraqi antiquities (Rothfield 2009: 43–46). When Ashton Hawkins, one of the leaders of the ACCP, succeeded in having an op-ed piece published before the start of the war, as previously described, and Arthur Houghton, another ACCP leader, subsequently succeeded in setting up meetings with the State Department and the Department of Defense, this engendered distrust in the archaeological community as to what plans to privatize much of the Iraqi economy would mean for Iraq's cultural heritage. As Lawrence Rothfield describes, this distrust further hampered efforts of the cultural community to communicate with Pentagon and military war planners in the lead-up to the Gulf War.

for an expanded market, though, did not relate to the problems of the museum or of the looting of archaeological sites during the chaos of the immediate post-war period. Rather, these arguments seemed to be particularly simplistic attempts at a logic that would surely confuse and mislead the public.

Unintended Beneficial Consequences

While the damage caused to the archaeological heritage of Iraq cannot be overstated, and the field of Mesopotamian studies has suffered a serious blow, some beneficial results came from this disaster, and these should largely be attributed both to the archaeologists who kept this issue in the public consciousness and to the members of the media who allowed the story to be told and kept the public interested. We can identify at least three positive consequences: the enactment of legislative and other measures to prohibit trade in looted Iraqi cultural materials, United States ratification of the 1954 Hague Convention on the Protection of Cultural Property in the Event of Armed Conflict, and the founding of the U.S. Committee of the Blue Shield, which works with the U.S. military and comparable bodies in other nations to further the cause of protecting cultural property during armed conflict.

Prohibition on Trade in Looted Iraqi Cultural Materials

A month after the news of the looting of the Iraq Museum and other cultural repositories in Iraq, Representative Phil English (R-PA) introduced a bill, the Iraq Cultural Heritage Protection Act, H.R. 2009, on May 7, 2003. In light of the looting of Iraq's cultural repositories, the destruction of the documentation of the Iraq Museum's inventory, the incipient looting of archaeological sites, and Iraq's inability to bring a request for import restrictions under the Convention on Cultural Property Implementation Act,[2] Congressman English's proposed legislation

---

2. The Convention on Cultural Property Implementation (CPIA) is the domestic legislation by which the United States implements the 1970 UNESCO Convention on the Means of Prohibiting and Preventing the Illicit Import, Export and Transfer of Ownership of Cultural Property (19 U.S.C. §§2601–13). Among other provisions, the CPIA provides a mechanism by which other nations that are party to the 1970 UNESCO Convention can ask the United States to impose import restrictions on designated categories of archaeological and ethnological materials. Several criteria must be satisfied before these restrictions can be imposed, including a requirement that the cultural patrimony of the requesting nation is in jeopardy from the pillage of archaeological materials. Despite the fact that Iraq was and continued to be a party to the 1970 UNESCO Convention, it still could not bring a request under the CPIA because, at first, there were no diplomatic relations between the two nations and, subsequently, under the Bremer Coalition Provisional Authority, it was not clear whether a U.S. administrator could present such a request. In addition, the burdensome process required for a CPIA request did not seem feasible in light of the ongoing chaos in Iraq.

was intended to provide a quick method of preventing looted Iraqi archaeological materials from entering the United States (Gerstenblith
and Hanson 2008). The art market community, including the Association of Art Museum Directors, quickly marshaled its lobbying forces to
oppose H.R. 2009.

By late May 2003 and while H.R. 2009 was stalled in the House, the
international community took action to ban trade in illegally exported
cultural materials from Iraq. All goods, including cultural objects, from
Iraq had been barred from entry into the United States since August of
1990 under the general sanctions imposed pursuant to Security Council
Resolution 661 of August 1990 and Executive Orders 12722 and 12744.
United Nations Security Council Resolution 1483, passed on May 22,
2003, called for the lifting of those sanctions. However, it also provides
in paragraph 7 that the Security Council

> [d]ecides that all Member States shall take appropriate steps to facili-
> tate the safe return to Iraqi institutions of Iraqi cultural property and
> other items of archaeological, historical, cultural, rare scientific, and
> religious importance illegally removed from the Iraq National Mu-
> seum, the National Library, and other locations in Iraq since the adop-
> tion of resolution 661 (1990) of 6 August 1990, including by establish-
> ing a prohibition on trade in or transfer of such items and items with
> respect to which reasonable suspicion exists that they have been il-
> legally removed, and calls upon the United Nations Educational, Sci-
> entific, and Cultural Organization, Interpol, and other international
> organizations, as appropriate, to assist in the implementation of this
> paragraph.[3]

This resolution was adopted under Chapter VII of the United Nations
Charter and is therefore legally binding on all UN Member States. This
provision calls on all Member States to prohibit trade in and to adopt
other means to ensure return to Iraq of all cultural objects, not just
those taken from the museums and other public institutions, but also
those taken from other locations including archaeological sites.

On May 23, 2003, the day after UNSCR 1483 was passed, the United
States lifted trade sanctions on goods from Iraq by granting a general license for these goods. However, Iraqi cultural property and other items
of archaeological, historical, cultural and religious importance were ex-
empted from this general license, meaning that the prohibition on import of and trade in such objects remained in force.

A more permanent means of prohibiting import of stolen or illegally
removed Iraqi cultural materials was provided by passage of the Emer-
gency Protection for Iraqi Cultural Antiquities Act (EPIC Antiquities

---

3. United Nations Security Council (SC), Resolution 1483, "The Situation between Iraq and Kuwait," May 22, 2003. On-line: http://daccess-dds-ny.un.org/doc/
UNDOC/GEN/N03/368/53/PDF/N0336853.pdf?OpenElement.

Act) in late 2004. Senator Charles Grassley, Republican of Iowa and then chair of the Senate Finance Committee, introduced S. 1291 in June 2003. This legislation authorized the President to exercise his authority under the CPIA to prohibit import of archaeological and ethnological materials from Iraq under a streamlined process and, in particular, without need for Iraq to bring a request under the CPIA for import restrictions. This legislation is notable for broadening the CPIA definitions of the archaeological and ethnological materials of Iraq so that they would be in accord with UNSCR 1483. The legislation also removed the usual five-year limit for import restrictions, thus allowing these restrictions to remain in effect indefinitely.

S. 1291 was ultimately enacted with minor modifications. The only remarks on the legislation came from Senator Grassley when he proposed the amendment in the Senate and again in the Senate conference report:

> The purpose of this bill is simply to close a legal loophole which could allow looted Iraqi antiquities to be brought into the U.S. If Congress does not act to provide the means for establishing an interim ban on trade, the door may be opened to imports of looted Iraqi antiquities into the United States. Already the press has reported allegations that European auction houses have traded in looted Iraqi antiquities. The last thing that we in Congress want to do is to fail to act to prevent trade in looted Iraqi artifacts here in the United States. (Grassley 2004)

Import restrictions under this legislation finally went into effect in April 2008. The reference, although brief, in Senator Grassley's statement to media reports as providing some of the impetus for this legislation was highly significant and illustrates the beneficial role that the media played in bringing about this legislation to prevent the United States from becoming a haven for looted archaeological objects from Iraq.

Other nations took similar steps to ban the trade in Iraqi cultural materials that were illegally exported any time after August 1990. Those nations include the United Kingdom, under Statutory Instrument 2003 No. 1519,[4] and Switzerland, under the Ordinance on Economic Measures against the Republic of Iraq of 28 May 2003, SR 946.206,[5] as well as the European Union under European Union Council Common Position 2003/495/CFSP of 7 July 2003, Article 3, OJ L 169/72.[6] The swift and meaningful action taken by these nations in light of the looting of the Iraq Museum demonstrates that the world community can be

---

4. Available on-line: http://www.legislation.gov.uk/uksi/2003/1519/contents/made.

5. Available on-line: http://www.ifar.org/upload/PDFLink49be847020290Iraq%20Ordinance%20(French).pdf.

6. Available on-line: http://eur-lex.europa.eu/LexUriServ/LexUriServ.do?uri=OJ:L:2003:169:0072:0073:EN:PDF.

united in attempting to prevent the trade in illegal cultural materials, at least in those few situations where sufficient public attention is brought to bear, largely as the byproduct of media efforts. Scholars have attributed both a decrease in looting after 2004 and at least a temporary diminution in Iraqi archaeological objects available for sale on the international market to these legislative efforts (Stone 2008a: 138; Stone 2008b; Brodie 2006: 214–17; Brodie 2008: 2).

Ratification of the 1954 Hague Convention

The 1954 Hague Convention on the Protection of Cultural Property in the Event of Armed Conflict was the first international treaty to address exclusively cultural property.[7] Based on the earlier Hague Conventions of 1899 and 1907 that codified rules of warfare and adopted in the aftermath of the cultural devastation of World War II, the 1954 Hague Convention was intended to establish principles for protecting cultural property, including sites, monuments and repositories of cultural objects, during armed conflict and for preventing looting and smuggling of these objects from occupied territory.

The Hague Convention begins with a preamble asserting the universal value of cultural property whereby all people are diminished when cultural property, situated anywhere in the world, is damaged or destroyed. In setting out the justifications for the Convention, the Preamble states that the nations join the Convention,

> Being convinced that damage to cultural property belonging to any people whatsoever means damage to the cultural heritage of all mankind, since each people makes its contribution to the culture of the world;
> Considering that the preservation of the cultural heritage is of great importance for all peoples of the world and that it is important that this heritage should receive international protection[.]

The phrasing of the preamble draws on a tradition that imposes obligations on nations to care for the cultural property within their borders during both peacetime and military conflict.

In Article 1, the Convention defines cultural property to include

> movable or immovable property of great importance to the cultural heritage of every people, such as monuments of architecture, art or history, whether religious or secular; archaeological sites; groups of buildings which, as a whole, are of historical or artistic interest; works of art; manuscripts, books and other objects of artistic, historical or archaeological interest; as well as scientific collections and important collections of books or archives.

---

7. For the full text of the Hague Convention, cited extensively below, see http://portal.unesco.org/en/ev.php-URL_ID=13637&URL_DO=DO_TOPIC&URL_SECTION=201.html.

Also included in the definition are buildings whose purpose is to preserve or exhibit cultural property, including museums, libraries, and archives, as well as refuges specifically intended to shelter cultural property during armed conflict.

The core principles of the 1954 Hague Convention are the requirements to safeguard and to respect cultural property. Article 3 defines the safeguarding of cultural property: nations have the obligation to safeguard cultural property by preparing during peace to protect it from "the foreseeable effects of an armed conflict." Article 4 addresses the respect that should be shown to cultural property during armed conflict and imposes primarily negative obligations—that is, actions that a nation is required to refrain from taking. The first provision calls on nations to respect cultural property located in their own territory and in the territory of other parties to the Convention by refraining from using the cultural property "for purposes which are likely to expose it to destruction or damage" during armed conflict and by refraining from directing any act of hostility against such property. The next paragraph provides a waiver of these obligations where "military necessity imperatively requires such a waiver." The Convention is unclear as to what is meant by military necessity. While there have been some attempts to define it, there is no universal agreement, and it has been argued that the waiver significantly undermines the effectiveness of the Convention.

The third paragraph of Article 4 had received virtually no commentary or interpretation until after the looting of the Iraq Museum. The provision states that parties to the Convention "undertake to prohibit, prevent and, if necessary, put a stop to any form of theft, pillage, or misappropriation of, and any acts of vandalism directed against, cultural property." When read literally, it seems to impose an obligation on nations to prevent *any* form of theft or pillage, even if carried out by the local population. However, for reasons that I have explained more fully elsewhere (Gerstenblith 2006: 308–11), this provision most likely refers only to an obligation to prevent acts of theft, pillage and misappropriation carried out by members of the nation's own military. In particular, because there is no caveat limiting the obligation only to what is feasible or practical under the circumstances and given the post-World War II context in which the Convention was written, it seems very unlikely that the drafters intended to impose a blanket obligation to prevent theft and pillage during conflict. However, it is perfectly reasonable to expect nations to control the conduct of their own military and to punish those who violate such restrictions. The final provisions of Article 4 prohibit the requisitioning of cultural property and acts of reprisal taken against cultural property.

Article 5 turns to the obligations of an occupying power. The primary obligation of an occupying power is to support the competent national authorities of the occupied territory in carrying out their obligations to

preserve and safeguard its cultural property. The only affirmative obligation imposed is to take "the most necessary measures of preservation" for cultural property damaged by military operations and only if
the competent national authorities are themselves unable to take such
measures. The primary value promoted by this provision is one of non-
interference—in other words, the occupying power should interfere as
little as possible with the cultural heritage of occupied territory and
only when the local authorities are unable to do so. Any actions taken
by the occupying power should be done only in concert with the competent national authorities whenever and to the extent possible.

The Convention provides special protection for centers with monuments, immovable cultural property, and repositories of moveable cultural property (Articles 8–11); but this mechanism has rarely been used.
Cultural property under special protection is immune from acts of hostility except in cases of "unavoidable military necessity" or if the property or its surroundings are used for military purposes. Article 6 provides for the marking of cultural property with the Blue Shield symbol,
as outlined in Article 17. Article 7 requires parties to the Convention to
introduce military regulations and instructions to ensure observance of
the Convention and to foster a spirit of respect for the culture and cultural property of all peoples. It also requires nations to establish, within
their armed forces, services or specialist personnel whose purpose is to
secure respect for cultural property and to cooperate with the civilian
authorities responsible for safeguarding cultural property.

The First Protocol, which prohibits illegal export of cultural objects
from occupied territory and seeks to facilitate return of such objects at
the end of occupation, was also adopted in 1954. The Second Protocol
was finalized in 1999 and came into effect in 2004. The Second Protocol
clarifies and strengthens several sections of the main Convention and,
among other provisions, requires States Parties to create a criminal of-
fense, including command responsibility, for serious violations of the
Second Protocol and of the main Convention. At this time, 125 nations
have joined the main Convention, 101 have joined the First Protocol,
and 62 have joined the Second Protocol. All three instruments received
significant attention during the 2003 Gulf War, particularly because
two of the central military powers involved in the conflict, the United
States and the United Kingdom, were not parties to the Convention,
although they had signed it in 1954.

Although the Hague Convention was largely based on instructions
given by General Eisenhower to United States forces during World
War II, and the United States was one of the first nations to sign it, the
United States failed to ratify the Convention because of objections from
the military as Cold War tensions increased.[8] Only with the fall of the

---

8. Signing of an international convention indicates that a nation intends to ratify
the convention and will not act contrary to the spirit of the convention. However, a

Soviet Union did the military review the Convention and withdraw its objections. President Clinton transmitted both the main Convention and the First Protocol to the Senate Foreign Relations Committee in March 1999. The transmittal was accompanied by a recommendation from the State Department that the United States opt out of the first part of the First Protocol. In early 2007, the State Department listed the Convention and First Protocol on its treaty priority list. In April 2008, the Senate Foreign Relations Committee held hearings on only the main Convention and unanimously recommended ratification to the full Senate. On September 25, 2008, the Senate voted to give its advice and consent on ratification to the main Convention. The First Protocol was considered by neither body. On March 13, 2009, the United States deposited its instrument of ratification and immediately became a party under Article 33, which allows ratification to be given immediate effect for nations currently engaged in armed conflict.

The United States' ratification was subject to four understandings and one declaration. The First Understanding states that the level of protection to be accorded to property under special protection, as provided in Articles 8–11 of the Convention, is consistent with existing customary international law. The Second Understanding clarifies that the action of any military commander or other military personnel is to be judged based on the information that was reasonably available at the time an action was taken. The Third Understanding clarifies that the rules of the Convention apply only to conventional weapons and do not affect other international law concerning nonconventional weapons, such as nuclear weapons. The Fourth Understanding states that the provisions of Article 4(1) requiring Parties "to respect cultural property situated within their own territory" means that the "primary responsibility for the protection of cultural objects rests with the Party controlling that property, to ensure that it is properly identified and that it is not used for an unlawful purpose." Finally, the Declaration states that the Convention is self-executing, meaning that it does not require any implementing legislation. But the Declaration also notes that the Convention does not confer any private rights enforceable in U.S. courts (United States Senate 2008).

Ratification of the Convention may have relatively little direct impact on the conduct of the U.S. military because the U.S. government took the position that its military already complies with the core provisions of the Convention as a matter of customary international law. However, ratification raises the status and awareness of cultural property within the military, and concerns for preservation should therefore be incorporated into earlier stages of military planning. Article 7 of the

---

nation is legally bound to the terms of a convention only after ratifying or otherwise acceding to it, unless the provisions of the convention are deemed to be part of customary international law.

Convention also requires States Parties to train their military in cultural preservation awareness and to maintain cultural heritage professionals within their military forces. This could lead to greater recruitment efforts by the United States of such professionals into the military. Finally, ratification demonstrates to other nations that the United States will take cultural heritage preservation more seriously in the planning and conduct of future military operations.

In May 2004, on the 50th anniversary of the Convention, the United Kingdom announced that it would move toward ratification of the main Convention and both the First and Second Protocols. Unlike the United States, which ratified only the main Convention, because the United Kingdom proposed to ratify the Second Protocol, it was necessary to adopt implementing legislation. Such legislation, the draft Cultural Property (Armed Conflicts) bill, was introduced into Parliament in 2008 and provided for the creation of two criminal offenses—one for serious breaches of the Second Protocol, and the other for breach of the First Protocol by dealing in cultural property unlawfully exported from occupied territory knowingly or with reason to suspect that the property has been unlawfully exported. However, in considering how to implement the Convention's requirement for preparing during peacetime for the protection of its domestic cultural property in case of armed conflict, Parliament became bogged down in the enormity of the task. Parliament has therefore failed to act on the implementing legislation, and prospects for ratification are unclear at this time.

The United States' ratification was part of an almost 20-year process that began in the early 1990s with the collapse of the Soviet Union and the gradual withdrawal of objections to the Convention by the U.S. military. Prospects for ratification were also significantly enhanced when the Democratic Party regained its majority in the United States Senate after the 2006 election. However, the impetus for ratification came from the military, which seemed to recognize the damage done to its reputation through the negative publicity from the looting of the Iraq Museum and the difficulties inherent in coalition action when the individual members of a military coalition are subject to differing international treaty obligations, as well as a general public awareness of these issues. Once again, the damage done to Iraq's cultural heritage during and as a result of the 2003 Gulf War, and, indirectly, the media's attention to this played a role in bringing about a beneficial consequence.

Founding of the U.S. Committee of the Blue Shield and the Blue Shield Movement

A third beneficial consequence of the looting of the Iraq Museum was expansion of the international Blue Shield movement and the founding of the United States Committee of the Blue Shield (USCBS) by retired Major Corine Wegener, who had worked on the reconstruction of the

Iraq Museum for close to a year between 2003 and 2004. The 1954 and earlier Hague Conventions provided for the marking of cultural property that was to be protected during armed conflict. The symbol that was eventually adopted is a blue-and-white shield, composed of three triangles and one diamond at the bottom. In 1996, several international cultural organizations joined to create the International Committee of the Blue Shield (ICBS) and a mechanism for the creation of national Blue Shield committees (Cole 2008: 67).

The purpose of the Blue Shield committees is to advocate for ratification of the 1954 Hague Convention, to work with the various militaries to train their members and assure adequate presence of cultural heritage professionals within the military, and to coordinate cultural heritage preservation in areas of armed conflict and natural disaster. The Blue Shield committees are supposed to be able to respond to these situations with the same emergency-response capabilities of established humanitarian organizations such as the Red Cross (Wegener 2008: 165). As Wegener explains,

> Humanitarian NGOs are routinely allowed access to a military theater of operations by the United States because they provide services for which the military has scant resources. They also usually have established their credibility with the military prior to the conflict by clearly demonstrating a professional capability to assist without becoming a logistical or security burden. In fact, military units often invite NGOs to training exercises to provide realism and coordination for future real world missions. . . . [A]n NGO hoping to advocate for the protection of cultural property during armed conflict could work to establish and maintain military contacts during peacetime so that it would later be invited into the military planning process. (Wegener 2008: 165)

The founding of the USCBS provides considerable potential for avoidance of the same kind of damage to cultural heritage in future conflicts in which the United States is engaged. The USCBS, as well as other organizations, is committed to the training of military units, especially the Civil Affairs units that are tasked with providing noncombat services to the military. Changes within the United States military also raise the possibility that the military as a whole will take cultural heritage protection more seriously and will take it into account from initial phases of military planning through combat and stability operations and postconflict reconstruction (Jackson 2008: 51–57).

Although it is still too early to judge the effectiveness of the Blue Shield movement fully, several recent conflicts have provided an opportunity for initial assessment. The Libyan bombing campaign, which began in March 2011, was the first test of the United States' commitment to cultural heritage protection since its ratification of the Hague

Convention, although the avoidance of targeting of cultural sites was already observed by the United States as part of customary international law. USCBS coordinated with archaeologists who are specialists on Libya as well as the ICBS to compile a list of site coordinates for important Libyan cultural heritage sites. USCBS then passed this list on to contacts within the U.S. Department of Defense just prior to the start of the NATO No-Fly-Zone bombing campaign. USCBS supplied the same information to Blue Shield national committees in other NATO countries and they shared this information with their own military contacts (Association of National Committees of the Blue Shield and the International Military Cultural Resources Working Group 2011). Libyan sources have credited this list with preserving cultural heritage from any significant damage during this campaign (NATO 2012). The Association of National Committees of the Blue Shield and the International Military Cultural Resources Working Group sent assessment teams to Egypt and to Libya to provide the first reports on damage to cultural heritage sites and museums during the events of the "Arab spring."

Although not a part of its formal mission to protect cultural property during armed conflict, the ICBS and the various national committees have also engaged in numerous projects to assess and conserve cultural property that was damaged by natural disasters. Their projects have included providing assistance in Italy after earthquakes, in Dresden after floods, in Japan following the earthquake and tsunami in 2011, and Haiti after the 2010 earthquake. In Haiti, the USCBS, in partnership with the Smithsonian, has been particularly engaged in providing conservation work for damaged paintings and murals (Kurin 2011).

The 2003 Gulf War had disastrous consequences for the cultural and archaeological heritage of Iraq. Recognition both within the United States government and among the worldwide community of these consequences also led to some beneficial, albeit entirely unintended, advances in efforts to protect cultural heritage. The media played a significant role in both the good and the bad. Inaccurate reporting and conclusions drawn only to advance political and art market–related financial motives were used in attempts to delegitimize some of those who worked hardest to preserve Iraq's cultural heritage and to dismantle Iraq's legal regime that aimed to protect its heritage. The advances that were made in legal and institutional structures may not counterbalance the irretrievable losses to Iraq's archaeological heritage, but they should help to assure that this sort of disaster will not occur in the future.

References

Aaronovitch, D.
2003   Lost from the Baghdad Museum: Truth. *The Guardian*, June 10: 5.
Association of National Committees of the Blue Shield and the International
        Military Cultural Resources Working Group
2011   Mission Report: Civil-Military Assessment Mission for Libyan Heri-
        tage, Nov. 12–16. On-line: http://blueshield.de/libya2-report.html.
Banerjee, N., and Garen, M.
2004   Saving Iraq's Archaeological Past from Thieves Remains an Uphill
        Battle. *New York Times*, April 4: A16.
Bogdanos, M.
2004   The Casualties of War: The Truth about the Iraq Museum. *American
        Journal of Archaeology* 109: 477–526.
2008   Thieves of Baghdad. Pp. 109–34 in *The Destruction of Cultural Heritage
        in Iraq*, ed. P. G. Stone and J. Farchakh Bajjaly. Woodbridge, UK: Boydell.
Brodie, N.
2006   The Plunder of Iraq's Archaeological Heritage, 1991–2005, and the Lon-
        don Antiquities Trade. Pp. 206–26 in *Archaeology, Cultural Heritage,
        and the Antiquities Trade*, ed. N. Brodie, M. M. Kersel, C. Luke, and K.
        W. Tubb. Gainesville: University of Florida Press.
2008   The Market in Iraqi Antiquities 1980–2008. Unpublished report.Avail-
        able on-line: https://www.stanford.edu/group/chr/cgi-bin/drupal/files/
        Market%20in%20Iraqi%20antiquities%20(2008)%20txt.pdf.
Cole, S.
2008   War, Cultural Property and the Blue Shield. Pp. 65–71 in *The Destruc-
        tion of Cultural Heritage in Iraq*, ed. P. G. Stone and J. Farchakh Bajjaly.
        Woodbridge: Boydell.
Farchakh, J.
2003   Le Massacre du patrimoine irakienne. *Archeologia* 402: 14–31.
Farchakh-Bajjaly, J.
2008   Who Are the Looters at Archaeological Sites in Iraq? Pp. 49–61 in *An-
        tiquities under Siege: Cultural Heritage Protection after the Iraq War*,
        ed. L. Rothfield. London: AltaMira.
Garen, M.
2004   The War within the War. *Archaeology* 57: 4, 28–31.
George, D.
2008   The Looting of the Iraq National Museum. Pp. 97–107 in *The Destruc-
        tion of Cultural Heritage in Iraq*, ed. P. G. Stone and J. Farchakh Bajjaly.
        Woodbridge, UK: Boydell.
Gerstenblith, P.
2006   From Bamiyan to Baghdad: Warfare and the Preservation of Cultural
        Heritage at the Beginning of the 21st Century. *Georgetown Journal of
        International Law* 37: 245–351.
2007   Controlling the International Market in Antiquities: Reducing the
        Harm, Preserving the Past. *Chicago Journal International Law* 8:
        169–95.
Gerstenblith, P., and Hanson, K.
2008   Congressional Responses to the Looting of Iraq's Cultural Property. Pp.
        103–15 in *Antiquities under Siege: Cultural Heritage Protection after
        the Iraq War*, ed. L. Rothfield. London: AltaMira.

Grassley, C.
   2004   Floor Statement. *Congressional Record*, S 2188, March 4.
Hawkins, A., and Anderson, M.
   2002   Preserving Iraq's Past. *Washington Post*, November 29: A43.
Jackson, R.
   2008   Cultural Property Protection in Stability Operations. *Army Lawyer*
           425: 47–57.
Jehl, D., and Becker, E.
   2003   A Nation at War: The Looting; Experts' Pleas to Pentagon Didn't Save
           Museum. *New York Times*, April 16: B5.
Jenkins, I.
   2001   The Elgin Marbles: Questions of Accuracy and Reliability. *Interna-
           tional Journal of Cultural Property* 10: 55–69.
Krauthammer, C.
   2003   Hoaxes, Hype and Humiliation. *Washington Post*, June 11: A29.
Kurin, R.
   2011   *Saving Haiti's Heritage: Cultural Recovery after the Earthquake.*
           Washington, DC: Smithsonian Institution.
Lawler, A.
   2003   Beyond the Looting: What's Next for Iraq's Treasures? *National Geo-
           graphic* (October). Available on-line: http://ngm.nationalgeographic
           .com/features/world/asia/iraq/iraqi-antiquities-text.html.
Liu, M., and Dickey, C.
   2004   Unearthing the Bible. *Newsweek*, August 30: 32.
Merryman, J. H.
   1985   Thinking about the Elgin Marbles. *Michigan Law Review* 83:
           1881–1923.
Merryman, J. H., and Elsen, A.
   1998   *Law, Ethics and the Visual Arts.* 3rd ed. London: Kluwer Law
           International.
NATO
   2012   Protecting Libya's Heritage. January 4. On-line: http://www.nato.int/
           cps/en/SID-65C15F94-D3CDC3FF/natolive/news_82441.htm.
Neils, J.
   2001   *The Parthenon Frieze.* Cambridge: Cambridge University Press.
Nicholas, L.
   1994   *The Rape of Europa: The Fate of Europe's Treasures in the Third Reich
           and the Second World War.* New York: Knopf.
Rothfield, L.
   2009   *The Rape of Mesopotamia: Behind the Looting of the Iraq Museum.*
           Chicago: University of Chicago Press.
Shanks, H.
   2003   Iraq's Looted Treasures Should Be Bought Back—On the Market. *The
           Scotsman*, April 17: 15.
St. Clair, W.
   1998   *Lord Elgin and the Marbles: The Controversial History of the Parthe-
           non Sculptures.* Oxford: Oxford University Press.
   1999   The Elgin Marbles: Questions of Stewardship and Accountability. *In-
           ternational Journal of Cultural Property* 8: 391–521.

2006   Imperial Appropriations of the Parthenon. Pp. 65–97 in *Imperialism, Art and Restitution,* ed. J. H. Merryman. Cambridge: Cambridge University Press.

Stone, E. C.
2008a   Patterns of Looting in Southern Iraq. *Antiquity* 82: 125–38.
2008b   Archaeological Site Looting: The Destruction of Cultural Heritage in Southern Iraq. Pp. 65–80 in *Catastrophe! The Looting and Destruction of Iraq's Past,* ed. G. Emberling and K. Hanson. Chicago: University of Chicago Press.

Tierney, J.
2003   Did Lord Elgin Do Something Right? *New York Times,* April 20: §4:10.

United States Senate
2008   110th Congress, 2d Session Executive Report 110–26. September 16. Available on-line: http://frwebgate.access.gpo.gov/cgi-bin/getdoc.cgi?dbname=110_cong_reports&docid=f:er026.pdf.

Webb, T.
2002   Appropriating the Stones: The "Elgin" Marbles and English National Taste. Pp. 51–96 in *Claiming the Stones, Naming the Bones: Cultural Property and the Negotiation of National and Ethnic Identity,* ed. E. Barkan and R. Bush. Los Angeles: Getty Research Institute.

Wegener, C.
2008   Assignment Blue Shield: The Looting of the Iraq Museum and Cultural Property at War. Pp. 163–73 in *Antiquities under Siege: Cultural Heritage Protection after the Iraq War,* ed. L. Rothfield. London: AltaMira.

PART 2

Archaeology and the Media

Fabulous Finds or Fantastic Forgeries?
The Distortion of Archaeology by the Media and Pseudoarchaeologists, and What We Can Do About It

Eric H. Cline

In an op-ed in the *Washington Post* on Sunday, March 14, 2009, David Shaywitz described what happened when a group of British researchers linked eating cereal for breakfast with giving birth to sons (rather than to daughters). The attention lavished on the story by the media was immediate and far-flung, including a story in the *Economist*, which advised women to "skip breakfast for a daughter, eat up your cereals for a son" (cited in Shaywitz 2009: A15). The link between breakfast preferences and gender of newborns was subsequently shown to be incorrect for, as Shaywitz pointed out, "a lot of science . . . cannot withstand serious scrutiny. . . . more than half of published scientific research findings can't be replicated by other researchers" (Shaywitz 2009: A15). The media, however, paid little attention to the revised findings, for the lack of a link was far less interesting than the original suggestion.

We find similar situations every year in archaeology, for the junk science that is practiced by many pseudoarchaeologists and amateur enthusiasts not only cannot withstand serious scrutiny, but in many cases the "results" themselves are not really results at all. However, when gratuitous claims of amazing finds, especially concerning Noah's Ark, the Ark of the Covenant, and Sodom and Gomorrah, are first made, they are featured prominently in the media—but subsequent rebuttals are given little or no attention.

Professional archaeologists have to face the reality of the situation, which is that the media are going to keep reporting these stories because they sell newspapers and get people to watch TV or click on internet

Author's note: I would like to take this opportunity to thank Eric and Carol Meyers, Erin Darby, and everyone else involved in organizing the conference. All Web sites listed below were last accessed and the links still active on August 29, 2012.

links. Whereas they are not nearly as interested in later negative responses, reporters almost always seek immediate reactions that can be
used in the original story. So, we have to decide what we are going to do
about this and how to turn it to our advantage.

Beginning on a positive note, I would argue that we have, in fact, already taken the first steps toward retaking our field, not least of which
is the very conference for which this essay was prepared. Back in late
September 2007, I published an op-ed piece in the *Boston Globe* saying
that we had to reclaim our field from the pseudoarchaeologists and junk
scientists (Cline 2007a: E1–2). I had reached the breaking point after
doing research for a book (Cline 2007b); I was increasingly incensed at
the amount of misinformation being published by amateur enthusiasts
and pseudoarchaeologists on the internet and elsewhere (Cline 2007b:
ix–xv). In part because of that op-ed piece, which was essentially meant
as a call to arms, a series of sessions at the annual conventions of the
American Schools of Oriental Research (ASOR), the Society of Biblical
Literature (SBL), and the Archaeological Institute of America (AIA) have
dealt with media issues. Similarly, this conference at Duke has as its
stated objective "to outline better methods of communication between
archaeologists, media representatives, and non-specialist audiences."[1]
These are important steps, but I hope that we are not speaking in an
echo chamber and preaching to the choir here today. Nevertheless, that
may be to the good, for it is the members of the choir who need to continue aggressively working on these better methods of communication.

Progress Made in Taking Back Our Field

A "War Room"

The participants in an ASOR session entitled "*Archaeology and the
Media: How to Put the Record Straight*," held in November 2008, decided that it was necessary to set up a "war room" in order to respond
immediately to false claims by pseudoarchaeologists, amateur enthusiasts, and junk scientists. Jodi Magness pioneered this approach in March
2007 when, after being called numerous times by different journalists
seeking her reaction to the Talpiyot Tomb fiasco, she wrote a lengthy
response, posted it on the web, and thereafter directed reporters to that
response, from which they were able to quote (Magness 2007).

To that end, a blog linked to the ASOR Web site now functions to
respond to and combat erroneous and extravagant claims reported by
the media. For instance, in February 2009, Robert Cargill of UCLA and
I each responded to articles appearing in print and on the Web widely
reporting Randall Price's claim to know the location of Noah's Ark and

---

1. See the official announcement of the Duke Symposium on Archaeology, Politics, and the Media at http://fds.duke.edu/db?attachment-110--0-view-790.

announcement that he would be involved in an excavation to uncover it in the summer of 2009 (Cline 2009b; Cargill 2009). Price is the executive director of the Center for Judaic Studies at Jerry Falwell's Liberty University. Price stated in late January 2009 that the location of Noah's Ark had been verified by a shepherd who said he had climbed on it when he was a boy (Associated Press 2009; Desrets 2009). According to the Associated Press, during a preliminary trip in late 2008, Price and his colleagues "found the spot . . . but it now is covered by an estimated 60-foot-deep pile of boulders" (Associated Press 2009). One team member had already told Fox News, "there will be discovery. The only thing that's holding us back is to finance the machinery that we need" (Associated Press 2009). The expedition clearly made a priori conclusions, as so many such groups often do.

Price responded immediately to our blog postings, attempting to justify and clarify his statements. Interestingly, at the same time as Price was using the media to promote his expedition and agenda, he also complained—via the ASOR blog—that the media had seized on one small portion of his overall interview and that it went viral without his intending it to do so:

> I would like to clarify for the record that the Ark Search LLC expedition was not seeking national publicity or funds when its planned work was announced in the Fox News piece. I gave the original story to a local reporter for a local paper as part of an interview concerning the archaeological field work of our newly instituted program in field archaeology. . . . The interviewer learned of my survey of the site on Mt. Ararat this past October and hoping to raise from the local community some funds for the planned summer excavation I gave them some of the material. I did not approve of the paper's focus on the Noah's Ark expedition and its spread to national exposure. I have repeatedly declined any and all request for interviews from the media on this subject, even though they offered the means to raise needed excavation funds.[2]

This may be an example of the media seizing on the sexiest part of an otherwise nondescript interview and running with it, but it may just as easily—and perhaps more likely—be an example of a junk scientist

---

2. See Price's comment/response at http://asorblog.org/?p=84. However, see also the relevant posts on *YouTube*: http://www.youtube.com/watch?v=u0lH86JD3PA; http://www.youtube.com/watch?v=d-WkutWclWA&feature=related; and http://www.youtube.com/watch?v=W6vLrvzr4wI&feature=related. Note that, upon returning from the expedition, in early September 2009, Price posted an on-line message at http://www.worldofthebible.com/Arch_update.html (since removed) stating that, while they had little to show for their efforts so far, apart from lost toenails and a "mysterious situation" whose details could not be divulged, they needed still more monetary donations so that they could return to the alleged site.

peddling his wares to a gullible media and general public. At the very least, this episode served notice that ASOR archaeologists are not going to be passive about these pronouncements. As I wrote in my response to Price, "I will be watching with interest to see whether you are actually conducting 'organized archaeological work . . . at a site connected with a documentary account' or whether you are aiding and abetting a group of untrained amateur enthusiasts practicing pseudo-archaeology."[3] Joe Zias similarly wrote: "it's time that those of us in the profession put an end to this manipulation in the hunt for fame and fortune. These 'expeditions' are more in the category of Amazing Dis-Grace than the world of archaeology, biblical or otherwise, and we must put forth more effort at bringing this to an end."[4]

A similar episode took place in late February and early March 2009, when media sources reported that Klaus Schmidt, a German archaeologist, had claimed a link between the site of Gobekli Tepe in Turkey and the Garden of Eden. No fewer than four television journalists contacted me, including one from the BBC, so I decided to look into the matter, if only to be able to answer preliminary questions over the telephone. When I looked closely at the media reports, I first noticed that they all could be traced back to a single story written by Tom Cox, which appeared in the *Daily Mail* on February 28, 2009 (Knox 2009a). That same story was re-released on March 5,[5] with the only change being in the name of the author—Tom Cox was now Tom Knox—and a little blurb in italic type at the end of the article said that Tom Knox's novel on a similar topic was being published by Harper Collins that same week. In other words, the so-called newspaper account was apparently nothing more than hype for Knox's new book (Knox 2009b).[6] Did Schmidt really think that Gobekli Tepe is the Garden of Eden? Or was he unwittingly being used by the media and especially by a journalist hawking a book?

Doing further research, I found that a similar story, written by a journalist named Sean Thomas, had appeared much earlier, in October 2006 (Thomas 2006). This, then, seemed to indicate that Schmidt either really does believe the Gobekli Tepe–Garden of Eden link or is simply not adverse to the publicity that it generates (Curry 2008). However, it turned out that Sean Thomas, Tom Cox, and Tom Knox are all the same person—"Tom Knox" being a pseudonym for Sean Thomas—so that the original 2006 article, the more recent 2009 one, and the 2009

---

3. See, again, comments/responses posted at http://asorblog.org/?p=84.

4. Ibid.

5. Note that the first several comments made by readers at the Web site are dated to February 28, that is, to the original version of the story, which has been replaced.

6. Others have noticed this too; see http://dailygrail.com/Hidden-History/2009/3/Goebekli-Tepe-Fiction.

novel (based in part on Thomas's experiences in reporting on Gobekli Tepe) are all apparently written by the same enterprising journalist.[7]

Gobekli Tepe is indeed an important site, perhaps having significant implications for understanding the Neolithic Revolution (ca. 10,000 B.C.E.). However, to link it to the Garden of Eden is both unnecessary and unscientific. As Michael Homan, ASOR Co-Vice President for Programs at the time and the original moving force behind the ASOR blog, wrote there: "While it is truly an amazing site with great implications for understanding the Neolithic Revolution, it's not Paradise" (Homan 2009). A more colorful response came from an on-line posting written by a reader in France: "Although a very important archaeological discovery, claiming it to be the mythical Garden of Eden is as likely as it being Superman's Fortress of Solitude."[8]

We are apparently left with the question of whether Schmidt really does believe that Gobekli Tepe is the Garden of Eden or has been used by a journalist who simply smelled a good story and a cash payout regardless of its link to the truth. Unfortunately, Schmidt has not responded to Homan's blog posting. However, it is telling that in Thomas's 2006 article, and again in the November 2008 *Smithsonian* magazine article by Andrew Curry, Schmidt is quoted as saying that Gobekli Tepe is "the world's oldest temple" but does not link it to the Garden of Eden; Thomas is the one who does that, elevating a fascinating site into the "realms of the fantastical" (Curry 2008; Knox 2009a). And in Cox's/Knox's/Thomas's 2009 article (Knox 2009a), Schmidt is actually quoted as saying "Gobekli Tepe is not the Garden of Eden," although he also says, perhaps now to his everlasting regret, "(but) it is a temple in Eden." In short, this seems to be a prime example of the distortion of archaeology by the media, in this case specifically by Cox/Knox/Thomas.

However, the story came to a close on March 18, 2009, when the Deutsches Archäologisches Institut (DAI) issued the following press release:

> On February 28th the *Daily Mail* published an article by Tom Cox, in which Prof. Dr. Klaus Schmidt, leader of the Göbekli Tepe excavations, is cited as follows: "Göbekli Tepe is a temple in Eden." On the basis of this, the author formulates several conclusions about the biblical paradise, Adam and Eve and other events connected to the Book of Genesis in the Old Testament. Several German- and Turkish-language newspapers and radio stations of German and Turkish language have picked up on the contents of the article since its publication. "Tom

---

7. See http://www.amazon.co.uk/Genesis-Secret-Tom-Knox/dp/0007284144 and "Book Review: The Genesis Secret by Tom Knox" on the *Monsters and Critics* Web site: http://www.monstersandcritics.com/books/mystery/reviews/article_1464554. php/Book_Review_The_Genesis_Secret_by_Tom_Knox.

8. See the "Comments" section of Knox 2009a.

Cox" or "Tom Knox" is a pseudonym of the British journalist Sean
Thomas, who used the article to get publicity for his thriller "Genesis
Secret", which is due to appear in March in English and simultane-
ously in German. Since Sean Thomas is using a falsified version of an
interview with Klaus Schmidt made in fall 2006, he presents a distortion of the scientific work of the German Archaeological Institute.
The German Archaeological Institute (DAI) distances itself from these
statements and reserves the right to take legal action against further
dissemination of the story in connection with the work of the DAI at
Göbekli Tepe. Klaus Schmidt neither in an interview nor on any other
occasion made the above mentioned statements.[9]

The DAI is to be commended for its rapid response in issuing a press
release denying the claims made by this specific journalist.

Working with the Media

The participants in the subsequent AIA session, held in January 2009
and entitled "Taking Back Our Field: Archaeology and the Media," decided that communication between professional archaeologists and the
media should be improved, so that better and more accurate stories are
written and published. Several of us have now begun to do this by cultivating our contacts at various media outlets. A prime example is the
recent case of Raphael Golb, son of Norman Golb, Dead Sea Scrolls
scholar at the University of Chicago. After initial reports that the Dis-
trict Attorney's office in New York had arrested the younger Golb on
March 5, 2009, the *Chronicle of Higher Education* ran a long and detailed front-page story using all of the evidence that had been amassed
by Robert Cargill (Kolowich 2009).[10] The story most likely would not
have appeared, at least not there and then, were it not for our active
cultivation of contacts such as these in the media.[11]

Since the AIA session, several instances of the egregious misuse of
the data—the media seizing on the parts of a story that they like and
ignoring the rest—have appeared. In such cases, archaeologists should
respond by working with the media rather than simply complaining
about being misunderstood and misquoted. The best recent example
comes from someone who attended the AIA session: Simon James of the
University of Leicester in England. At another AIA session, he gave a
paper on the Sasanian Persian siege of the Roman fortress city of Dura-
Europos, Syria, in 256 C.E. One part of his paper concerned the possible
use of poisonous gas, which he hypothesized had been used against the

---

9. See the official Web site for the Deutsches Archäologisches Institut, http://
www.dainst.org/index_9631_en.html.
10. See also Robert R. Cargill, "Who Is Charles Gadda?" On-line: http://www
.bobcargill.com/who-is-charles-gadda.html.
11. See now Grace 2010 on the conclusion of the trial, which resulted in the con-
viction of Raphael Golb on multiple counts.

Roman defenders during mining operations, involving a tunnel dug under the city wall, conducted by the Persians as part of their siege tactics. On his return home to England, he found that, although the poisonous gas episode was but one part of his paper, the media had seized on this and ignored the rest of his presentation. With characteristic understatement, he commented that this generated considerable media interest.[12]

Moreover, James immediately utilized what he had just heard at the AIA media session, in particular Jodi Magness's suggestion of creating a Web page about one's work. He did exactly that, presenting his data there in more detail; in a general e-mail sent just days after the AIA session, James wrote:

> I have been somewhat taken aback by the media interest in my AIA presentation on the Dura siege, which has made the national newspapers here. . . . Much of the coverage has been somewhat garbled, so following the discussion at another AIA session on the media, I have quickly created a web-page with the press release text, pictures, captions and credits so people can get a more direct and accurate version of what I actually said.[13]

Indeed, the subsequent stories reported in the media were more accurate than those that first appeared, indicating that taking a proactive approach can certainly be effective, even if one is at first caught unaware by the media focusing on a minor, albeit interesting, point.

Still Needs Work—What Is Not Said

Although there have been some positive steps, there is still much more to be done. For instance, sometimes more damaging than what is said by the media is what is not said. Consider Hershel Shanks and the report of archaeological discoveries in his magazine *Biblical Archaeology Review* (*BAR*). Striving to be at the forefront in reporting new archaeological discoveries, the magazine sometimes reports claims that are unconfirmed or still disputed; one example is Eilat Mazar's claims to have found David's palace and Nehemiah's wall in the City of David (Ir David) excavations (Mazar 2009).[14] Another prominent example is

---

12. For example, "The Final Stage of Dura: Ancient 'Chemical Warfare'?" on-line: http://www2.le.ac.uk/departments/archaeology/research/projects/roman-soldiers-in-the-city-dura-europos-syria-1/the-final-siege-of-dura-ancient-chemical-warfare?searchterm=dura; see previously "Early Chemical Warfare Comes to Light," on-line: http://www.sciencenews.org/view/generic/id/39814/title/Ancient_chemical_warfare_comes_to_light; http://www.medicalnewstoday.com/articles/135586.php; http://www.world-science.net/othernews/090116_chemical.htm.

13. Personal communication by e-mail, January 15, 2009.

14. The claim by Mazar that she has found King David's palace in Jerusalem has been discussed and dismissed by Finkelstein et al. 2007: 142–64; other archaeologists

the saga of Oded Golan, who was placed on trial in Israel for the possible forgery of antiquities. Shanks followed this trial diligently, with multiple postings on the Biblical Archaeology Society Web site and in *BAR* magazine.[15] And yet, there was at least one curious omission in his reporting of one of Golan's supposed forgeries: an inscription called the Jehoash Tablet because of its reference to King Jehoash, a king of Judah in the 9th century B.C.E.

In March 2008, Bob Simon reported on *60 Minutes* that an Egyptian man called Marko Sammech said that he had carved the text into the Jehoash Tablet for Golan. "I inscribed several stone slabs that looked just like this for Golan," Marko remarked. "Yeah, but I mean, he presumably gave you the text," [producer Michael] Gavshon asked. "Yes, Golan brought me the text and I carved it onto the tablet," Marko replied." The story was subsequently widely reported in the media and became a part of the ongoing saga when the man (perhaps at the behest of the Egyptian authorities) refused to go to Israel to testify in the trial against Golan (Simon 2008; see also Burleigh 2008 and Cline 2009a). While this may well have been the smoking gun in the case and could have tilted the judge's opinion in favor of a guilty verdict against Golan, no mention whatsoever of this appeared either on *BAR*'s Web site or in the magazine for more than three years, despite the fact that new articles and dispatches about other aspects of the case appeared regularly in both places.[16]

I believe that *BAR* should have introduced such testimony into the debate far earlier, even if it flew in the face of Shanks's contention that the objects are genuine. However, *BAR* is a privately-produced publication and Shanks can publish what he wishes. This raises a dilemma for archaeologists. How are we to deal with such an issue, in which a publication reaching thousands of lay readers might not present the entire story? Is this an issue to be taken up on the ASOR blog? Or is there some other, or better, way to address this so that *BAR*'s readers will learn the full story?

Where Do We Go from Here?

In 2008, I published a light-hearted piece in *Near Eastern Archaeology (NEA)* about archaeology and the media. Originally written in 2005, well before I had become outraged during the process of writing my *From Eden to Exile* book, it was meant simply to run as a side-bar to a

---

are awaiting further evidence before evaluating her claims.

15. E.g., Shanks 2008.

16. It was only in the May/June 2011 and the July/August 2011 issues of his magazine, more than two years after this conference and more than three years after it aired, that Shanks finally mentioned the *60 Minutes* piece, only to call it into question; see Shanks 2012: 31, 65 n. 2, with reference to the two earlier pieces.

larger story on archaeology and Hollywood. In the end, it appeared as a stand-alone piece in the *NEA*'s Forum section, with responses from Neil Asher Silberman and Cornelius Holtorf and a final statement from Ann Killebrew (Cline et al. 2008: 172–80).

I offered a few broad suggestions about working together with television producers on topics of real interest and value; and I pointed out that the codes of ethics written for AIA, ASOR, and SAA (Society for American Archaeology) all state that the knowledge and expertise of scholars should be brought to the public. If Holtorf is correct in his claim that archaeology is a brand (Holtorf 2006), then we archaeologists should be working together to protect that brand, just as George Lucas and Steven Spielberg fiercely protect the Indiana Jones franchise and Microsoft and Coca-Cola protect their brands (Cline et al. 2008: 179). As others at the Duke conference have suggested, perhaps we should create something akin to the "Good Housekeeping Seal of Approval," to be awarded to TV shows, newspaper articles, and Internet blogs and postings that are accurate and balanced.

In April 2009, Paul Flesher, Director of the Religious Studies Program at the University of Wyoming, published a long response to our combined *NEA* "Forum" articles on the Bible and Interpretation Web site. He suggested that archaeologists might draw on the expertise of people in university departments of English, theater, journalism, and communication and form teams to help create our own "interesting and filmable story" (Flesher 2009). He also proposed using the Internet as a means of communicating archaeological discoveries to the public, saying that excavators could bring bloggers with them or could film their own excavations.

I had already done just this at Megiddo: in 2008, my students were each requested to post one blog entry per week on our Web site (we did it again in 2010); and in 2006, a filmmaker—Jesse Krinsky—came to Megiddo to capture our activities 24/7 for three weeks. This endeavor resulted in a 5-minute trailer placed on our Megiddo Web site,[17] in addition to a 30-minute movie. Many other excavations maintain an active Web presence, which will surely help to provide accurate information to the media.

Flesher ended his response by urging archaeologists to ask: "How does archaeology communicate its message to the public and what are the best media forms for that task?" (Flesher 2009). Along those lines, the words of Seth Kahan, a consultant for Visionary Leadership in the Washington DC area, are relevant.[18] Among other advice that Kahan gave in a seminar held in Washington DC was, first and foremost, the necessity of expressing one's ideas in a compelling, easy-to-communicate

---

17. "The Megiddo Expedition" Web site: http://megiddo.tau.ac.il/.
18. Seth Kahan, http://visionaryleadership.com/.

statement—what some call the "elevator pitch" (that is, can you convey your idea to a listener in the time it takes to ride an elevator from the ground floor to the top floor?)—because that is what is going to take to answer a question in a sound bite or to pitch or to explain an idea to the media. The second most important thing to do is to identify the people who can present our vision, ranging from leaders within ASOR, SBL, and AIA, to the practical visionaries, the public faces presenting factual archaeological material, and the strategic partners who can help form the alliances that are necessary to make things happen.

So, I end my essay with a simple statement and a leading question since, as David Shaywitz said in the op-ed piece already cited, "Researchers are unlikely to become less self-serving—just as reporters are unlikely to become less opportunistic in their hunt for news" (Shaywitz 2009: A15).

My statement is that what we have been doing in the past year or two has worked to a certain extent, and we can already see tangible results. For instance, I was contacted by, and appeared on, both *Good Morning America* and the *Fox News Channel* in April 2010, to present a response to new claims that Noah's Ark had been found by a Hong Kong evangelical group on Mt. Ararat.[19] But we need to do more, much more, such as making the Web sites of archaeological societies like ASOR more accessible to the public and posting a list of archaeologists, with their areas of specialty, who are willing to work with the media. Most universities have such a media-friendly webpage naming scholarly experts in various areas; why not archaeological societies?

And my question is as follows: Where do we go from here? It is time for the choir to sing . . . and I am all ears.

---

19. ABC News Video, "Was Noah's Ark Found?" April 28, 2010, http://abcnews.go.com/GMA/videønoahs-ark-found-10496395 and Fox News Video, "Where's the Actual Site?" April 29, 2010, http://video.foxnews.com/v/4171840/wheres-the-actual-site/.

References

Associated Press
    2009   Virginia Man to Search for Noah's Ark in Turkey. *Fox News*, February 2. On-line: http://www.foxnews.com/story/0,2933,486684,00.html.
Burleigh, N.
    2008   *Unholy Business: A True Tale of Faith, Greed and Forgery in the Holy Land*. New York: HarperCollins.
Cargill, R.
    2009   Yet Another Ark Quest: Randall Price, Liberty University, and Pseudo-scientific Religious Fundamentalism. *The Official Blog of Robert R. Cargill*, February 10, 2009. On-line: http://bobcargill.wordpress.com/2009/02/10/yet-another-ark-quest-randall-price-liberty-university-and-pseudo-scientific-religious-fundamentalism/.

Cline, E. H.
2007a Raiders of the Faux Ark. *Boston Globe,* September 30, E1–2.
2007b *From Eden to Exile: Unraveling Mysteries of the Bible.* Washington, DC: National Geographic Books.
2009a *Biblical Archaeology: A Very Short Introduction.* New York: Oxford University Press.
2009b Adrift again on Noah's Ark. *ASOR Blog,* February 10. On-line: http://asorblog.org/?p=84
Cline, E. H.; Silberman, N. A.; and Holtorf, C.
2008 Forum: Archaeologists and the Media. *Near Eastern Archaeology* 71: 172–80.
Curry, A.
2008 Gobekli Tepe: The World's First Temple? *Smithsonian Magazine Online,* November. http://www.smithsonianmag.com/history-archaeology/gobekli-tepe.html.
Desrets, C.
2009 Lynchburg Man Looking for Noah's Ark. *The News and Advance,* February 5. On-line: http://www.newsadvance.com/lna/news/local/article/lynchburg_man_looking_for_noahs_ark/13000/.
Finkelstein, I.; Herzog, Z.; Singer-Avitz, L.; and Ussishkin, D.
2007 Has King David's Palace in *Jerusalem* Been Found? *Tel Aviv* 34: 142–64.
Flesher, P. V. M.
2009 How Should Archaeology Reach Its Public? *The Bible and Interpretation,* April. On-line: www.bibleinterp.com/articles/paul.shtml.
Grace, M.
2010 Manhattan Lawyer Raphael Golb Convicted of Lmpersonating, Harassing NYU Dead Sea Scrolls professor. *Daily News,* October 1. On-line: http://www.nydailynews.com/ny_local/2010/10/01/2010–10–01_dead_sea_troll_is_convicted_for_impersonating_nyu_prof.html.
Holtorf, C.
2006 *Archaeology Is a Brand! The Meaning of Archaeology in Contemporary Popular Culture.* Oxford: Archaeopress.
Homan, M. M.
2009 Archaeologists and Journalists: Please Stop Finding the Garden of Eden! *ASOR Blog,* March 1. On-line: http://asorblog.org/?p=93.
Knox, T.
2009a Do These Mysterious Stones Mark the Site of the Garden of Eden? *Daily Mail Online,* March 5. On-line: http://www.dailymail.co.uk/sciencetech/article-1157784/Do-mysterious-stones-mark-site-Garden-Eden.html.
2009b *The Genesis Secret.* New York: HarperCollins.
Kolowich, S.
2009 The Fall of an Academic Cyberbully. *The Chronicle of Higher Education* 55/28, March 20, A1. On-line: http://chronicle.com/weekly/v55/i28/28a00101.htm (subscription required for access).
Magness, J.
2007 Has the Tomb of Jesus Been Discovered? *Biblical Archaeology Review,* March 5. On-line: http://www.bib-arch.org/scholars-study/jesus-tomb-02.asp.

Mazar, E.
    2009   The Wall That Nehemiah Built. *Biblical Archaeology Review* 35/02, March/April. On-line: http://www.bib-arch.org/bar/article.asp?PubID =BSBA&Volume=35&Issue=2&ArticleID=7.

Shanks, H.
    2008   Hershel Shanks: Trial Reaching Climax? *Biblical Archaeology Review*, February 6. On-line: http://www.bib-arch.org/debates/antiquities-trial -01.asp.

    2012   "Brother of Jesus" Inscription Is Authentic! *Biblical Archaeology Review* 38/4 (July–August) 26–33, 62–65.

Shaywitz, D. A.
    2009   When Science Is a Siren Song. *Washington Post*, March 14, A15.

Simon, B.
    2008   The Stone Box and Jesus' Brother's Bones. CBS news broadcast, March 23. Accessed November 2, 2010. Available on-line: http://www .cbsnews.com/stories/2008/03/20/60minutes/main3954980.shtml.

Thomas, S.
    2006   Digging for History at Gobekli Tepe, Turkey. *The First Post.* October 17. On-line: http://www.thefirstpost.co.uk/1410,features,history-in -turkey-gobekli-tepe-garden-eden-klaus-schmidt.

Dealing with the Media
Response to Eric H. Cline

JOE ZIAS

Eric Cline's opening paragraph includes an alarming quotation from David Shaywitz's *Washington Post* op-ed statement: "more than half of published scientific research findings today cannot be replicated by other researchers." I would argue that the percentage of faulty claims is even higher in today's world of biblical archaeology, where so many clamor for media recognition and instant acclaim, if not also fame and fortune. The media are replete with bogus claims of arks, the tomb of Jesus, the blood of Jesus, and John the Baptist's baptismal site, to name just a few. None of these has any creditability among serious scholars, as many of the papers in this volume explain. Thus, Cline's 2007 *Boston Globe* op-ed piece (Cline 2007a), which called on archaeologists "to reclaim our field from the pseudo-archaeologists and junk scientists," is a declaration long overdue. For the past three decades I have been arguing the same with little or no success, telling colleagues that a lesson should have been taken from the days of Eric von Däniken.[1] Von Däniken is an out-and-out hustler, without any formal education, who once did prison time for embezzlement. We archaeologists initially ignored him, believing that no one would be "dumb enough" to accept his foolishness. We were wrong, for he has become today synonymous with archaeology for many.

When I read Eric Cline's excellent book, *From Eden to Exile: Unraveling Mysteries of the Bible* (2007b), in which he exposes much of the pseudoarchaeology that has plagued the profession, my one criticism was that he was not aggressive enough in criticizing the media and scholars who abuse it. His well-founded attack on the "evangelical biblical maximalists," whose archaeological/scientific paradigm reminds one of the phrase "God said it, I believe it, and that settles it," was one of the strongest arguments in the book. Unfortunately, the

---

1. Part of von Däniken's best-selling and heavily plagiarized book *Chariots of the Gods?* (1970) was written while he was incarcerated. He exploits well-known archaeological data to substantiate his belief that aliens were responsible for many impressive archaeological discoveries.

pseudoarchaeologists still receive the lion's share of the media attention. Now Cline's essay in this volume makes amends, in my opinion, by presenting a more aggressive and critical challenge to the media and to those few self-serving colleagues who abuse the media. One of Cline's statements in his oral presentation of the paper at the Duke conference (but not published here) in particular stands out: "My personal feeling is that while I did not get into the field of archaeology to become a policeman, if that's what it takes to protect the integrity of our field, then so be it." This sentence should be a call to colleagues that, unless we accept Eric Cline's position, it will only get worse.

I also want to note that Cline's reference in his oral presentation to *Biblical Archaeology Review (BAR)* as "a privately produced publication with Shanks reporting only what he wants to" is well taken, for many scholars regard *BAR* as having contributed to many of the current credibility problems of biblical archaeology. The so-called "updates" in *BAR* are usually out of date or ignore important issues, despite Shanks's declaration (1975) to "further the interests of archaeology" and be committed to "accuracy and things interesting." By his selectivity, this commitment to accuracy seems often to be a chimera.

I could give my own examples, to add to what Cline has provided, of media distortions and selective reporting; but perhaps my response to his essay will be more useful if I draw on my experiences to provide suggestions for what scholars can do to avoid or remedy many of the problems they face in dealing with the media.

Where Does One Go from Here?
Some Guidelines for Scholars

1. A famous newsroom maxim cautions reporters as follows: "If your mother says she loves you, check it out." This is even more important, in today's world of New Journalism, for biblical scholars asked to appear in the media, especially television documentaries. Scholars should ask to see the script and then the final proposal when it is available. All too often the script is written by someone outside the profession with no experience in or knowledge of archaeology, often with embarrassing results. Every poorly conceived documentary produced lessens the chance of a later, well-conceived documentary on that topic; film producers will rightfully say "It's already been done before." The bad often drive out the good, as shown by the many substandard documentaries being produced today.

2. Scholars should search the internet for everyone with whom they will be working on a documentary. If their resumes are not posted online, they should be requested so their qualifications and experience can be checked. Recently, I was contacted by a producer doing something on the Essene *War Scroll* from Qumran, and he was not all that forthcoming

about his past experience. By researching him him, I learned that much of his experience had been in the world of producing pornography.

3. Scholars should insist on knowing who else will appear in the program, for this will provide a clue about the real intention/agenda of the producer.

4. Scholars should be paid for their efforts. The "holy mantra" in the film business is "this is a low-budget production." If a project is truly that low budget, then it probably cannot be made. Scholars should be wary of the oft-repeated claim that a project is "investigative journalism" (that is, "I ain't gonna pay you because it's news"), which is a ploy used even by some high-profile film makers as a ruse not to pay academics. Many of these documentaries, some with budgets of four to five million dollars, have nothing to do with investigative journalism—and even less to do with biblical archaeology—but are purely commercial enterprises. The film on the Talpiyot Tomb (the so-called "Jesus Tomb"), which did not pay all the scholars who appeared in it, is a good example.[2] To be sure, one never or rarely gets paid for a news broadcast. But scholars must be careful to determine whether an interview is really for a news item. I once traveled to New York along with colleagues to be interviewed for NBC's *Dateline*. The producers claimed that it was a news program, and none of us was paid. I later checked the program's Web site and found that it is not categorized as news but rather "entertainment."

What sort of honorarium should scholars expect? In 2010, free-lance videographers using their own equipment, who are virtually a dime a dozen in the open market, make upwards of $2000 per day. To expect an academic to work for anything less is unjustifiable, although receiving the same fees as a videographer seems unlikely. One way of dealing with this is simply to request that they make a donation to a research fund, which academics can use for their work. This would be a win-win situation for the producers, for they can write it off as a donation at the end of the year.

5. Today many freelance producers and directors are outsourced by some major film companies. These freelancers try to enter the world of documentaries and begin their careers by showing executives in the film business that they can do it for less. Scholars should be wary of working with these independent producers, whose credibility and expertise are often questionable and who cannot guarantee that they will create a quality product. Recently I was asked to work with one of these people and turned him down; he subsequently advertised on Craigslist for an expert on Qumran and secured the services of pseudo-scholar Vendyl Jones and two other virtually unknown people. That is how bad it can get.

---

2. See my critique of the whole "Jesus Tomb" enterprise (2007).

6. Scholars should avoiding falling into the category of Arthur Koestler's "academic whores" (Koestler 1972), willing to appear in each and every documentary as if being on the "screen" will enhance one's career. Based on my three decades of experience in this field, I can attest that appearing in films does little to advance one's professional career. However, it may mean selling a few more books, which is why publishers may pressure academics to participate in these endeavors.

7. Scholars should not sign any release, particularly confidentiality/ non-disclosure agreements, without knowing the goals of a documentary. It is important to say "No, I'm not interested" if it is not clear what the project is all about; otherwise, participation may compromise the integrity of the profession.

8. Scholars should perhaps follow the advice James F. Strange, an archaeologist and a professor at the University of South Florida, who told me that he urges colleagues to tape their interviews and have the producer sign a written agreement that any of a scholar's ideas that remain in the documentary, even if the interview itself ends up on the cuttingroom floor, must be given full attribution in the documentary. This is particularly important in dealing with U.S. film makers, whose highprofile narrators may take a scholar's ideas and use them as their own.

9. Scholars should insist on financial transparency; they should learn who is financing a documentary. This issue is important, unless one is willing to compromise one's integrity and that of the profession by cooperating in endeavors funded by organizations or institutions with which a scholar would not want to be connected.

10 Perhaps scholars should establish their own code of ethics, like the Hippocratic oath in medicine, the ethics code in the legal profession, or the non-obligatory code recently established for students receiving the MBA from Harvard's School of Business.[3] Such a document would provide archaeologists and scholars of biblical, Jewish, and Christian antiquity with guidelines for acting in a responsible and ethical manner.

11. Scholars should subject documentaries to peer review. For a number of years I have been toying with the idea of establishing a small committee of experienced archaeologists and biblical scholars who will critique documentaries and, if they pass accepted academic standards, be given a seal of approval, similar to the American "Good Housekeeping Seal of Approval." The committee would award an ASA (Archaeological Seal of Approval) to worthwhile documentaries. It would decide whether a documentary meets accepted academic standards. This committee, composed of American and Israeli scholars with years of media experience, would provide information to networks about whether a documentary should be broadcast.

---

3. Leslie Wayne, "A Promise to Be Ethical in an Era of Immorality," *New York Times*, May 29, 2009. http://www.nytimes.com/2009/05/30/business/30oath.html?scp=1&sq=mba%20code%20of%20ethics&st=cse.

References

Cline, E. H.
  2007a   Raiders of the Faux Ark. *Boston Globe,* September 30, E1-2.
  2007b   *From Eden to Exile: Unraveling Mysteries of the Bible.* Washington, DC: National Geographic Books.
Däniken, E. von
  1970   *Chariots of the Gods? Unsolved Mysteries from the Past,* trans. M. Heron. New York: Putnam.
Koestler, A.
  1972   *The Call-Girls: A Tragi-comedy with Prologue and Epilogue.* London: Hutchinson.
Shanks, H.
  1975   Introducing BAR. *Biblical Archaeology Review* 1: 16.
Zias, J.
  2007   Viewers Guide to Understanding the Talpiot Tomb "Documentary" to Be Aired on the Discovery Channel: Deconstructing the Second and Hopefully Last Coming of Simcha and the *BAR* Crowd [accessed June 1, 2012]. Online: http://www.joezias.com/tomb.html.

The Talpiyot Tomb and the Bloggers

MARK GOODACRE

An Early Success

When the sensationalist documentary *The Lost Tomb of Jesus* was first broadcast, in a two-hour slot on the Discovery Channel at 9:00 p.m. on March 4, 2007, several bloggers "live blogged" the event (Goodacre 2007b), commenting on the documentary as it aired. By this point, Discovery's publicity machine had already been in full force for several days. The project was launched with a dramatic press conference and two major Web sites, the snazzy "official" site (Talmor Media 2007) as well as Discovery Channel's own site (Discovery Channel 2007–10). Bloggers began commenting on this material as soon as it went public, with all the speed that the still-young medium encourages (Williams 2007a).[1] By the time the documentary aired, the bloggers had already put major question marks against the claims being made by Simcha Jacobovici and the other program makers.

One of the most prominent criticisms, right at the beginning, related to the use of statistics. The case for the identification of the Talpiyot Tomb with the family of Jesus of Nazareth is based largely on statistics. The cluster of names found in this tomb is said to correspond to a remarkable degree with the names of Jesus and his family. Before the documentary had aired, I was highly sceptical of the statistical case (Goodacre 2007a), not least because it appeared to rely on a dubious identification between the name "Mariamēnē" and Mary Magdalene while at the same time failing to take seriously important contrary evidence, "Judas son of Jesus," and ignoring the non-match "Matia."

Simcha Jacobovici had hired a top statistician, though; and surely, he argued, his expertise should be taken seriously. The statistician in

---

1. A companion book for the series was released at the end of February 2007 (Jacobovici and Pellegrino 2007), but it made no impact on the blogosphere in this early period. The instant and immediate access to the key materials made possible on the internet effectively marginalized the book's contribution, though in due course highly critical reviews of the book did appear; see especially Reed 2007.

question was Dr. Andrey Feuerverger, Professor of Mathematics and Statistics at the University of Toronto. I wrote the following:

> Clearly he knows *a lot* more about statistics than most of us, and I would not dream of trying to second guess him. But he revealed a very important piece of information at the press conference, that he is not an expert on the New Testament or archaeological data, so he was *working with the data given to him* by the programme makers. The relevance of this is that a significant and fatal bias was introduced into the analysis before it had even begun.
>
> One can view the data that was given to Feuerverger on the Discovery Web site, in the PDF packet of documentation, where the grounds for the statistical analysis are given. It is clear from this that the task he was given was to work out the probability of a certain cluster of names occurring, where in each case all known examples of the given name in the given period were divided into all known naming possibilities in the given period. And the names he worked with were Jesus son of Joseph, Mariamne, Maria and Joseph. The name Matia was initially factored in too, and then removed "since he is not explicatively mentioned in the Gospels". But the problem is not just that Matia is not mentioned as a family member in the Gospels, it is that the greater the number of non-matches, the less impressive the cluster becomes. Or, to put it another way, it stops being a cluster of striking names when the cluster is diluted with non-matches. Mariamne needs to be taken out of the positive calculation and instead treated as a non-match; Matia needs to be treated as a second non-match; Judas son of Jesus needs to be treated as contradictory evidence. These three pieces of data together detract radically from the impressiveness of the given cluster. (Goodacre 2007a, referencing Discovery Channel 2007–10)

In an attempt to make the point by extending and reapplying an analogy that Simcha Jacobovici was fond of, I continued:

> At the risk of labouring the point, let me attempt to explain my concerns by using the analogy of which the film-makers are so fond, the Beatles analogy. This analogy works by saying that if in 2,000 years a tomb was discovered in Liverpool that featured the names John, Paul and George, we would not immediately conclude that we had found the tomb of the Beatles. But if we also found so distinctive a name as Ringo, then we would be interested. Jacobovici claims that the "Ringo" in this tomb is Mariamēnē, whom he interprets as Mary Magdalene and as Jesus's wife, which is problematic (see Mariamne and the "Jesus Family Tomb" and below). What we actually have is the equivalent of a tomb with the names John, Paul, George, Martin, Alan, and Ziggy. We might well say, "Perhaps the 'Martin' is George Martin, and so this is a match!" or "Perhaps John Lennon had a son called Ziggy we have not previously heard about" but this would be

special pleading and we would rightly reject such claims. A cluster of names is only impressive when it is a cluster that is uncontaminated by non-matches and contradictory evidence.

In short, including Mariamne and leaving out Matia and Judas son of Jesus is problematic for any claim to be made about the remaining cluster. All data must be included. *You cannot cherry pick or manipulate your data before doing your statistical analysis.* (Goodacre 2007a, referencing Goodacre 2007c and Goodacre 2007d and links found there).

This post appeared on Thursday, March 1, three days before the documentary aired. The date stamp of 1:45 a.m. is typical in the bloggers' world, in which speedy publication is key; and losing sleep can be the only way of ensuring that a post has the timely impact that makes it worthwhile. There will always be time for the measured, assured, detailed response in due course. On this occasion, the timeliness of the post contributed to the momentum that was building all over the blogosphere (Williams 2007b, 2007c). Within 24 hours, I was able to post a follow-up (D'Mello 2007a) based on a helpful but technical e-mail from Joe D'Mello, who was concerned about some of the claims being made on the Discovery Channel Web site.

D'Mello was offering a fresh perspective on the data. Where I and others (Pahl 2007) were questioning the data that had been fed to Feuerverger, D'Mello could see that there were problems also in the interpretation of the statistical calculations. D'Mello was disputing the following claim that appeared prominently on the Discovery Channel Web site:

A statistical study commissioned by the broadcasters (Discovery Channel / Vision Canada / C4 UK) concludes that the probability factor is 600 to 1 in favor of this tomb being the tomb of Jesus of Nazareth and his family.

D'Mello was clear that this conclusion was not justified by the data. I invited him to write a guest post for me (D'Mello 2007a); and at the same time he wrote to Feuerverger and Discovery. Within two days, now the day of the broadcast itself, D'Mello had secured important corrections from Feuerverger, including the following:

In this respect I now believe that I should not assert any conclusions connecting this tomb with any hypothetical one of the NT family. The interpretation of the computation should be that it is estimating the probability of there having been another family at the time whose tomb this might be, under certain specified assumptions. (D'Mello 2007b).

Again, I published the material in my blog (D'Mello 2007b), and again it was not the end of the story. Within a week, by March 10, D'Mello had secured an agreement that there should be an adjustment on the

Discovery Web site itself (D'Mello 2007c), a correction that duly appeared three days later, on March 13 (D'Mello 2007d) and then throughout the site by the end of the week, on March 16 (D'Mello 2007e). The most significant of the changes was the following one (D'Mello 2007e), straightforwardly represented in synopsis format:

Original Claim	*Revised Claim*
Dr. Andrey Feuerverger, professor of statistics & mathematics at the University of Toronto, has concluded a high statistical probability that the Talpiyot Tomb is the JESUS FAMILY TOMB.	Dr. Andrey Feuerverger, professor of statistics at the University of Toronto, has concluded (subject to the stated historical assumptions) that it is unlikely that an equally "surprising" cluster of names would have arisen by chance under purely random sampling.

The second statement is, of course, significantly more cautious and nuanced than the first.[2] It is a small adjustment, but it is significant; and it is a change that came about because of sustained, accurate and speedy blog activity.

After the major flurry of activity surrounding the release of *The Lost Tomb of Jesus* in February and March 2007, the blog activity slowed down; and aside from occasional posts, the issue was forgotten, by many, for the rest of the year.[3] Controversy reignited briefly in January 2008 as the result of the "Third Princeton Theological Seminary Symposium on Jewish Views of the Afterlife and Burial Practices in Second Temple Judaism: Evaluating the Talpiot Tomb in Context." This conference took place in Jerusalem in January 2008; and although there was no significant representation from the blogging community,[4] the blogs subsequently became the means by which a major statement was

---

2. Although the original version of the statement disappeared from the Discovery Web site, it can still be read in Jacobovici and Pellegrino 2007 (p. 114): "When he did all that, he got a 'P factor' (probability factor) of 600 to one in favor of the tomb belonging to Jesus of Nazareth." The claim is also present, though less clearly, on the official site (Talmor Media 2007; see on-line http://www .jesusfamilytomb.com/evidence/probability/jesus_equation.html). Later writers assumed that the original statement "came to be attributed to Feuerverger" (Lutgen 2009) rather than that Feuerverger himself changed his mind in the light of the discussion in the blogosphere.

3. Activity on the blogs briefly resumed in order to comment on new articles: Evans and Feldman 2007 (comment in Goodacre 2007h), and Kilty and Elliott 2007 (comment in Goodacre 2007i, with further references there).

4. Occasional bloggers Stephen Pfann (Pfann 2007–8) and James Tabor (Tabor 2007–10) were present, but they do not appear to have been invited in their specific capacity as bloggers. Tabor was one of the major contributors to the original documentary and a key voice speaking in favor of the identification of the Talpiyot Tomb with Jesus' family.

disseminated (Aviam et al. 2008; Duke University Religion Department 2008).

Meanwhile, the statistical case was now being properly written up by the scholar at the center of the discussion. Andrey Feuerverger produced a detailed, peer-reviewed article (Feuerverger 2008a and 2008b) in which some of the claims were more nuanced even if many of the historical problems remained.[5] There were informed responses from other experts including a well-informed, critical refutation by Randy Ingermanson (Ingermanson 2008a and 2008b). The blogs occasionally reported this activity (for example, Tabor 2008), but the intensity of posts that had marked the earlier controversy had now dissipated, apparently for the long term.

But in the early days of the controversy over the Talpiyot Tomb, when energy levels were high and the media attention unrelenting, it is worth remembering the important contributions made by the academic blogs, not least because it illustrates one of the upsides of the blogging phenomenon. By providing informed comment in an up-to-the-minute way, the blogs can, on occasions like this, hold the media to account, exposing problematic claims and faulty logic,[6] at just the moment when uninformed but intelligent members of the public are looking for reliable comment. It was this combination of speed and accuracy that made the impact of blogging so significant. The reactions were instant, at the very time that the eye of the media was on the blogging community and when Discovery wanted to avoid as much as it could of the criticism that was building up against them. The reactions were informed and accurate, and the blogging revolution was encouraging connections between biblical scholars and statisticians.

A Change in Tone

This early success, whereby accurate and knowledgeable blogging led to changes in several of the claims made on the Discovery Channel Web

---

5. Unfortunately, Feuerverger's article apparently remains ignorant of some of the important discussions that took place in the blogs in the year before the publication of the article, and his article is much weaker because of it. His discussion of the Mariamēnē inscription (Feuerverger 2008a: 6–7), for example, does not take into consideration Pfann's suggestion that the reading should be *Mariame kai Mara* (Pfann 2007), and it accepts the specious identification of this ossuary with Mary Magdalene (Feuerverger 2008: 20–21) on the basis of the misreading of Francois Bovon's article on the *Acts of Philip* (Bovon 2003). I pointed out the error in my blog (Goodacre 2007f), and Bovon himself later repudiated the identification (Bovon 2007). Feuerverger's presentation of "a brief NT genealogy" (2008: 13–14) is full of undocumented assertions of dubious historical value.

6. This has been a valuable emphasis in Jim Davila's *Paleojudaica* blog (Davila 2003–10). Davila writes, for example, that "All too frequently, discussion of media and other public treatments of biblical studies requires the correction of serious errors" (Davila 2005b); see also Davila 2005a.

site, was symptomatic of a larger trend according to which the early, bold, and far-reaching statements gave way to something much more cautious. Indeed, the Discovery Channel appeared progressively to distance themselves from claims that at first they had embraced. The press conference on Monday, February 26, 2009 (still available to view online at Discovery Channel 2007–10), at which the case was first made, showed a remarkable degree of confidence in the importance of the alleged discovery. The president and general manager of the Discovery Channel began the press conference by announcing:

> You are joining us here for what might be one of the most important archaeological finds in human history. In the hills of Jerusalem, archaeologists have discovered a tomb, a two thousand year old tomb, which contains significant forensic evidence, and some potentially historic consequences. . . . I would like to briefly discuss how this momentous find came about and how it comes to be before you today (Discovery Channel 2007–10).

And James Cameron, who came to the microphone next, told the story of his involvement with the documentary, which he went on to produce. He said, "literally this is the biggest archaeology story of the century." And so it goes on.[7] But this robust beginning gave way, quite quickly, to a more cautious tone.

The reaction in the blogosphere, as well as in other media outlets, demonstrated very quickly that the vast majority of scholars assessing the case were not finding it convincing. Unlike Cameron, who said that as a layman he had found the case "pretty darn compelling" (Discovery Channel 2007–10), the experts were finding the case completely unpersuasive.[8] The statistical case was crumbling as scholars began to notice how much weight had been placed on the claim that "Mariamēnou Mara" was a unique way of identifying Mary Magdalene, a claim that appeared to be based on a misreading of François Bovon's analysis of the *Acts of Philip*. I called attention to this before the documentary aired (Goodacre 2007f), and others made similar points—including Tony Chartrand-Burke, whose *Apocryphicity* blog specialized in noncanonical Christian materials (Chartrand-Burke 2007, and Richard Bauckham (Bauckham 2007).

Bauckham himself is not a blogger, but he was guest-posting on his colleague Jim Davila's blog, *Paleojudaica* (Davila 2003–10), an ideal

---

7. Notice similar comments by James Cameron in the preface to Jacobovici and Pellegrino 2007.

8. The major exceptions here were James Tabor, an enthusiastic supporter of the identification (see p. 59 n. 4 above), and James Charlesworth. Charlesworth was at the press conference and was quoted in the press as saying that "a very good claim could be made that this was Jesus' clan." He later clarified in a statement that, by "clan," he meant "extended family group" (Goodacre 2007e and relevant links there).

forum for this kind of contribution. *Paleojudaica* has the greatest pedigree of all the biblical studies blogs;[9] it has a "no-frills" approach, with
news reports and occasional critical comments designed to hold the
media to account. Once again, bloggers were adding guest posts from
experts to enhance their own efforts, and the effect was pretty dramatic.

When the documentary aired on Sunday, March 4, Discovery added
an extra program that followed on immediately afterwards—a studio
discussion, hosted by Ted Koppel, called *The Lost Tomb of Jesus: A
Critical Look*. The first half of the program was a debate between Simcha Jacobovici and James Tabor, representing the case for the defense,
and Jonathan Reed and William Dever, representing the case for the
prosecution. Jacobovici was fairly defensive throughout, perhaps not
surprisingly in view of some hostile questions from Koppel, who suggested on several occasions that he had quoted people out of context.
There were barbed comments too from Jonathan Reed, who called the
program "archaeoporn." The second half of the program was devoted to
"religious responses" and included Darrell Bock and David O'Connell
alongside Jacobovici and Tabor. Some at the time saw the scheduling
of this program as an opportunity for Discovery to imply some critical
distancing from the claims made in the documentary, claims that they
had been heartily endorsing only a week earlier. When the first repeat
of *The Lost Tomb of Jesus* was dropped from Discovery's schedules, it
began to look as if they were indeed feeling less confident about the
documentary than they had at first.

It was not only the bloggers, then, who were playing a role in holding the program makers to account. Other key events included the appearance of Eric Meyers with Simcha Jacobovici, engaging in heated yet
reasoned debate, on the Diane Rehm show on March 5,[10] the morning
after the documentary aired. In only the recent past, radio appearances
and newspaper op-eds would have been the only major public venues for
providing critiques of programs like this. Now the blogging revolution
had changed all that; and the reactions were thorough, detailed, varied,
and fast.

The Talpiyot Tomb provided the first major test for the bloggers in
the area of academic biblical studies and its related disciplines, and it is
a test that they passed with flying colors. The contrast with the earlier
and similar story, the James Ossuary, only a few years earlier in 2002,
is telling. At that point, blogging was only in its infancy, and in biblical

---

9. *AKMA's Random Thoughts* (Adam 2003–10) predates *Paleojudaica* by several
months, but its subject matter ranges widely, and Adam only occasionally posts on
biblical studies.

10. A recording of the interview can be found on the official Web site of *The
Diane Rehm Show*: http://thedianerehmshow.org/shows/2007-03-05/jesus-family
-tomb-story.

studies it was nonexistent.[11] The James Ossuary story took some time to unravel; and, although furiously debated on the then-more-popular e-lists,[12] the latter did not attract the same degree of expertise or the same degree of publicity now reached by the blogs. Indeed, two occasional bloggers were themselves involved directly with the Talpiyot Tomb project: Darrell Bock, who was highly critical of the documentary's claims, and James Tabor, who remained sympathetic and provided a sane if lonely voice speaking up for Jacobovici.

When Bloggers Fail to Make an Impact

It may be a little too easy to celebrate blogging successes in relation to this story. This was an occasion when several expert voices spoke up quickly and accurately and created a strong wall of opinion that had the effect of seriously undermining the claims made by the filmmakers. But it is not always so straightforward. Indeed, the kinds of successes witnessed on this occasion are the exception rather than the rule. It is much more common for academic bloggers to be ignored by the media, even when they are pointing out errors and inaccuracies that are actually embarrassing those making the claims. A clear example of this occurred in relation to a lengthy and fairly detailed blog post I wrote entitled "Jesus Family Tomb Website: Errors and Inaccuracies" (Goodacre 2007g).

I published the post on March 11, 2007, a week after the documentary aired, and it took some time to write. It was one of those posts with which other bloggers will be familiar, the post that keeps expanding and that makes one ask repeatedly, "Is this really worth the effort?" The post concerns the "official" Web site for *The Lost Tomb of Jesus* at www.jesusfamilytomb.com (Talmor Media 2007). This Web site, more slick, more snazzy, and far more detailed than Discovery's site (Discovery Channel 2007–10), had gone on-line at the same time, the end of February. But unlike Discovery's site, it was riddled with errors and inaccuracies.

Some of the errors were simply careless and sloppy, such as confusing *Acts of Philip* with the *Gospel of Philip*, mistaking "AC" for "AD," and mentioning Jesus at age thirteen being with "local rabbis" rather than at age twelve being at the Jerusalem temple. Others, though, were more substantial. Several claims about the Talpiyot Tomb discoveries were

---

11. See previous note. Jim Davila's *Paleojudaica*, the pioneer, began in March 2003. My *NT Blog* began six months later in September 2003, though then under the name *NT Gateway Weblog*. The *NT Gateway Weblog* and the *NT Blog* became separate entities in February 2009.

12. For an annotated list of academic e-lists in the area of biblical studies, see my *NT Gateway: E-Lists*, on-line: http://www.ntgateway.com/tools-and -resources/e-lists/.

so badly stated that they amounted to misleading information, such as
the assertion that one of the ossuaries actually read "Mary Magdalene,"
alongside other familiar difficulties such as the misreading of François
Bovon's analysis of Mary in the *Acts of Philip*.

The most remarkable elements on this site, though, were not so
much these misguided and inaccurate statements, but entire sections
consisting of historical fiction. The site claims, for example, that the
Gospel of Thomas was "suppressed by Christian authorities due to the
status allotted to Mary of Magadala [*sic*] as master" and that "the Essene Gospel of Peace" is "one ancient manuscript discovered in the Secret Archives of the Vatican." Perhaps the most striking example of this
type of material is a section of the site headed "The Gospels Nazarene:
The Gospel of the Holy Twelve," which is breathtaking on a site aspir-
ing to be doing something resembling academic history:

> The Gospel of the Nazarenes or the Gospel of the Holy Twelve is con-
> sidered to be the original Gospel or one of the first complete written
> manuscripts of the original word of Jesus. The term "Nazarene" is
> used by some to refer to early Jewish followers of Christianity in con-
> nection with the ancient Essene sect of Judaism which Jesus is often
> associated with. The original Gospels of Nazarene are said to have
> been written by St. John, who passed the manuscript along to a trusted
> friend in 70 A.D. following his arrest.
>
> In the nineteenth century, the Gospel of the Holy Twelve was re-
> discovered by a friar. However, since its exposure to Church Author-
> ities in Rome, it has remained hidden in the Vatican archive, which
> some say is due to newly discovered content that would discredit the
> Church and the Council of Nicea (Talmor Media 2007).

There is, of course, no historically reliable information here of any kind.

Since it was greatly to the discredit of the "Jesus Family Tomb" project that material such as this appeared on their site, I thought it worthwhile to draw attention to it. I documented each of the errors and inaccuracies that I could find, linking to the page in question, quoting the
problematic material, and explaining where the errors lay. I suspected
that a still-more-careful reading would reveal many more errors, inaccuracies, and fictions; but my list gave the site's authors—I thought—a
head start on where to find the most egregious and embarrassing difficulties. I hoped that they would take the list seriously and amend their
site accordingly. They did not. Each error still remains on the site to
this day.[13]

This somewhat depressing example of blogging without impact provides a sobering contrast to the successful blogging surveyed earlier.

---

13. James Tabor (personal communication, March 13, 2007) noted that he had reported this list to those responsible for the site but no adjustments were made, either
then or in the subsequent three years.

Perhaps it could be said that examples such as this remind bloggers of the potential for wasting time on sites that are driven by commercial concerns and that are uninterested in honest intellectual engagement. Academics all too easily fall into the naive belief that people will want to set the record straight, that they will want to eliminate disreputable and ignorant statements, and that accuracy, precision, and nuance matter.[14] One cynical comment on the blog post in question noted that, while the link to the *Gospel of Philip* was inaccurate, the links to "Buy the DVD" and "Buy the book" were working without trouble.

Nevertheless, posts such as this still have value. When a glitzy site retains misinformation on a large scale, there is value in the academic bloggers' publicly setting out the errors and inaccuracies involved. If "googlization" democratizes the process of attaining knowledge, one of the values of the process is that any researcher looking for material on "the Jesus family tomb" will quickly come into contact not only with the glitzy, commercial, error-ridden official site but also the mundane, noncommercial, accurate academic blogs.

As in other areas—politics, religion, journalism—the blogs have empowered experts who have something intelligent, well researched, and cogent to say. When we are using the medium thoughtfully, they can place us in a surprisingly influential position, even when those with the money, the staff, the time, and the publicity might at first seem to be formidable opponents. In spite of our failures, it is a responsibility worth taking seriously.

---

14. Cf. Paula Fredriksen on the difficulties she and others had in corresponding with Icon Productions about the script for the *The Passion of the Christ* (directed by Mel Gibson in 2003): "In retrospect, we also functioned with a naïveté that is peculiar to educators: the belief that, once an error is made plain, a person will prefer the truth" (Fredriksen 2003: 27; see Goodacre 2004 for context).

References

Adam, A. K. M.
2003–10 *AKMA's Random Thoughts*. On-line: http://akma.disseminary.org/.
Aviam, M.; Graham Brock, A.; Dobbs-Allsopp, F. W.; Elledge, C.; Gibson, S.; Hachlili, R.; Kloner, A.; Magness, J.; McDonald, L.; Meyers, E. M.; Pfann, S.; Price, J.; Rollston, C.; Segal, A.; Seow, C.-L.; Zias, J.; Zissu, B.
2008 The Talpiot Tomb Controversy Revisited. *NT Blog*, January 21. On-line: http://ntweblog.blogspot.com/2008/01/talpiot-tomb-controversy -revisited.html.
Bauckham, R.
2007 The Alleged "Jesus Family Tomb." *Paleojudaica*, March 2. On-line: http://paleojudaica.blogspot.com/2007_02_25_paleojudaica_archive. html#117283555211644646.

Bovon, F.
2003   Mary Magdalene in the *Acts of Philip*. Pp. 75–89 in *Which Mary? The Marys of Early Christian Tradition*, ed. F. S. Jones. Leiden: Brill.
2007   "The Tomb of Jesus." *SBL Forum*. On-line: http://sbl-site.org/publications/article.aspx?articleId=656.

Chartrand-Burke, T.
2007   The Jesus Tomb and the Acts of Philip. *Apocryphicity*, February 26. On-line:http://www.tonyburke.ca/apocryphicity/2007/02/26/the-jesus-tomb-and-the-acts-of-philip/.

Davila, J. R.
2003–10 *Paleojudaica*. On-line: http://paleojudaica.blogspot.com/.
2005a   Assimilated to the Blogosphere: Blogging Ancient Judaism. *SBL Forum*. On-line: http://sbl-site.org/Article.aspx?ArticleID=390.
2005b   Enter the Bibliobloggers. Paper presented at the Society of Biblical Literature Annual Meeting, Computer Assisted Research Group, November 20. Available on-line: http://www.st-andrews.ac.uk/divinity/rt/otp/abstracts/enterthebibliobloggers/.

D'Mello, J.
2007a   The Correct Interpretation of Dr. Andrey Feuerverger's 1:600 Odds Calculation. *NT Blog*, March 2. On-line: http://ntweblog.blogspot.com/2007/03/correct-interpretation-of-dr-andrey.html.
2007b   The "Jesus Family Tomb" Statistics: Further Developments. *NT Blog*, March 4. On-line: http://ntweblog.blogspot.com/2007/ 03/jesus-family-tomb-statistics-further.html.
2007c   Adjustments to Discovery Website Statistics Claims. *NT Blog*, March 10. On-line: http://ntweblog.blogspot.com/2007/03/adjustments-to-discovery-website.html.
2007d   Correction on Discovery Tomb Website. *NT Blog*, March 13. On-line: http://ntweblog.blogspot.com/2007/03/correction-on-discovery-tomb-website.html.
2007e   Discovery Website Adjusts Tomb Claims. *NT Blog*, March 16. On-line: http://ntweblog.blogspot.com/2007/03/discovery-website-adjusts-tomb-claims.html.

Discovery Channel
2007–10 *The Lost Tomb of Jesus*. On-line: http://dsc.discovery.com/convergence/tomb/tomb.html.

Duke University Religion Department
2008   The Talpiot Tomb Controversy Revisited. *Duke University Religion Department Blog* January 21, 2008. http://dukereligion.blogspot.com/2008/01/talpiot-tomb-controversy-revisited.html

Evans, C., and Feldman, S.
2007   The Tomb of Jesus? Wrong on Every Count. *Biblical Archaeology Review*. March 11. On-line: http://www.bib-arch.org/debates/jesus-tomb-02-b.asp

Feuerverger, A.
2008a   Statistical Analysis of an Archaeological Find. *Annals of Applied Statistics* 2: 3–54.
2008b   Rejoinder of: Statistical Analysis of an Archeological Find. *Annals of Applied Statistics* 2: 99–112.

Fredriksen, P.
2003   Mad Mel: The Gospel according to Gibson. *The New Republic*, July 28 and August 4: 25–29.
Goodacre, M.
2004   The Stolen Script. *NT Blog*, February 25. On-line: http://ntweblog .blogspot.com/2004/02/stolen-script.html.
2007a   The Statistical Case for the Identity of the "Jesus Family Tomb." *NT Blog*, March 1. On-line: http://ntweblog.blogspot.com/2007/03/statis-tical-case-for-identity-of-jesus.html.
2007b   The Lost Tomb of Jesus: Live Blog. *NT Blog.* March 4. On-line: http:// ntweblog.blogspot.com/2007/03/lost-tomb-of-jesus-documentary-live .html.
2007c   The Beatles and the Jesus Family Tomb. *NT Blog*, February 27. On-line: http://ntweblog.blogspot.com/2007/02/beatles-and-jesus-family -tomb.html.
2007d   Mariamne and the "Jesus Family Tomb." *NT Blog*, February 28. On-line: http://ntweblog.blogspot.com/2007/02/mariamne-and-jesus -family-tomb.html.
2007e   James Charlesworth on the "Jesus Family Tomb": Follow-up. *NT Blog*, March 10. On-line: http://ntweblog.blogspot.com/2007/03/james -charlesworth-on-jesus-family-tomb_10.html.
2007f   Mariamne, Mary Magdalene and Mary of Bethany. *NT Blog*, March 11. On-line: http://ntweblog.blogspot.com/2007/03/mariamne-mary -magdalene-and-mary-of.html.
2007g   Jesus Family Tomb Website: Errors and Inaccuracies. *NT Blog*, March 11. On-line: http://ntweblog.blogspot.com/2007/03/jesus-family-tomb -website-errors-and.html.
2007h   New Article on the Talpiot Tomb. *NT Blog*, May 15. On-line: http://ntweblog.blogspot.com/2007/05/new-article-on-talpiot-tomb .html.
2007i   Talpiot Tomb Statistics Article. *NT Blog*, September 10. On-line: http://ntweblog.blogspot.com/2007/09/talpiot-tomb-statistics-article .html.
Ingermanson, R.
2008a   Analysis of Andrey Feuerverger's Article on the Jesus Family Tomb. *Ingermanson.com.* On-line: http://www.ingermanson.com/jesus/art/ stats3.php.
2008b   Discussion of: Statistical Analysis of an Archaeological Find. *Annals of Applied Statistics* 2: 84–90.
Jacobovici, S., and Pellegrino, C.
2007   *The Jesus Family Tomb: The Discovery, the Investigation, and the Ev-idence That Could Change History.* New York: HarperCollins.
Kilty, K. T., and Elliott, M.
2007   Probability, Statistics and the Talpiot Tomb. June 10. On-line: http:// www.lccc.wy.edu/Media/Website%20Resources/documents/ Education%20Natural%20and%20Social%20Sciences/tomb.pdf.
Lutgen, J.
2009   The Talpiot Tomb: What Are the Odds? *Bible and Interpretation.* On-line: http://www.bibleinterp.com/articles/tomb357926.shtml.

Pahl, M.
    2007   The "Jesus Tomb." *The Stuff of Earth*, February 26 [accessed February 26, 2007]. On-line: http://michaelpahl.blogspot.com/2007/02/jesus-tomb.html.

Pfann, S.
    2007   Mary Magdalene Is Now Missing: A Corrected Reading of Ossuaries CJO 701 and 108. On-line: http://www.uhl.ac/MariameAndMartha.pdf.
    2007–8 *The View from Jerusalem.* On-line: http://www.uhl.ac/blog/.

Reed, J.
    2007   Review of Simcha Jacobovici and Charles Pellegrino, *The Jesus Family Tomb: The Discovery, the Investigation, and the Evidence That Could Change History. Review of Biblical Literature.* On-line: http://www.bookreviews.org/bookdetail.asp?TitleID=5934.

Tabor, J.
    2007–10 *TaborBlog*: The Talpiot Jesus Family Tomb Category. On-line: http://jamestabor.com/category/talpiot-jesus-family-tomb/
    2008   Feuerverger's Paper on Talpiot Tomb Statistics Published. *TaborBlog*, April 6. On-line: http://jamestabor.com/2008/04/06/feuervergers-paper-on-talpiot-tomb-statistics-published/.

Talmor Media
    2007   *Jesus Tomb *Official Site* The Lost Tomb of Jesus.* On-line: http://www.jesusfamilytomb.com/.

Williams, T.
    2007a The Jesus/Talpiot Tomb: Around the Blogosphere. *Codex: Biblical Studies Blog*, February 26. On-line: http://biblical-studies.ca/blog/2007/02/26/the-jesustalpiot-tomb-around-the-blogosphere/.
    2007b Jesus/Talpiot Tomb: Thursday Roundup. *Codex: Biblical Studies Blog*, March 1. On-line: http://biblical-studies.ca/blog/2007/03/01/jesustalpiot-tomb-thursday-roundup/.
    2007c Jesus/Talpiot Tomb: Monday Update. *Codex: Biblical Studies Blog*, March 5. On-line: http://biblical-studies.ca/blog/2007/03/05/jesustalpiot-tomb-monday-update/.

From Ossuary Epigraphs
to Flickering Pixels
A Response to Mark Goodacre

A. K. M. Adam

Mark Goodacre's excellent presentation on the role of bloggers in the debate over the Talpiyot Tomb offers a helpful insight into one scholar's experience in pushing back against the mudslide of errors in popular media treatment of an archaeological controversy.

I would like to add to his account at a couple of points. First, he assesses his own lack of influence far too harshly when he describes his "Jesus Family Tomb Website: Errors and Inaccuracies" blog post (Goodacre 2007) as a failure. No one could reasonably fault him for others' ignoring his careful work on Talpiyot inaccuracies. But second, I would like to underscore a point that Mark made in passing, namely, that while he led the way as an on-line Talpiyot skeptic, he was accompanied and supported by a crowd of responsible scholars all along. I say this not to diminish Mark's importance but to call our attention to one element of on-line scholarship that often escapes notice: the influence and value of an on-line presence increases as it extends outward through interconnected nodes. Even as Mark's presentation concentrated on his own reporting, the value of his reports increased with every link that another scholar made to Mark's Web site. This is one way Google recognizes and ranks the pages that it finds; if Google's spiders detect a number of people who agree with Mark and link to his page, Mark's page becomes that much more prominent and rises in Google's rankings. By the same token, if we all decline to link to the *Jesus Family Tomb* site, Google interprets that lack of linkage as a sign that the site is less important; it then sinks in Google's rankings. The expressed support of Mark's colleagues raises his Web page to prominence, even if the rest of us do not

Author's note: I want thank Carol and Eric Meyers, Erin Darby, and all involved in gathering this conference.

contribute specific critiques of inaccurate archaeological claims, and even if popular media do not notice.

Moreover, the more scholars who participate in on-line interaction, the richer will be the pool of available examples of technical reasoning for our students and for our broader audiences to read. That's especially valuable because, despite the hundreds of years of hermeneutical discourse since Schleiermacher, what we actually *do* as archaeological interpreters and as biblical interpreters still remains under-theorized and hard to understand. We need only look to our students' papers for evidence; they often have a very difficult time writing an exegetical paper, no matter how many books we give them, no matter how many step-by-step guides we provide. The capacity to interpret responsibly is something that we have picked up by banging our heads against it persistently, until gradually our minds take on the contours of a biblical scholar's mind or an archaeologist's mind. But outsiders frequently find mystifying the processes and logics by which we form our conclusions. An on-line presence such as Mark's blog, like the blogs of many of our colleagues, can helpfully display the thinking-through process that grounds our assessments of phenomena such as the Talpiyot Tomb. If we can point students and broader audiences toward that sort of informal technical discussion, we can perhaps give the world a clearer sense of how archaeologists and biblical scholars work through their interpretive problems.

But the more important point of my response to Mark's presentation concerns its somewhat limited field of view. Although he titled his presentation "The Talpiyot Tomb and the Bloggers," he tells us mostly about *one* blog: his own. Now, his blog gave us admirable insight into his thoughts and actions as the Talpiyot controversy unfolded, but blogs constitute only one of many different digital media. The transforming shift that accompanies the advent of digital communication technology impinges on archaeology and politics not solely by means of individual scholars' carefully reasoned weblogs but also by the seemingly endless stream of blogs and various other modes of Web presence that interact to produce the soup or stew or mud of public discourse on these topics. It behooves us as scholars and spokespeople to bear in mind that it is not just someone as reputable and judicious as Mark with whom we are interacting—but *everyone*.[1] And in that light, the prospect of a system of certification, which some speakers this afternoon have proposed, strikes me as a project doomed to cumbersome procedures with minimal impact. I am sympathetic to the project of developing some way of communicating the relative credibility of Web enterprises; there are already several technical steps we could take to help move toward

---

1. Media theorist Clay Shirky (2008) titled his recent book on the internet's impact on culture and social dynamics *Here Comes Everybody*.

this goal (though this is not the occasion to begin a discussion of various tags and flavors of HTML). But I think that certification would be a disproportionately awkward and ineffective means for attaining the outcomes we desire.

Moreover, the field of digital media extends very far beyond only blogs, as Annabel Wharton's presentation notes.[2] If we take account of all the various modes of digital technology that affect our work as scholars of antiquity, we have to realize that the very ground is shifting under our feet. The contributions to this volume discuss archaeology, politics, and media as though the media environment for the future into which we are moving were relatively stable: technical journals, popular journals, newspapers, broadcast journalism, films, documentaries, pot-boiling sensationalism. This perspective stares resolutely back into the past century and neglects the extent to which all of these elements of media culture have already begun a transformational change. Just adding "blogs" to the mix does not even *begin* to address what is happening all around us. If, as Milton Moreland argues,[3] the public now draws most of its archaeological conclusions from sensational books and film documentaries, we should be all the more alert to take advantage of this opportunity to engage vigorously with the emerging future digital media ecology, lest in our dealings with digital media we fall far behind yet again and end up playing catch-up to a new generation of media entrepreneurs.

To illustrate with just one example of what I am talking about, Mark's survey of bloggers' responses to Talpiyot and his criticism of the corporate *Jesus Family Tomb* Web site omits all mention of *Wikipedia*, which—as it turns out—reports very reasonably on the controversy. The main article,[4] which (in late 2009) showed up first in a Google search for "Talpiyot Tomb" (followed immediately by the Duke Religion Department blog on the topic [Aviam et al. 2008]; Joe Zias's "Viewers Guide" [Zias 2007] turned out to be fourth in the search results), reports on the sensational claims made on behalf of the tomb without according those claims any credence. The Wikipedia article allots much more space to the academic resistance to the "Jesus Family Tomb" theory than to the tomb itself.

I do not mean to submit that *Wikipedia* will be the savior of truth and probity in the digital media environment; I merely wish to observe that one much-maligned source of on-line information suggests that Mark and other critics have not failed at all. They are the prevailing

2. Annabel Wharton, "History and Fiction: Comments on Morag M. Kersel's 'The Power of the Press,'" pp. 84–88 in this volume.

3. Milton Moreland, "The Future of the Hisorical Documentary: Scholarly Responses to History Channel Meets *CSI*," pp. 109–122 in this volume.

4. See the *Wikipedia* entry "Talpiot Tomb," on-line: http://en.wikipedia.org/wiki/Talpiyot_Tomb.

party according to what is by many measures the most visible arbiter of digital intelligence.

But our students and our audiences seek knowledge not only through *Wikipedia* and scholars' blogs; they also communicate and learn from YouTube, Twitter, MySpace, Facebook, IRC conversations, podcasts, vlogs, blogs, and various multiuser virtual worlds. If we think that all these manifestations of digital media and the transforming effect they have on our audiences' mode of learning will not affect our practice of archaeological and biblical scholarship and pedagogy, I suggest we take this assumption to the recorded music industry, the broadcast news industry, television and movies, and to the newspaper industry—and ask how this assumption is working out for them.

References

Aviam, M.; Graham Brock, A.; Dobbs-Allsopp, F. W.; Elledge, C. D.; Gibson, S.; Hachlili, R.; Kloner, A.; Magness, J.; McDonald, L.; Meyers, E. M.; Pfann, S.; Price, J.; Rollston, C.; Segal, A. F.; Seow, C.-L.; Zias, J.; Zissu, B.

    2008   The Talpiot Tomb Controversy Revisited. *NT Blog*, January 21. Online: http://ntweblog.blogspot.com/2008/01/talpiot-tomb-controversy -revisited.html.

Goodacre, M.

    2007   Jesus Family Tomb Website: Errors and Inaccuracies. *NT Blog*, March 11. On-line: http://ntweblog.blogspot.com/2007/03/jesus-family-tomb -website-errors-and.html.

Shirkey, C.

    2008   *Here Comes Everybody*. New York: Penguin.

Zias, J.

    2007   Viewers' Guide to Understanding the Talpiot Tomb "Documentary" to Be Aired on the Discovery Channel. On-line: http://www.joezias .com/tomb.html.

The Power of the Press
The Effects of Press Releases and Popular Magazines on the Antiquities Trade

Morag M. Kersel

In December of 2007, *Time* magazine published an article by journalist Maria Baugh, entitled "Antiquities: The Hottest Investment." This article appeared just days after the New York office of Sotheby's auction house sold the Guennol Lioness for a record-shattering U.S. $57.2 million. Declaring that although "the sculpture is just three and a half inches tall and looks like a female body-builder with a lion's head," there was no question that "the 1948 purchase of the Guennol Lioness by Alistair Bradley Martin was a brilliant investment" (Baugh 2007). Antiquities and art appear to be the next hot investment, yielding up to a 10-percent return and esthetically more appealing in your curio cabinet than a stock certificate, which may or may not be worth the paper it's printed on. When Baugh asked whether the "average Joe" could actually afford to participate in the market, experts in the dealer community hastened to assure that buying antiquities is not just sport for the very rich.

> The good news is that it is possible for the individual investor to buy antiquities—and for a surprisingly moderate amount. For under U.S. $10,000 a year one could acquire two to four quality pieces with good provenance (object history, which includes a history of ownership) that you could expect would not only hold their value but actually appreciate in value,

blogged John Ambrose (2007), director of the antiquities shop *Fragments of Time*.

Responses to the report in *Time* magazine came from both sides of the debate over the trade in archaeological artifacts. Predictably, the archaeological community was outraged over what they considered to be a flippant disregard for the importance of archaeological context and the commodification of antiquities. In a letter to the editor of *Time*, Claire

73

Smith (2007), president of the World Archaeological Congress (WAC) stated: "many of our members . . . read this article with utter disbelief." She continued: "It is difficult to describe or imagine the degree of destruction that takes place in order to find one small object worthy of the antiquities market." WAC asked *Time* magazine to run stories to counter the damage done by this article—which they have thus far chosen not to do.

A year later in the December 2008 Antiquities Auction at Sotheby's in New York, lot 27, a Cycladic figurine of the Spedos variety, sold for U.S. $1,022,500, reinforcing the trope of art as the next big investment, even during a recession. Recently, while conducting ethnographic research on the trade in antiquities, I was stunned to come into contact with the anonymous purchaser of the Cycladic figurine. When I asked about the piece and the motivations behind its acquisition, the collector remarked that it was a "safe investment," one that could later be sold at a greater profit when the economy bounced back. And, like the Guennol Lioness, the Cycladic figurine has a pristine provenance, adding to the increased investment potential and assurance of authenticity. "Better than the stock market at the moment, and there are no Bernie Madoffs[1] in the mix," stated the buyer.

In March of 2009 at the annual European Fine Art Foundation (TEFAF) Art and Antiquities fair in the Netherlands, the volume of sales in the Classical Antiquities and Egyptian Works of Art section was high, with a large number of purchases made at less than U.S. $70,000[2]—lending support to the notion of the purchasing power of the "average Joe." At TEFAF, long-time antiquities dealers Jerome Eisenberg, Rupert Wace, and James Ede all reported stronger than expected sales of classical antiquities. Market analysts attributed the strength in sales in spite of the shaky economy to the "Yves Saint Laurent effect." Prior to the sale at Christie's auction house of the collection of recently deceased fashion designer Yves Saint Laurent, an in-depth feature article appeared in the pages of *Vanity Fair* (Collins 2009). The article served as a de facto auction catalog, for images depicted Yves Saint Laurent and his partner Pierre Bergé among the belongings to be auctioned off later that year. The weakened economy notwithstanding, the Yves Saint Laurent sale at Christie's Paris auction house earned a record breaking US $507 million—a record for a single-owner collection (Gleadell 2009). The question on the minds of market analysts was whether this sale revived confidence in the antiquities market or whether the sale was a one-off phenomenon of celebrity. Like the TEFAF, the Yves Saint Laurent collection was a virtual cabinet of curiosities appealing to all types of

1. Bernard Madoff, former financier, was convicted of defrauding thousands of investors out of billions of dollars in a ponzi scheme.
2. See the *Artdaily.org* review of the TEFAF fair (Artdaily.org 2009).

collectors; and both venues defied all market expectations, suggesting that antiquities are "safer" than an IRA or the stock market, given the current economic climate. The antiquities market might be touted as a sure thing and a safe investment; but without knowing the exact archaeological find spot (the provenience), can the investor ever be certain that the artifact being purchased is real?

Missing from these popular articles on the benefits of investing in the antiquities market are considerations of the damage done to the ancient landscape as a result of looting in search of saleable items; the value of a particular piece to historians and archaeologists is as much in its context as in the object itself. Research amply illustrates the connection between the demand for archaeological material and the looting of archaeological sites to meet growing demand (see Fincham 2009 for further discussion). There is a finite supply of material, but with articles such as the piece in *Time Magazine* promoting antiquities as available to all pocket books and glossy cover stories on the fashionable collections of celebrities providing a pastiche of credibility to the antiquities market, there are an increasing number of investors interested in owning ancient art.

The question for investors is what, if anything, scientific context contributes to the monetary value of an object. At a recent panel on Heritage Issues and the Middle East hosted by the Boston University Art Law Society and The Lawyers' Committee for Cultural Heritage Preservation, Jane Levine, compliance officer for Sotheby's, stated that solid provenance was definitely adding value to the purchase price of antiquities (Levine 2009). The comment was in response to a question regarding the purchase price and provenance of the Guennol Lioness. The Sotheby's catalog entry describes the Guennol Lioness as "said to have been found at a site near Baghdad," but we will never know for certain. Nor will we know of any associated artifacts and structures found with or near this artifact. Was it from a funerary context, a domestic context, or a cultic context? Was it buried alongside a child, a woman, or a dog? Was it found inside a pot or in the foundation of a building? The trade claims that this piece has an impeccable provenance because it has been in private collections since 1931 and on display and "accessible" to the public in the Brooklyn Museum since 1949. But now that a private collector has acquired the piece, will it ever be accessible again for the enjoyment of the international community?

The preceding examples attest to the impact of the press—more specifically, popular magazines—on the trade in antiquities. Equally as influential are the policy statements and press releases of professional organizations and their representatives. In June of 2008, the Association of Art Museum Directors (AAMD) released the findings of their "2008 Report of the AAMD Subcommittee on the Acquisition of Archaeological Materials and Ancient Art" (AAMD 2008). The new report goes

beyond earlier efforts by formally recognizing the United Nations Educational, Cultural, and Scientific Organization (UNESCO)'s 1970 "Convention on the Means of Prohibiting and Preventing the Illicit Import,
Export, and Transfer of Ownership of Cultural Property" (UNESCO
1970) as a threshold date for the acquisition of archaeological material.
The report *encourages* members not to acquire material that cannot be
proven to have been outside the country of origin before 1970 or that
does not have proof of legal exportation after 1970. The AAMD will
dedicate a section of its Web site to the on-line publication of museum
acquisitions of ancient material. Their goal is to make the information
"readily and publicly accessible" (AAMD 2008). Their aim is increased
transparency in the marketplace—no acquisitions without legal proof of
exportation and a database of all acquisitions.

While the new AAMD recommendations for its member museums
are to be commended, this statement in its report is troubling: "The
AAMD affirms the value of licit markets for the controlled sale of ancient art and archaeological materials as an effective means of preventing looting" (AAMD 2008). The AAMD is expressing its support for a
legal market in antiquities as a way to prevent the illegal excavation
of sites, providing their imprimatur for a controlled sale of antiquities.
The topic of my Ph.D. dissertation (Kersel 2006b), *A License to Sell: The
Legal Trade in Antiquities in Israel*, was the licit market for antiquities in Israel (legally sanctioned by the Israeli government) and whether
the legal market had any effect on archaeological looting. My study
concluded that the legal availability of archaeological material has led
to continued looting in Israel, Jordan, and the Palestinian Territories
(Kersel 2006b)—the ever-increasing demand due to tourism or as investments has led to a need for more artifacts in the market, which has led
to increased looting. Numerous studies based on examples from all over
the world (Al Hamdani 2008; Kersel 2006a; Kersel, Luke, and Roosevelt
2008; Luke and Henderson 2006; Roosevelt and Luke 2006; Yahya 2008)
have illustrated the causal relationship between the demand for archaeological material and the looting of archaeological sites, but this fact
is often overlooked in the debate over "who owns the past" and is not
addressed in the recent report of the AAMD.

Rather than simply criticize or vilify collectors (and by collectors I
include low-end tourists and high-end connoisseurs, as well as museums and educational institutions), I intend to demonstrate that those
who support a position of free-trade in antiquities, regardless of the
damage to the archaeological landscape, are waging a much more successful public relations campaign in the media than those in the realm
of archaeology.

Recently, the debate in antiquities has been reduced to nationalist
and so-called internationalist positions—pitting those who believe in
the uninhibited movement of archaeological material against those

who would like to retain it within the borders of the nation in which it was originally found (for further discussion, see Bauer 2008). The term *cultural internationalist*, first proposed by Stanford lawyer John Henry Merryman (1986), is actually a misnomer, as this view of cultural property is not really internationalist and should more appropriately be termed a free-market approach. The term *internationalist* conjures up positive connotations, providing access to all. Rather than being internationalist in approach, the free-market position, in this context, advocates for the unfettered movement of cultural material in the marketplace—those who can afford to purchase the artifacts are allowed access. The international exchange of free-market goods is primarily a flow of objects from less-developed nations to collectors, generally with access to capital. The exchange is usually financial, not intellectual. Perhaps recognizing that the term *cultural internationalist* was passé, or needed rebranding, this position has now taken on the moniker *cosmopolitanism*, with very influential academics and museum professionals (such as James Cuno, president and CEO of the J. Paul Getty Trust, and Princeton intellectual Kwame Anthony Appiah) leading the debate.

For the purposes of the cultural internationalists, the cosmopolitanism of Appiah (2006) is a dynamic concept in which we all have obligations that are based on a respect of other customs and beliefs that have meaning and value. The cosmopolitan argument used in the antiquities trade is that if exposure to art is valuable to a society, then we should want everyone to experience it, echoing the internationalist mantra "art as ambassador" first introduced by Paul Bator (1982) and embodying the free market stance.

Nationalists are primarily comprised of archaeologically rich nations and those, including some archaeologists, who emphasize a relationship between cultural objects and national identity, culture, and history.

A third position, one that is often conflated with the nationalist group and typically held by anthropologists, archaeologists, and ethnographers, places primary emphasis on the contextual information associated with cultural objects, highlighting the acquisition of information about the human past through relationships and proper scientific documentation. As Patty Gerstenblith (2001: 221) argues, "today, ever more sophisticated scientific techniques, as well as interdisciplinary methods of analysis are available and routinely used in the reconstruction of past civilizations." Anthropologist Richard Handler (1992) forcefully maintains that to have meaning objects must be surrounded by other objects, by words, or by human activity. The question of archaeological context is often overlooked by the dealing and collecting communities and is elided in popular magazine articles and press releases encouraging the legal trade in antiquities. The issue of archaeological context is something that the lay public (often consumers of archaeological material) are unaware of or see as insignificant.

Not only is there no discussion of the causal relationship between the demand for archaeological artifacts and the looting of sites, but there is also an active denial from the internationalist/cosmopolitanist camp. Cuno (2006: 29) has stated: "when an antiquity is offered to a museum for acquisition, the looting, if indeed there was any, has already occurred. . . . Museums are havens for objects that are already, and for whatever reason, alienated from their original context. Museums do not alienate objects." The AAMD press release encouraging the use of a legal market for acquiring artifacts rejects the characterization of looted antiquities as stolen property. Their position is that, once artifacts reach the market, they are already long divorced from their past and should be available for consumption. In fact, museums are giving these "orphans" a good home. Gerstenblith (2007: 187) deconstructs the cosmopolitanist position to "if the trade in looted artifacts were no longer criminalized, then the black market would largely disappear." Yet evidence indicates that the looting of sites continues whether there is a legal market or an illegal underground black market (Kersel 2006b). The real issue here is the harm caused by the trade (legal or illegal) in undocumented artifacts.

One of the research questions I asked respondents[3] while conducting interviews for my doctoral research concerned the relationship between the demand for artifacts and the looting of archaeological sites—as well as thefts from museums and private collections. The question was whether there existed any correlation between them. More than 70 percent of the total respondents (66 out of 94) declared that there was a causal relationship: the demand for archaeological artifacts in the marketplace results in the looting of archaeological sites.

Four of the six stakeholder responses (archaeologists, government employees, miscellaneous, and dealers) supported the position that a legal market does not act as a deterrent to looting, and some asserted that the market may and does actually stimulate looting. The museum professional group is evenly divided over the issue. The only set of stakeholders who supported the hypothesis that a legal trade will diminish looting (the assertion of those who support a free-market in antiquities) was the collecting community, which is an interesting comment on their ability to avoid discussions involving the origins of the artifacts they are considering for purchase.

Although 46 percent of the dealers interviewed felt that there was no relationship between looting and the sale of archaeological material, 54

---

3. Over the course of 14 months I interviewed various individuals with an expressed interest in the legal trade in antiquities. The interviewees included dealers, collectors, archaeologists, government employees, museum professionals and a miscellaneous group, which included architects and conservators. See Kersel 2006b for a full description of the methodology.

Table 1. Stakeholder Group Positions on the Link between Demand and Looting

Stakeholder Group	Yes	No	Total
Archaeologists	95%	5%	100%
Collectors	33%	67%	100%
Dealers	54%	46%	100%
Government Employees	100%	0%	100%
Miscellaneous	60%	40%	100%
Museum Professionals	50%	50%	100%

percent fully admitted to a connection between the two spheres of the economy. Consider these comments of dealers:

> If a tourist comes into my store and wants a figurine from the Iron II period and I don't have one I ask some of my fellow shop owners. If they don't have one I call my "middleman" in Hebron to ask if he as any in his storeroom. Within days I have one in my shop. I don't ask too many questions, but I do ask for the location of the find because lots of tourists want to know the name of the archaeological site that the figurine came from (Dealer 19).

and:

> I get the catalogues from the major auction houses and I check eBay and I monitor what is selling. Right now inscriptions are hot, anything with an inscription is a good seller but I don't have many pieces. I am always on the lookout for inscriptions; I make sure that my contacts in the territories know that I can easily move inscriptions (Dealer 27).

Testimony from archaeologists and government employees as well as dealers clearly illustrates the link between consumer demand for archaeological material and the looting of archaeological sites. The legal market for antiquities in Israel does not diminish looting and may in fact contribute to greater mining of archaeological sites for saleable items.

Traditionally, when engaging with the trade in looted artifacts, most legal and/or protective measures are directed at looters, who are considered the source of the problem. The reasons for this are manifold. The identification of culprits in the fight against the looting of sites is much easier than identifying a nameless purchaser on eBay or at an auction house. Excavating without a permit is illegal in most countries, while the purchasing of archaeological material with dubious provenance (ownership history) or provenience (known archaeological find spot) is not illegal per se, however ethically suspect it is. Protecting borders against the import and export of archaeological material is easier than developing social programs aimed at reducing consumer predilection. Curbing demand enters the tricky terrain of social policy, values, and education, while curbing supply relies on the use of force, coercion, and law enforcement (Naím 2005). Local and national governments have enforced laws, arrested illegal excavators, and fined middlemen; but consumers go unpunished and sometimes are unaware of the crime, which they are abetting. A redirection of efforts is required if any headway is to be made in the cessation of looting (see Kersel 2008 for further discussion).

The presence of looted artifacts in the marketplace is predicated on the willingness of consumers to purchase unprovenienced artifacts, turning a blind eye to the thorny question of archaeological find spot and object history. Euphemisms such as "from the collection of Swiss gentleman" or "a family heirloom" litter the pages of auction catalogs and are endemic to eBay and other Internet sites. Purchasers of artifacts should be asking more questions and should be held accountable when they don't. If the AAMD supports a legal trade as a solution to looting, then they should mandate that their members ask the sticky questions surrounding ownership history and archaeological find spot.

Those in the archaeological community are not blameless in the fight against purchasing artifacts with suspect backgrounds. A stronger case should be made in the popular press regarding the connection between supply (looting) and demand (collecting) or about the importance of archaeological context (Fincham 2009). Most visitors to museums, art galleries, and heritage sites see artifacts that are decontextualized and divorced from their find spot, and yet they can still admire them and learn something about them as *objets d'art*. Scholars publish in obscure journals and scholarly volumes to secure jobs, grants, and tenure; but these sources are often inaccessible to the readers of *Time*, *Vanity Fair*, or *Archaeology*. Funding agencies do not support investigations into market analyses of the trade in antiquities—it is not "hard science" or excavation. It is difficult to conduct this type of research with no institutional support. If we scholars used the popular press and media in the ways the dealer and collector community does, perhaps we would have greater impact on changing the way the acquiring public thinks about the social lives of the artifacts they are buying.

A recent popular article in *Archaeology* magazine linking the looting of archaeological sites to methamphetamine addicts, who "loot sites for artifacts they can sell or trade for more drugs" (Patel 2009: 45), went a long way to dispelling the sanitized notion of the "antiquities road show" piece found in your grandmother's attic. As Justin Jennings and Adrienne Rand (2008: 29) argue, "social marketing—the use of marketing principles and techniques to advance social ideas, causes and/or behaviors—is the necessary next step in the fight against illicit antiquities." By employing the negative associations of phenomena such as drugs, marketing can change consumer tastes. This type of initiative—negative associations, such as between smoking and cancer—has been demonstrably successful in anti-smoking campaigns. This behavior modification is the result of advocacy campaigns focused on social persuasion rather than criminal sanctions.

The purchase of antiquities may be a good, safe investment; but what's missing from the investment equation is recognition of the effects of demand for archaeological artifacts on the archaeological record—demand for artifacts can lead to the destruction of archaeological sites due to unauthorized, unscientific, and unsupervised excavations. The Guennol Lioness and the Spedos Cycladic figurine are now in the hands of private collectors who may or may not choose to exhibit or allow public access to these extraordinary artifacts. If one of the basic tenets of the art-as-ambassador position is access for all, isn't supporting a legal trade where objects routinely disappear from the public realm into the private sphere the antithesis of cosmopolitanism?

Antiquities remain an investment opportunity available to all—the Internet profoundly changed the collecting of archaeological material, and recent market results attest to the lure of the artifact. An active, dynamic market characterized by legal and illegal asymmetries, unequal power among the stakeholders, and secrecy has the propensity to leave the consumer in an uninformed and unfavorable situation—buying unprovenienced artifacts. A system with greater lucidity and oversight, coupled with an advocacy program aimed at presenting incontrovertible evidence connecting archaeological site destruction from looting with consumer demand, could go a long way to ameliorate this inauspicious predicament. We in the archaeological community need to be more active in countering the personal benefits of owning antiquities. We need to wage our own campaigns against the collecting of unprovenienced archaeological material in the pages of popular magazines as well as in our professional organizations. We must present the complete picture of the consequences of regarding antiquities as hot investments.

References

AAMD (Association of Art Museum Directors)
  2008   New Report on Acquisition of Archaeological Materials and Ancient Art Issued by Association of Art Museum Directors, AAMD Press Release, June 4. http://www.aamd.org/newsroom/documents/2008ReportAndRelease.pdf.

Ambrose, J.
  2007   The Time Magazine Article: Thoughts That Didn't Make It into the Article on Collecting Antiquities. *Antiquities and Ancient Art*, December 15. On-line: http://antiquities.blogs.com/antiquities/2007/12/the-time-magazi.html.

Appiah, K. A.
    2006   *Cosmopolitanism: Ethics in a World of Strangers*. New York: W. W.
            Norton.
Artdaily.org
    2009   TEFAF Maastricht 2009 Confirms Art Market Remains Solid. *Artdaily
            .org: The First Art Newspaper on the Net*, March 24. On-line: http://
            www.artdaily.org/section/news/index.asp?int_sec=2&int_new=29771
            &b=TEFAF%20Maastricht.
Bator, P.
    1982   An Essay on the International Trade in Art. *Stanford Law Review* 34:
            275–384.
Bauer, A.
    2008   New Ways of Thinking about Cultural Property: A Critical Appraisal
            of the Antiquities Trade Debates. *Fordham International Law Journal*
            31: 690–724.
Baugh, M.
    2007   Antiquities: The Hottest Investment. *Time*, December 12.
Brodie, N.; Kersel, M. M.; Luke, C.; and Tubb, K. W., eds.
    2006   *Archaeology, Cultural Heritage, and the Antiquities Trade*. Gaines-
            ville: University Press of Florida.
Collins, A. F.
    2009   The Things Yves Loved. *Vanity Fair*, January: 76–83.
Cuno, J.
    2006   View from the Universal Museum. Pp. 15–33 in *Imperialism, Art and
            Restitution*, ed. J. H. Merryman. Cambridge: Cambridge University
            Press.
Fincham, D.
    2009   The Fundamental Importance of Archaeological Context. Pp. 1–12 in
            Art and Crime: Exploring the Dark Side of the Art World, ed. N. Char-
            ney. Westport, CT: Greenwood.
Gerstenblith, P.
    2001   The Public Interest in the Restitution of Cultural Objects (Symposium,
            Ownership and Protection of Heritage: Cultural Property Rights for the
            21st Century). *Connecticut Journal of International Law* 16: 197–246.
    2007   Controlling the International Market in Antiquities: Reducing the
            Harm, Preserving the Past. *Chicago Journal of International Law*,
            Summer: 169–94.
Gleadell, C.
    2009   Saint Laurent Sale: Yves Gives the Market a Shot in the Arm. *The
            Daily Telegraph*, March 3: 24.
Hamdani, A. al
    2008   Recovering the Past: Protecting and Recording our Archaeological Her-
            itage in Southern Iraq. *Near Eastern Archaeology* 71: 221–30.
Handler, R.
    1992   On Valuing Museum Objects. *Museum Anthropology* 12: 21–28.
Jennings, J., and Rand, A.
    2008   Stemming the Tide: How Social Marketers Can Help Fight against
            Looted Antiquities. *SAA Archaeological Record* 8: 28–31.

Kersel, M. M.
2006a   From the Ground to the Buyer: A Market Analysis of the Illicit Trade in Antiquities. Pp. 188–205 in Brodie et al. 2006.
2006b   *A License to Sell: The Antiquities Trade in Israel.* Ph.D. dissertation, University of Cambridge.
2008   A Focus on the Demand Side of the Antiquities Equation. *Near Eastern Archaeology* 71: 230–33.

Kersel, M. M.; Luke, C.; and Roosevelt, C. H.
2008   Valuing the Past: Perceptions of Archaeological Practice in Lydia and the Levant. *Journal of Social Archaeology* 8: 299–320.

Levine, J.
2009   Heritage Issues in the Middle East. Panelist presentation at the Boston University Art Law Society and The Lawyers' Committee for Cultural Heritage Preservation Panel Discussion, Boston, MA.

Luke, C., and Henderson, J. S.
2006   The Plunder of the Ulúa Valley, Honduras and a Market Analysis for Its Antiquities. Pp. 147–72 in Brodie et al. 2006.

Merryman, J. H.
1986   Two Ways of Thinking about Cultural Property. *The American Journal of International Law* 80: 831–53.

Naím, M.
2005   *Illicit: How Smugglers, Traffickers and Copycats Are Hijacking the Global Economy.* New York: Doubleday.

Patel, S.
2009   Drugs, Guns, and Dirt: Methamphetamine Fuels a New Epidemic of Looting. *Archaeology* 62: 45–47.

Roosevelt, C. H., and Luke, C.
2006   Looting Lydia: The Destruction of the Archaeological Landscape in Western Turkey. Pp. 173–87 in Brodie et al. 2006.

Smith, C.
2007   Letter to *Time* Magazine. *World Archaeological Congress Web Site,* December 21. On-line: http://www.worldarchaeologicalcongress.org /activities/submissions/265-letter-to-time-magazine.

UNESCO (United Nations Educational, Cultural, and Scientific Organization)
1970   Convention on the Means of Prohibiting and Preventing the Illicit Import, Export, and Transfer of Ownership of Cultural Property. *United Nations Educational, Cultural, and Scientific Organization Web Site.* On-line: http://portal.unesco.org/en/ev.php-URL_ID =13039&URL_DO=DO_TOPIC&URL_SECTION=201.html.

Yahya, A.
2008   Managing Heritage in a War Zone. *Archaeologies: Journal of the World Archaeological Congress* 4: 495–505.

History and Fiction

Comments on Morag M. Kersel's
"The Power of the Press"

Annabel Wharton

A number of the presentations made in the conference "Archaeology, Politics, and the Media" carry an explicit moral charge. They promise their audience a critical investigation of the ethics of archaeology. One of those papers, Morag M. Kersel's "The Power of the Press: The Effects of Press Releases and Popular Magazines on the Antiquities Trade" describes the corrosive effects on archaeology wrought by the trade, legal as well as illegal, in ancient artifacts.

Kersel's essay proves what Aristotle knew to be the case in the 4th century B.C.E. and what we, at the end of the first decade of the 21st century, have painfully relearned: the financial market, as a mechanism for producing profit, is ethically problematic.[1] Her argument for the complicity of the market in the theft of artifacts offers a refinement and a confirmation of a broad, well-established, popular suspicion of the art market. In February, 2009, National Public Radio sponsored a debate entitled "On Ethics: Is the Art Market Worse Than the Stock Market?"[2] Before the debate the live audience was almost equally divided among those in favor of the motion, those opposed, and those undecided. At the end of the debate, the majority had been persuaded that the art market was indeed less ethical than the stock market.

Aristotle regarded profit from investment as usury and therefore as unnatural and unethical; those of us who have suffered in the current economic collapse displace that moral outrage from the market to the market's greedy and corrupt manipulators. But Kersel locates the evil of the antiquities market not in its unearned gain (as Aristotle might

---

Author's note: I am grateful to Prof. Kalman Bland for his careful reading of this note and his comments on it.

1. See Aristotle, *Politics* 3:23.

2. For a synopsis of the debate and its participants, as well as a link to a sound file of the original debate, see "On Ethics, Is Art Market Worse than Stock Market?" on the NPR Web site: http://www.npr.org/templates/story/story.php?storyId=100557165.

have) or even in the unscrupulousness of dealers (as the NPR audience did). Rather, she identifies the ethical egregiousness of the operation of the market with its abuse of history. Decontextualizing an artifact, she reminds us, robs it of its history. The act is felonious morally as well as legally. Kersel's piece ends with a plea to archaeologists to oppose the market in artifacts and thereby work to salvage history.

As a supplement to Kersel's conclusion, I offer two gentle prods. First, though academics might disdain the globalized market, we should not pretend that we can much affect it. Second, history is not what it used to be. All of us at the conference and no doubt most of this volume's readership are, I assume, devoted to history. We struggle to produce honest versions of it. But we cannot afford to be naive about the object of our affection. We live in a post-historical moment. History—so august, so real, so confident in the 19th and early 20th centuries—has lost its authority. It has been reduced to a cultural ornament or, worse, to the stuff of political opportunism. We can neither dismantle the market nor ensure history's chastity.

Of course, we are not entirely powerless. We may not be able to put a halt to those who strip an artifact of its true history in order to put it on the market. But we can at least expose those who produce faux history for the sake of increasing an object's value.

One example of such an abuse of history in the service of venality may serve to make my point. The Tomb of King David, located outside Zion Gate south of the Old City of Jerusalem, is rather like the Garden Tomb of Jesus beyond Damascus Gate on its opposite, northern side. Both are recognized by all competent archaeologists and historians as faux, and both are treated by some religious fundamentalists as authentic. It is well known that the Garden Tomb was a Protestant invention of General George Gordon, martyr of Khartoum, in the 19th century (Monk 2002: 18–33).

The sources of the fabrication of King David's tomb are more obscure—and this is certainly not the place identify them (but see Wharton forthcoming). I will simply document the abuse of history perpetrated by the site's present occupiers: the Diaspora Yeshiva, put in place in 1968 by the Ministry of Religious Affairs of the State of Israel. The quotation that follows is taken from the "Visitor's Guide" of the Diaspora Yeshiva's *Tomb of David* Web site[3]; I have added interlinear comments in brackets.

> You have now entered the holy site of Mt. Zion. [Zion in Davidic times was associated with the southeast hill, now known as the City of David, not the southwest hill, now mislabeled "Mount Zion."[4]]

---

3. See http://s105753740.onlinehome.us/Clients/davidstomb/Visitors-guide.htm.
4. For an accessible overview of the archaeological understanding of Zion, see Mazar, Cornfeld, and Freedman 1975.

The structures you see about are built upon foundations that go back
to biblical times. . . . [The earliest excavated floor level in the complex has been dated to the 1st or 2nd century c.e. (Pinkerfeld 1960).]
The spirit and personality of King David can be sensed all around.
Visitors can feel his humility, his humanity, his joy and his towering
faith, which made him G-d's anointed one. King David united the Jewish People. He built Jerusalem and the foundation of our Holy Temple.

For more than a thousand years Jewish tradition has identified
Mount Zion as being the last resting place of King David and his descendants, the Kings of Judah. [Since the 9th century c.e.? Before the
early 7th century, Christians had identified the lower level of this
building (now the Tomb) as the site of the Washing of the Feet and
the room upstairs as the Cenacle, the place of the Last Supper.[5]] The
fearless Jewish traveler, Benjamin of Tudela, traveled from his native
Spain to visit Jerusalem in the 12th century. [Benjamin was on his way
to Baghdad.] His chronicles tell the story of how King David's Tomb
and the other royal graves were discovered. [Benjamin, in relating an
Ali-Babesque tale told to him by a local rabbi of an event that had supposedly occurred 15 years before he visited Jerusalem, explicitly states
in his account that the site was hidden from sight from the time of its
purported discovery until the present.[6]] . . .

You are now standing in the presence of a huge stone monument,
hewn of a single piece of black Granite. [The cenotaph has been dated
to Crusader times.] It blocks the way to the cave wherein King David
lies buried. [There is no evidence whatsoever of the building's association with a burial cave. On the contrary, the distinguished Jewish
archaeologist who examined and published the building identified it
as a Roman-period synagogue—any association with a tomb would
have made such an ascription impossible (Pinkerfeld 1960: 42–43).]

The misrepresentations in this blurb are egregious. Rabbis entrusted
with the education of youth should show a greater respect for truth.

This "visitor's guide" is a very small part of the yeshiva's Web site.
The domain is, in fact, largely devoted to the description of the yeshiva's collection of objects associated with the tomb. Among these artifacts are a pre-State [pre-1948] cloth tomb-covering, a "two-hundred-
year-old magical and mystical charity box," a "stone well cover to King
David's well of blessings and miracles," and three wooden, pointed-arch
window frames "of transforming light" from the "tomb." The fact that
they are from the Gothic windows of the Cenacle goes unmentioned.[7]

---

5. The Christian associations of the building are codified by Sophronius of Jerusalem (1957; trans. Wilkinson 2002).

6. Benjamin of Tudela 1907: 24–25, 38–41. For a discussion of Benjamin of Tudela's identification of the location of the Tomb of David and a refutation of those who
use that account to support any claims of tomb's authenticity, see Arce 1963.

7. E.g., the "King David's Heritage" section of the *David's Tomb* Web site:
http://s105753740.onlinehome.us/Clients/kingdavidsheritage/index.html [accessed

These artifacts are offered by the yeshiva for sale:

> In order to help facilitate, promote and maintain the growth of our institutions on Mount Zion, to protect and guarantee the Historical Jewish Ownership of this Holy Place and bring back the dignity and glory of King David it has now been deemed necessary to sell the above mentioned one of a kind artifacts.[8]

The contribution requested for their acquisition is over $65 million.[9]

The yeshiva's ahistorical authentication of the tomb provides its commodities with a mythologized sacrality, apparently in an effort to increase their market value.[10] The yeshiva's reworking of history thus makes the institution vulnerable to accusations of venality as well as appalling scholarship. It remains unclear to me what we, as academics, can do more generally to staunch the bleeding away of a history that set limits on the fables told about the past.[11] But this brief note suggests how we might collectively work to reveal those inflicting wounds on the body of history.

One final point. The success or failure of our shared mission to salvage what we can of history in this post-historical moment depends, I believe, on our willingness to exploit all the tools available to us to make our case. In the essays presented in this conference on archaeology and the media, only one, on blogging, was devoted to the digital media of our moment.[12] Other, extraordinarily creative media go unmentioned—from Web tools such as *Wikipedia* (which we should all be editing) to immersive worlds such as *Second Life* (www.secondlife. com), which has many active archaeological groups with wide lay audiences among its 16 million registered inhabitants. The digital is becoming an increasingly critical tool for the popular understanding of the world. We risk the loss of history entirely if those of us who care about it do not attend to how the past is rendered in the virtual universe. Digi-

---

August 11, 2008]; see the same texts with some variation, now available at http://kingdavidsheritage.com/.

8. See the homepage of the *David's Tomb* Web site: www.davidstomb.com.

9. See again the "King David's Heritage" section of the *David's Tomb* Web site at http://kingdavidsheritage.com/.

10. Of course, it also does a great deal of political work as well, as I discuss in Wharton forthcoming.

11. Mount Zion is indicative of modifications in the understanding of particular features of the urban topography produced by changes in the political control of a city. Under the Ottomans and the British, the "Tomb of David" was a Muslim holy place. The famous "status quo" of religious monuments, instituted in Jerusalem by the League of Nations with the establishment of the British Mandate in Palestine and nominally endorsed by the State of Israel, remains in place apparently only where it is convenient. See Her Majesty's Government of Great Britain 1977: 109. For charges of Judaizing the monuments of Jerusalem, see UNESCO 1981.

12. See Mark Goodacre's essay in this volume: "The Talpiyot Tomb and the Bloggers," pp. 56–68.

tal worlds provide a space for the broad circulation of archaeological
exposés as well as historical fictions. We should exploit it.

References

Arce, A.
    1963   El sepulcro de David en un texto de Benjamin de Tudela (1169). *Sefarad*
            23: 105–15.
Benjamin of Tudela
    1907   *The Itinerary of Benjamin of Tudela: Critical Text, Translation and
            Commentary*, trans. Marcus Nathan Adler. London: Henry Frowde.
Her Majesty's Government of Great Britain
    1977   Mandate to Great Britain over Palestine. Draft Submitted to the Coun-
            cil of the League of Nations, 1924. Final Draft Ratified, 1925. In *The
            Palestine Mandate, edited by Division of Near Eastern Affairs U.S. De-
            partment of State, 12–17*. Salisbury, N.C.: Documentary Publications.
Mazar, B.; Cornfeld, G.; and Freedman, D. N.
    1975   *The Mountain of the Lord*. Garden City, NY: Doubleday.
Monk, D.
    2002   *An Aesthetic Occupation: The Immediacy of Architecture and the
            Palestine Conflict*. Durham: Duke University Press.
Pinkerfeld, J.
    1960   David's Tomb. *Notes on the History of the Building: Bulletin of the
            Louis M. Rabinowitz Fund for the Exploration of Ancient Synagogues*
            3: 41–43.
Sophronius of Jerusalem
    1957   *Sophronii Anacreontica*. Opuscula: Testi per esercitazioni accade-
            mische 10–12. Rome: Gismondi.
UNESCO (United Nations Educational, Cultural, and Scientific Organization)
    1981   Jerusalem and the Application of the 21 C/Resolution4/14. On-line:
            http:unesdoc.unesco.org/images/0005/000572/057204eo.pdf.
Wharton, A.
    forthcoming   Jerusalem's Zions. *Material Religion* 9.
Wilkinson, J., ed.
    2002   Bishop of Jerusalem Sophronius, "Anacreonticon." Pp. 158–60 in *Jeru-
            salem Pilgrims before the Crusades*, ed. John Wilkinson. Warminster,
            UK: Aris & Phillips.

Confessions of an Archaeologist
Lessons I Learned from the Talpiyot Tomb
Fiasco and Other Media Encounters

Jodi Magness

In spring 2005, I participated in the filming of a high-budget, 10-part series on the life of Jesus called "Science of the Bible," which was broadcast on the National Geographic Channel. The main set was an ancient Galilean village that had been constructed from scratch outside Bodrum, Turkey. The film makers flew me twice from Israel to Turkey; and we shot an episode on "Jesus the healer" on the island of Kos. This experience was about as close as I have come to rubbing elbows with the rich and famous. The art director and production designer, Kim Hix, has won an Emmy and has to his credit a list of shows including *Desperate Housewives*. The program's director, James Younger, did extensive research on Jesus' life and was one of the best-informed film directors with whom I have worked. Nevertheless, one day in the faux Galilean village in Turkey, as we were shooting a reenactment of Jesus' Last Supper, I found myself looking at the camera and saying, "And this is what a Passover meal would have looked like at the time of Jesus"—while at the same time thinking, "We have no idea what a Passover meal looked like at the time of Jesus!" Thankfully, that take did not make it into the final version of the program.

I use this experience to show that even under the best of circumstances and working with the most responsible film makers or media people, scholars can be put in the position of saying things we do not believe or have our statements edited to mean something else. Furthermore, even the best reenactments convey only a general impression of the ancient world because our information is so incomplete; and even the highest quality documentary programs are not completely accurate.

Another of my experiences tells much the same story. A few years ago, I participated in the filming of an episode of *Battlefield Detectives* on the siege of Masada. I was interviewed because in 1995 I co-directed excavations in the Roman siege works at Masada, and also probably because they needed a female face in a field dominated by male scholars.

The British film team interviewed leading scholars and even an engineer about the construction of the Masada siege ramp. To reconstruct supply arrangements during the siege, they filmed me bringing water to Masada from the springs at Ein Gedi, 12 miles to the north. Despite the relatively high degree of accuracy of this production, there are a number of errors, including the use of ceramic jars instead of animal skins for bringing water from Ein Gedi and the depiction of their transport to Masada on pack animals instead of by boats on the Dead Sea. Because I had discussed these matters in advance with the producers, I assume these were conscious choices on their part, perhaps influenced by logistical considerations (e.g., it is easier to rent camels from Bedouin than boats on the Dead Sea).

This leads me to another story that is probably more illustrative of many of my colleagues' experiences. In March 2007, the Discovery Channel broadcast Simcha Jacobovici's widely hyped program claiming that the Talpiyot Tomb in Jerusalem is the tomb of Jesus and his family, mostly on the basis of the constellation of names inscribed on the tomb's ossuaries (see Jacobovici and Pellegrino 2007). The film's contents were shrouded in secrecy prior to its release, and everyone involved in its production (including the scholars interviewed) had to sign nondisclosure agreements. On the Monday before the film was broadcast (which was on a Sunday night; typical of this genre, it was shown at the Easter season), the Discovery Channel released a statement to the media for publicity purposes. That Friday (that is, three days before the media statement was released), a reporter from the Discovery Channel contacted me, seeking my comments and opinions about the program. The problem was that I knew nothing about the program at this point, as I had not been involved in its production, and the reporter knew almost nothing about it and could divulge even less. So we ended up having a meaningless conversation. Nevertheless, when the Discovery Channel released its statement to the media that Monday, I was quoted as follows: "Jodi Magness, associate department chair of religious studies at the University of North Carolina at Chapel Hill, told Discovery News that, based on the New Testament writings, 'Jesus likely lived during the first century A.D.'" (Viegas 2007).

In the following comments, I wish to contextualize contemporary media hype in a broader perspective and consider some of the problems facing archaeologists who work with the media. For better or worse, archaeology captures the public imagination as a romantic endeavor devoted to discovering lost treasure or revealing biblical secrets. Although there is some public interest in topics such as the Trojan War, few things excite the general public's interest as much as ancient Egypt (mummies, pharaohs' tombs, and pyramids) and anything relating to Jesus (but with relatively little interest in post-Pauline Christianity). In my opinion, many of today's media-related problems can be traced to the discovery of the Dead Sea Scrolls, which most people still think have something to do with Jesus. The slow rate of publication of the Dead Sea Scrolls, which led to charges that scholars and the Catholic Church conspired to hide secrets that could undermine Christianity, created the perfect storm. These events exacerbated several trends that have intensified since then: (1) a widespread perception that scholars conspire to hide from the public important new information or discoveries; (2) the notion that new archaeological discoveries can somehow prove, disprove, affirm, or undermine religious beliefs and especially the Christian faith; (3) the blurring of lines between academic and public discourse concerning new archaeological discoveries and interpretations; (4) the willingness and even eagerness of some scholars and archaeologists to use the media for publicity and self-promotion through claims of sensational finds; and (5) the multiplication of amateurs (including scholars trained in unrelated disciplines) who present themselves to the media and public as experts.

The World Wide Web has compounded these problems. The Web is a wonderful tool of democracy—a great equalizer that allows all voices to be heard. But disinformation is spread via the Web as easily as credible information, with little or no censorship or peer review. The Web has further blurred the lines between academic and public discourse because it is a forum in which new archaeological discoveries and interpretations are presented and discussed. Furthermore, the anonymous nature of Web postings provides a cover for negative attacks and discourse that would be unacceptable in scholarly forums.

Nevertheless, scholars can harness the Web to our advantage. Here, I provide one example. It began on that fateful Monday in March 2007, when the Discovery Channel announced the upcoming broadcast of Jacobovici's program on the Talpiyot Tomb. For the rest of the week immediately following the announcement, my phone rang off the hook with requests for interviews from the media, including the *Washington Post*, *Science* Magazine, Fox News, Anderson Cooper at CNN, Diane Rehm at NPR, Tom Brokaw from NBC, and innumerable smaller radio stations and newspapers from around the country. In addition, the editors of *Archaeology* magazine, a publication of the Archaeological Institute of America (AIA), sent me a copy of the film for immediate review. I had to decline most of these interviews due to prior commitments. Those that I did manage to squeeze into an overly full schedule were frustrating because it was impossible to explain in a sound bite of 60 seconds or fewer the complex reasons why the Talpiyot Tomb could not be the tomb of Jesus and his family. To make matters worse, in almost all cases the information that I managed to convey was cut and edited to only one or two sentences (or less), usually taken out of context. This is hardly a satisfactory way of responding to all of the errors and misinformation presented in a film-length TV program! By the end of that week,

frustrated with sound bites, I decided that the best way to respond was
to write an editorial aimed at a nonspecialist audience and post it on the
Web. Fortunately, the AIA, the Society of Biblical Literature (SBL), and
the Biblical Archaeology Society (BAS) immediately agreed to post my
piece.[1] This enabled me to refer everyone who contacted me after that
to the Web posting, which was widely read and therefore accomplished
its goal.

The Discovery Channel's program on the Talpiyot Tomb further
blurred the lines between archaeology as science and archaeology as
entertainment (is this archaeology as infotainment?). The tomb and ossuaries are authentic and were excavated legally by archaeologists under the auspices of the Israel Antiquities Authority. The final excavation report was published in 1996 in a scientific journal called `Atiqot
(Kloner 1996). So, unlike the so-called James ossuary, this is not a case
of an illegally excavated or forged find (for the James ossuary, see Magness 2005). Instead, this is an example of pseudo-science masquerad-
ing as science. The film's producer, Jacobovici, decided that Jesus and
his family were interred in the Talpiyot Tomb. Despite his lack of archaeological training and expertise, Jacobovici refused to listen to an
overwhelming majority of experts including the tomb's excavator, who
reject his claim. Jacobovici used his film-making skills, considerable
financial resources, and media contacts to present his view, bolstered by
a small but vocal number of academic supporters and an array of costly
scientific analyses. Of course, the scientific analyses—including DNA
analysis of the human skeletal remains—mean nothing unless one begins from the assumption that this is indeed the tomb of Jesus and his
family. Jacobovici's program received a disproportionate share of media
and public attention, as a check on Google quickly reveals.

The media frenzy was reignited when Professor James Charlesworth
of Princeton Theological Seminary sponsored a scholarly conference on
the Talpiyot Tomb in Jerusalem in January 2008. I hesitated to accept
an invitation to participate, fearing that attending would only further
legitimize Jacobovici's claim. In the end, however, I decided to participate, believing that this was the best way to refute publicly the claimed
identification (which I did). Nevertheless, I came away from the conference discouraged because, although all of the archaeologists who attended reject Jacobovici's claim, this is not how things were presented
to or by the media. Furthermore, I still feel that the very act of holding
a conference on the Talpiyot Tomb served to give an imprimatur of legitimacy to Jacobovici's claim—as if this was an issue that archaeologists had been debating, which was not the case. The claim about the
Talpiyot Tomb may have been the subject of much speculation by the

---

1. See Magness 2007, published on the AIA, SBL, and the *BAR* Magazine Web
sites.

media and the public, but from the start it was a nonstarter among archaeologists. A much more productive way to frame such a conference
might have been to discuss Jewish tombs and burial customs of the late
Second Temple period in general. After the conference, I co-authored
a statement with Professor Eric Meyers of Duke University (who also
attended), which we posted on Mark Goodacre's *New Testament Gateway* blog and which was picked up by other Web sites.[2] For a while,
there was a lively and sometimes nasty debate about the Talpiyot Tomb
on the Web, but thankfully the chatter seems to have died down.

What are some of the lessons learned from the Talpiyot Tomb fiasco?
In retrospect, I wish that the major professional organizations, including the American Schools of Oriental Research (ASOR), the SBL, and the
AIA had issued swift, strong, and unified statements responding to this
claim. Even if they did not wish to reject the claim outright, I feel that
these organizations have a responsibility to safeguard the professional
conduct of archaeology and related disciplines as scientific endeavors.
The manner in which we as professionals were being asked to respond
to a claim made on a *TV program* rather than in a peer-reviewed, scientific publication was outrageous. And we were asked to respond even
before the program had been broadcast! This sort of media circus erodes
archaeology's profile as a serious academic discipline in the eyes of both
the public and other disciplines. Finally, here is a case where scientific
inquiry was hijacked by someone with a nonacademic agenda. In other
words, it was a media-driven issue. Some of us devoted many days to responding to this claim in various forums, precious time that could have
been spent more productively on our own research agendas.

Much of the tension between archaeologists and the media stems
from our different goals. Archaeologists study the remains of material
culture to understand the past. We are not treasure hunters and we are
not allowed to keep what we find. In other words, we are not engaged in
archaeology for personal profit, nor are most of us involved in it to validate personal faith and beliefs. On the other hand, because for them the
bottom line is money, the media (especially television and film) capital-
ize on the public's fascination with events mentioned in the Bible and
the public's desire to find tangible proof of these events. Most members
of the media are interested not in scholarship for its own sake but rather
in topics that will make a profit. I have told numerous television people
who are at the beginning stages of producing a Jesus program that, although we do not have any archaeological remains definitely associated
with Jesus, we can reconstruct the world of Jesus with a fair degree of
accuracy. But this does not serve their purposes; they (or rather, the
public) want a physical part of Jesus, be it his shroud, his tomb, the
Holy Grail, or a piece of the cross. Because credible archaeologists are

2. See text of the statement at Aviam et al. 2008.

not interested in looking for Noah's Ark, the Ark of the Covenant, or remains associated with the Israelites' exodus from Egypt (for example), the usual program formula consists of interviewing a nonspecialist who claims to have made a sensational find related to some biblical person or event, which a scholar is brought in to refute. Usually the nay-saying scholar comes across as a skeptic who is too narrow-minded to entertain the possibility that someone from outside the ivory tower of academia made a valid new discovery, or even more sinister, who denies the validity of the discovery in order to keep this important information from the public.

Despite the difficulties and challenges inherent in dealing with the media, I believe that archaeologists have a responsibility to communicate our findings to the public. Because most people get their information from the media, we must learn how to communicate effectively. This means learning how to present complex issues and controversies in a sound bite, something most of us are unwilling and unable to do. Although some of our statements will be taken out of context and our views occasionally misrepresented, the alternative is to abandon the stage and allow others who are less qualified and knowledgeable to represent to the public the face of archaeology. I suggest that our professional organizations create permanent media committees (as ASOR has done) that will be proactive as well as reactive and will ensure that archaeological discoveries are presented accurately and responsibly to the public. Perhaps workshops offering training and advice to scholars about dealing with the media can be incorporated in the annual meetings. The organizers of this conference have done a great service by bringing these issues to the attention of scholars and the public and by setting us on the road toward a productive and hopefully long-term dialogue.

References

Aviam, M.; Graham Brock, A.; Dobbs-Allsopp, F. W.; Elledge, C. D.; Gibson, S.; Hachlili, R.; Kloner, A.; Magness, J.; McDonald, L.; Meyers, E. M.; Pfann, S.; Price, J.; Rollston, C.; Segal, A. F.; Seow, C.-L.; Zias, J.; Zissu, B.
  2008   The Talpiot Tomb Controversy Revisited. *NT Blog*, January 21. Online: http://ntweblog.blogspot.com/2008/01/talpiot-tomb-controversy-revisited.html.
Jacobovici, S., and Pellegrino, C.
  2007   *The Jesus Family Tomb: The Discovery, the Investigation, and the Evidence That Could Change History*. New York: HarperCollins.
Kloner, A.
  1996   A Tomb with Inscribed Ossuaries in East Talpiyot, Jerusalem. *ʿAtiqot* 29: 15–22.
Magness, J.
  2005   Ossuaries and the Burials of Jesus and James. *Journal of Biblical Literature* 124: 121–54.

2007   Has the Tomb of Jesus Been Discovered? On-line: *Archaeological Institute of America Web Site,* May 24: http://www.archaeological.org/news/279; *Society of Biblical Literature Web Site,* http://www.sbl-site.org/publications/article.aspx?ArticleId=640; and *BAR Magazine,* March 5: http://www.bib-arch.org/debates/jesus-tomb-02.asp.

Viegas, J.
2007   Jesus Family Tomb Believed Found. *Discovery Channel Web Site,* February 25. On-line: http://dsc.discovery.com/news/2007/02/25/tomb_arc.html?category=archaeology.

Popular Media, History, and the Classroom

Chad Spigel

In her essay, Jodi Magness vividly highlights some of the tensions that exist between historians of antiquity—including archaeologists, biblical scholars, and scholars of ancient Judaism and Christianity—and the popular media, which often sensationalize ancient history. She addresses important issues, such as the misuse or negative portrayal of scholars used as "experts," excessive media hype, and pseudoarchaeology. Recognizing the complex relationship between historians and those who work in the popular media, while acknowledging their different methods and goals, are important steps in correcting some of the problems, and Magness's essay certainly succeeds in this regard. Also, Magness's suggestion that scholars use popular media outlets to get their messages out should be taken seriously and actively pursued.

In the following pages, however, I want to turn away from the details of particular historical disputes and focus on more-general issues. That is, I want to focus on an issue—the concept of "completely accurate history" and how this relates to the role of "academic experts"—that Magness does not explicitly address and that has not received the attention I think it deserves in the scholarship on ancient Jewish and Christian history. Scholars who deal with the media have often been forced to devote their energies to correcting egregious misrepresentations of ancient literary and archaeological evidence in the popular media, and the underlying issue of accurate history is not directly addressed. In discussing it today, I also offer a suggestion about how academics can use an often-forgotten aspect of their expertise to deal with sensational historical claims and the irresponsible use of archaeological and literary evidence in the popular media. Although my comments can apply to any popular media outlet—television news, newspapers, magazines, and so on—my focus is on popular documentary films.

Completely Accurate History and Academic Experts

One important point in Magness's essay is that even the best historical documentary programs are not completely accurate. A question must be asked: is complete accuracy a fair expectation of documentary films or any form of popular media?

I ask this question because if we were to take a step back and think about it for a moment, it is unfair to expect *complete* accuracy even of historians. Most historians today agree that they do not tell history as it really was (*"wie es eigentlich gewesen"*), as Ranke suggested in the early 19th century. Rather, they tell how history may have been, based on how they choose to configure and interpret the available data. As E. H. Carr wrote nearly 50 years ago, "The belief in a hard core of historical facts existing objectively and independently of the interpretation of the historian is a preposterous fallacy, but one which it is very hard to eradicate" (Carr 1986: 6). In the case of ancient history, the fact that available sources are limited ensures that all writing of ancient history is based on incomplete data. Historians of antiquity should use *all* of the available sources, but *all* amounts to only a fraction of what would have been available were they living contemporaneously with their subjects. As Carr jokingly puts it, ancient historians only appear to be competent, "mainly because they are so ignorant of their subject" (Carr 1986: 9).

The fact that historians don't write *completely* accurate accounts—which doesn't mean they aren't accurate to some degree—is clear because there are always competing versions of the past. For example, two well-known and respected archaeologists—both participants in this conference—arrived at different historical conclusions, based on the same archaeological evidence, about the synagogues at Khirbet Shemaᶜ and Gush Ḥalav (Magness 2001a, 2001b; Meyers 2001). The point is not who interprets the evidence correctly or whether either is correct. The point is that academics do not always agree with each other's version of history, even when they use the same evidence and similar methods. History is interpretation. And because there is no past sitting out there with which to verify a particular interpretation of the evidence, competing interpretations must be allowed to exist side-by-side, each attracting supporters and detractors.

If historians cannot be expected to provide completely accurate histories, we certainly cannot expect completely accurate histories in documentary films. In fact, the idea that documentary filmmakers only present *their version* of history is generally acknowledged (Toplin 1988; Eitzen 2005); filmmakers do not necessarily think they are presenting completely accurate history. The problem is that, whereas academic historians are armed with tools for presenting opposing interpretations of evidence, such as footnotes and peer review, the limitations of video as a medium (most importantly, time limits) means that the audience of a documentary film is often left unaware of alternative interpretations. The lack of competing historical interpretations in most popular documentary films leaves the audience with the false impression that "history is a tidy operation, that it involves little more than laying out the chronology and 'getting the story straight'" (Toplin 1986: 1216).

This is where the academic "experts" who appear in many documentary films come into play and where the discrepancy between what historians are providing and what audiences think they are receiving can lead to miscommunication. Academic historians in the role of experts are not providing historical facts. Rather, they are providing their professional interpretations of the evidence; their expertise lies in historical interpretation. Magness's story about Passover in the time of Jesus is a perfect example. Yes, based on the available evidence, Passover in antiquity may have resembled her description, but behind the scenes she acknowledges that the evidence does not allow for a completely accurate understanding. Had her quotation about Passover been used in the film, the audience would likely have mistaken her historical interpretation for historical fact, even though the expert in this case did not consider this to be the case.

So, while scholars are indeed experts in their particular fields, they are not necessarily offering the sort of historical expertise expected by audiences. Historians offer historical interpretations, but audiences of popular documentary films think they are getting historical fact.

Academic Experts, Sound Bites, and the Classroom

In light of the issues of historical uncertainty and academic expertise, I would like to make two suggestions: first, a way scholars might better use their academic expertise when appearing in historical documentaries or other popular media; then, a way academic experts might take advantage of another area of their expertise, classroom teaching.

As Magness suggests, scholars must not only address the media when they are asked questions about history; they must also learn how to present complex issues in short sound bites. They are faced with the problem of what to include in the sound bite. Magness correctly points out that, although refuting misleading data is a crucial component of responding to misrepresentations of archaeology and history, it is often impossible to do in the allotted time. But lack of time is not the only problem with refuting irresponsible and highly unlikely historical conclusions. A number of years ago, Kenneth Feder, concerned with the "uncritical and often non-rational treatment" archaeology receives in the popular media (apparently, our current situation is not so unique), correctly noted that "the mere presentation of data in rebuttal to extreme claims is problematical . . . we must never allow our arguments to become couched in terms of 'our data' versus 'their data'" (1984: 535). The problem is that this strategy forces the viewer to make interpretive decisions about data and "facts," despite their lack of training. Instead, Feder suggests teaching about *how* archaeologists go about the task of attempting to explain the past. Perhaps, then, when asked to provide short sound bites about ancient history, experts should emphasize the role of interpretation inherent in writing ancient history. For example, while it might be a fact that an ossuary was found inscribed with the name *Jesus*, linking the ossuary with *the* Jesus of the New Testament is a historical interpretation of the evidence.

But Feder's suggestion goes beyond the issue of sound bites. In fact, his article (Feder 1984) is more concerned with an often-neglected area of academic expertise, classroom teaching, than with the sound bites problem. The results of a survey he conducted suggest the following: (1) undergraduate students are generally very interested in archaeology and related topics; (2) students also desire to learn about these subjects; (3) students are highly trusting of television as a source of factual data; (4) students also trust professors (slightly more than television) as a source of accurate information; and, perhaps most importantly, (5) students who had taken a course that had addressed sensational archaeological claims were less likely than students who had not taken such a course to agree with notions of the existence of ancient astronauts, Tutankhamun's curse, or Noah's Ark (Feder 1984: 527–32). Although students tend to trust television too much, they do "tend to believe teachers more than anyone else" (Feder 1984: 532). If the results of this survey still apply to today's students—and I think they do—the implication is that, despite the influence of television (and the internet), teachers "have a good chance at shaping what these students know about, and how they conceive of, the human past" (Feder 1984: 532).

Therefore, in addition to meeting the popular media in their arena with appropriate sound bites, scholars must also address the situation in the classroom by discussing popular misrepresentations of ancient history and also by explaining that reconstructing the past involves interpretation of limited data. Twenty years after conducting the survey, Kenneth Feder continues to teach a course at Central Connecticut State University that covers topics such as flying saucers, UFOs, and the lost continent of Atlantis. The sixth edition of the textbook for his class— *Frauds, Myths, and Mysteries: Science and Pseudoscience in Archaeology* (Feder 1990)—appeared in 2007.

Scholars of ancient Jewish and Christian history should also address popular (mis)representations of ancient history in the classroom.[1] We must remember that, as scholars, we are not only researchers; we are also teachers. Irresponsible uses of archaeological and literary evidence

---

1. I currently teach an undergraduate course titled "Digging for the Truth: Archaeology, the Bible, and Popular Media" at Trinity University in San Antonio. One text used in this course is Eric Cline's book *From Eden to Exile: Unraveling Mysteries of the Bible* (2007), which includes chapters on topics that are commonly found in popular television documentaries, such as Noah's Ark, Sodom and Gomorrah, and the Ark of the Covenant.

in the popular media provide teaching opportunities that should not be ignored. And while, as scholars, we may not have control of the popular media, we do have the opportunity to teach the future controllers of the popular media about ancient history.

References

Avery-Peck, A., and Neusner, J., eds.
  2001   *Judaism in Late Antiquity, Part 3*, vol. 4: *Where We Stand: Issues and Debates in Ancient Judaism.* Leiden: Brill.
Carr, E. H.
  1986   *What Is History?* London: MacMillan.
Cline, E. H.
  2007   *From Eden to Exile: Unraveling Mysteries of the Bible.* Washington, DC: National Geographic.
Eitzen, D.
  2005   Against the Ivory Tower: An Apologia for "Popular" Historical Documentaries. Pp. 409–18 in *New Challenges for Documentary*, ed. A. Rosenthal and J. Corner. 2nd ed. Manchester: Manchester University Press.
Feder, K. L.
  1984   Irrationality and Popular Archaeology. *American Antiquity* 49: 525–41.
  1990   *Frauds, Myths, and Mysteries: Science and Pseudoscience in Archaeology.* Mountain View, CA: Mayfield.
Magness, J.
  2001a   The Question of the Synagogue: The Problem of Typology. Pp. 1–48 in Avery-Peck and Neusner 2001.
  2001b   A Response to Eric M. Meyers and James F. Strange. Pp. 79–92 in Avery-Peck and Neusner 2001.
Meyers, E. M.
  2001   The Dating of the Gush Halav Synagogue: A Response to Jodi Magness. Pp. 51–70 in Avery-Peck and Neusner 2001.
Toplin, R. B.
  1988   The Filmmaker as Historian. *The American Historical Review* 93: 1210–27.

Scholars Behaving Badly
Sensationalism and
Archaeology in the Media

Byron R. McCane

You may think that you have heard this one before. In the Talpiyot
suburb of Jerusalem, a rock-cut Jewish tomb from the 1st century C.E. is
accidentally exposed by a building crew working on a house. Construction stops, and a team of archaeologists is called in. The tomb is carefully excavated. A top plan and sections are drawn. The tomb has a fore-
court, a small entrance blocked by a stone, and a single interior burial
chamber with niches carved into the walls. The finds include oil lamps,
cooking pots, perfume bottles, and one coin. In addition, limestone ossuaries are found in the niches and on the shelf around the burial chamber. Greek and Hebrew inscriptions on the ossuaries include the names
"Jesus," "Mary," "Simon," and "Matthew."

The tomb is a thoroughly ordinary, utterly typical Early Roman Jewish burial cave; there is no reason to connect it with Jesus of Nazareth
or anything else in the New Testament. But that is not the way this Talpiyot Tomb is treated in the media. The first news release goes like this:

"What is believed to be an eyewitness account of the death of Christ
has been discovered in the foundations of a house outside of Jerusalem. . . . The Greek writings are believed to be the work of a family of
Jewish disciples who stood among the multitudes at Calvary. A bitter
and moving lamentation, the account probably was written within a
few weeks of the crucifixion."

According to another report released that same day, the excavation
has uncovered "Hebrew-Greek inscriptions expressing lamentation by
Jewish disciples at the trial and crucifixion of Jesus." An international
news agency says that stone receptacles for bones have been found in
a cave near Jerusalem, with Hebrew, Greek, and Aramaic inscriptions.
Two of the receptacles, it adds, are marked with "pictorial representations of what happened to Christ."

All of this really took place—on Wednesday, October 3, 1945. The
news outlets were the *London Daily Herald*, the *New York Times*, and

Reuters, respectively (Kraeling 1946). It seems that *The Lost Tomb of Jesus* was not the first time someone used a 1st-century Jewish tomb in Talpiyot as the occasion for sensationalistic claims about archaeology and the Bible.

On September 10, 1945, Eliezer Lipa Sukenik, professor of archaeology at the Hebrew University in Jerusalem, began the excavation of the Talpiyot Tomb, assisted by his student, Nahman Avigad. It is a measure of Sukenik's accomplishment as an academic mentor that he was influential in developing the careers of two eminent archaeologists: Nahman Avigad, his student; and Yigael Yadin, his son. As the excavation of this tomb began, Sukenik had just turned 56; and his resume already included important fieldwork at Beth Alpha, Hammath-Gader, and Hadera. In two more years, he would become involved with the recovery and interpretation of the Dead Sea Scrolls. Excavating the Talpiyot Tomb took four days and proceeded according to form. But Sukenik's curiosity was piqued by a pair of ossuaries that were found side-by-side at the back of one of the loculus niches. Both bore inscriptions that included the Greek version of the name *Jesus*—one read, *iēsous iou* and the other *iēsous alōth*—and both bore *x*-shaped marks that Sukenik thought might be crosses. Of course he knew that the inscriptions most likely recorded the names of the deceased whose bones were collected in the ossuaries. But rather than staying with that idea, he argued instead that these inscriptions referred to Jesus of Nazareth. They were not names, he said, but "lamentations for the death of Jesus by some of his disciples." He argued further that the *x*-shaped marks were crosses, "a pictorial representation of the event, tantamount to exclaiming 'He was crucified'" (Sukenik 1947c: 365).

This interpretation was unsupported by the evidence in the tomb and unsupportable within the standard canons of archaeological interpretation of the time. Then as now, ossuary inscriptions were first to be interpreted as names; and then as now, *x*-shaped marks were first to be checked to see if they are indicators of the proper alignment of the ossuary's lid. It was a substantial error in judgment for Sukenik to propose such extraordinary interpretations for such ordinary finds. That an archaeologist of his experience and stature would do so provides a vivid example of how challenging this kind of work can be. All of us who have spent significant time in the worlds of archaeology and biblical studies can look back on similar (although perhaps less public) mistakes. For my part, I will always remember a paper that I submitted to the *Journal of Biblical Literature*. In it, I argued that the story of the raising of Lazarus in John 11 makes use of Jewish beliefs about the afterlife that are recorded in the Talmud. "The conceit of this article," wrote one of the reviewers, "might begin to be convincing if only the talmudic texts in question could somehow be shown to have something to do with first-century Judaism" (personal communication).

In addition, Sukenik's undue haste in trying to connect these archaeological finds with the biblical text may also have been influenced by the "biblical archaeology" movement that dominated the field in his day. The biblical archaeologists, led by eminent scholars such as William F. Albright and G. Ernest Wright, were confident that archaeology could and would confirm the substantial historicity of the biblical narrative (Dever 1997). To that end, they sought to dig (as a popular expression put it) "with a trowel in one hand and a Bible in the other," bringing together the finds in the dirt with the stories in the text. This strategy was certainly well-intentioned but ultimately counterproductive, for it produced a number of ill-considered and misguided interpretations. By the mid-1960s, biblical archaeology would give way to more productive theories and practices, but it was still widely popular when the Talpiyot Tomb was discovered in 1945. In sum, Sukenik was all too human: capable of erroneous judgments and influenced (perhaps unconsciously) by the prevailing intellectual and professional currents of his day.

When, however, news of the Talpiyot discoveries began to appear in the media, Professor Sukenik conducted himself in ways that stand out as a model of principled scholarship. First, on October 8—just five days after the earliest of the sensationalistic media announcements—he sat for an interview with the BBC in which he fully clarified the exact content and precise details of the Talpiyot Tomb and his interpretations (Kraeling 1946: 17). Subsequent media reporting on the tomb was far more accurate—and far less frequent. When exaggerations, misconceptions, and misrepresentations began to spread through the media, Sukenik took immediate and effective steps to ensure that the information available to the public was as clear and reliable as possible.

Second, Sukenik promptly published a full report on the tomb in a refereed academic journal in his field. Under the title, "The Earliest Records of Christianity," it appeared in the *American Journal of Archaeology* a year after the excavation of the tomb had been completed (Sukenik 1947c). Given the technologies of the time, the publication of his report was prompt. It was in every sense of the word a full report, including: a map of the location of the tomb, the top plan and sections, a detailed written description of the tomb, a detailed written description of the ossuaries, squeezes of the inscriptions, a catalog of the small finds, drawings of the pottery, and a concluding interpretive essay. With this report Sukenik presented his case to a jury of his peers, inviting their informed judgment on his work.

That informed judgment was, to put it mildly, overwhelmingly negative. The number of academics who found Sukenik's arguments convincing was very small. A steady stream of articles in refereed journals around the world criticized the idea that "the earliest records of Christianity" had been found. Reading those articles today, one is struck by the repetition of phrases such as "unjustifiable," "highly precarious," "gigantic inferences," "most debatable," "odd," and "by no means" (Bagatti 1950; Kane 1971; Kraeling 1946: 18; Willoughby 1949). Contradictory evidence piled up, and scholars arrived at a consensus that the inscriptions on the Talpiyot ossuaries were ordinary Early Roman Jewish names.

Sukenik received this wave of criticism without protest. As far as I have been able to ascertain, he never repeated those extraordinary claims about the Talpiyot Tomb. He was, above all else, a disciplined and productive scholar: in 1947 alone, he published two other articles in refereed journals, one on some previously unpublished coins from Aelia Capitolina and the other on the coins of John Hyrcanus (Sukenik 1947a, 1947b). Before long, he was deeply involved with the Dead Sea Scrolls. Taking the high road, Sukenik accepted the judgment of his peers; as a result, his mistaken interpretation of the Talpiyot Tomb has dwindled into insignificance, a tiny footnote in his long and distinguished career.

So *The Lost Tomb of Jesus* was not the first time that a perfectly ordinary Early Roman Jewish tomb in Talpiyot provided the occasion for wildly unreasonable claims about archaeology and the Bible. It is a troubling fact, however, that in recent years we have begun to see a sustained wave of this kind of egregious sensationalism. It now appears that roll-outs of (supposedly) earth-shattering archaeological discoveries are becoming a normal part of the media schedule, carefully timed to appear every year at Christmas and Easter. In our increasingly sophisticated digital culture, powerful forces are pressing us to get with this trend, to go with the flow, and (in so doing) to set aside an earlier generation's principled commitments to basic academic disciplines. More and more, we are being enticed to play a different game with a different set of rules. In 2002, the James ossuary was published in a popular magazine and announced in a national press conference before the guild of scholars ever had a chance to take a close look at it (Lemaire 2002). A television documentary and a popular book, with a national book tour, quickly followed (Jacobovici 2004; Shanks and Witherington 2003). Neither of the authors of that book was an experienced archaeologist. As soon as it was examined critically, of course, the inscription on the James ossuary was exposed as a modern forgery (Silberman and Goren 2003). But the money had been made. In 2004, the cave of John the Baptist appeared first as a popular book (Gibson 2004), to generally skeptical academic reviews (Murphy 2005; Scham 2004; Taylor 2005). In 2007, the lost tomb of Jesus went straight to broadcast and DVD, followed by a popular book (Jacobovici 2007; Jacobovici and Pellegrino 2008). After that event, public suspicions about archaeology and the Bible were so strong that a few months later, when Ehud Netzer announced the authentic discovery of Herod the Great's tomb, several friends and colleagues approached me to ask, "That's a fake too, right?"

The James ossuary, the cave of John the Baptist, and the lost tomb of Jesus: in each case, the announcement of the so-called "discovery" circumvented the standard scholarly disciplines of research, writing, and peer review. All of these sensational claims went straight to market, with a profit motive attached. As a result, public discussion was guided not by the disciplines of scholarship, but by the conventions of postmodern marketing. When responsible voices, including highly experienced field archaeologists, pointed out glaring errors of fact and logic, savvy promoters were ready with responses such as "Let's try to keep an open mind" and "We should hear both sides." "What are these scholars afraid of?" they seemed to hint darkly.

It is tempting, but mistaken, to suspect that the recent spate of sensationalism is caused by—and is the fault of—the media. If not for all those channels, we might be tempted to think, and all those producers and marketers, and all those Web sites, none of this ever could have happened. They are the ones, after all, with the cameras and the microphones and broadcasting equipment and sponsors. Yet that conclusion is unsupportable by the evidence. As a matter of fact, relatively few documentaries about archaeology and the Bible are sensationalistic. Most documentary film makers are careful and conscientious; they are trying to practice their craft in a way that will inform and entertain, not mislead. And they have certainly not invented the vibrant public interest in archaeology and the Bible. In a free society like ours, in which most people are religious or spiritual (or both), in which religion is regarded as a personal and private matter, and in which we watch television in the privacy of our homes, programs about archaeology and the Bible are going to earn high audience ratings—especially if they catch the eye, challenge the mind, and touch the heart.

In these changing circumstances, the behavior of Eliezer Sukenik can serve as a model for constructive and academically responsible engagement with an increasingly powerful media. Documentary film makers are doing what they are supposed to do in their business; all that is required is for all of us to do what we are supposed to do in ours. And we already know what that entails. In return for the privileges granted to us by the public (such as tenure and the opportunity to educate the next generation), we who teach on college and university campuses have been trained to act in accordance with a set of academic values, including intellectual rigor and critical thinking. Because we work in a subject area—religion—that is highly sensitive, it is our public responsibility to practice our craft in ways that are principled and disciplined. We have been trained, for example, to collect evidence in a fair and unbiased manner. We collect all the evidence, not just what can be used to support our hypotheses. In fact, we give special attention to evidence which appears not to support our hypotheses. We are trained to evaluate the evidence in an intellectually sophisticated way, constructing humanistic interpretations that cohere responsibly not only with the current state of scholarship in our disciplines, but also with centuries of knowledge in the study of history, philosophy, and culture.

In the field of archaeology and the Bible, we employ the most up-to-date methods of excavation and research, building on the accomplishments (but avoiding the errors) of earlier generations, especially biblical archaeology's overly hasty effort to connect text and artifact. We know better than to enter a tomb without an excavation permit, as the film crew did in *The Lost Tomb of Jesus*. We know better than to dig in order to try to prove or disprove anything in the Bible. On the contrary, we have been trained to unearth and interpret the material evidence of what was normal and typical in the ancient world, what biblical writers either did not think to mention or perhaps did not want to mention. And all along the way, we consistently adhere to those old-school disciplines of research, writing, and peer review. When we make mistakes (and we often do), we admit them, change our mind, and move on. Our adherence to these disciplines is a practical expression of our shared commitment to a set of intellectual virtues, and it is those virtues that give the public a reason to trust us.

In service to the public trust, we archaeologists and biblical scholars can and should cooperate with the media to inform, educate and—yes—entertain. There is (I sincerely hope) nothing inherently wrong with appearing on television in interviews and documentaries about our subjects. And when we do, it is our obligation to serve not as mouthpieces for our own pet theories, but as trustworthy experts on the current state of knowledge in our field. *Nova, Frontline,* CNN, National Geographic, the History Channel, and the Discovery Channel are not the appropriate venues for trotting out our own idiosyncratic hunches, off-the-cuff speculations, and extraordinary claims. Nor are they the settings in which we should range beyond the limits of our scholarly expertise. On the contrary, these programs and channels are (literally) *channels* through which we can introduce the general public to the current state of knowledge about archaeology and the Bible. My own view is that we should never present to the public through the media any ideas or theories which have not yet been vetted by the community of scholars. Put another way: if we could not get it published in peer-reviewed journals, notably the *Bulletin of the American Schools of Oriental Research* or the *Journal of Biblical Literature*, we should never say it in front of a camera when the little red light is on.

These scholarly disciplines deserve to be preserved and defended, because when they are abandoned and replaced by profit-driven sensationalism, the negative effects ripple outward far beyond the narrow fields of biblical studies and archaeology, and even farther beyond all those TV sets and living rooms. Irresponsible claims about archaeology and the Bible have the long-term deleterious effect of reinforcing exactly the wrong kinds of public attitudes about issues involving religion, politics, and the Middle East. A study by the Department of Religion at Rhodes College showed that during its brief heyday, the James ossuary became an early 21st-century relic, luring thousands of pilgrims with its promise of tangible proof for their most cherished religious hopes (Byrne and McNary-Zak 2009). In the blogosphere, *The Lost Tomb of Jesus* generated assertions that Christianity had been exposed as a fraud, to be accepted only by people who refused to listen to reason and evidence. In this way, sensationalism about the Bible and archaeology corrodes and degrades public attitudes toward some of the most important issues of our time. It disposes viewers toward black-and-white thinking and oversimplification. Worst of all, it invites the public to view the Middle East through a set of lenses that grossly distorts the current religious and political situation there. It implies that this rich and complicated region is actually a simple place, where religious battles can be won or lost, and so should be fought. It invites the public to conceive of the Middle East as an arena in which one side can prove itself right, and the other side wrong. Sensationalism about the Bible and archaeology miseducates the public about what the Middle East has been, and is today, thereby diminishing the prospects for what it might someday become.

References

Bagatti, B.
  1950   Resti Cristiani in Palestina Anteriori a Costatino? *Rivista di Archeologia Cristiana* 26: 119–20.
Byrne, R., and McNary-Zak, B., eds.
  2009   *Resurrecting the Brother of Jesus: The James Ossuary Controversy and the Quest for Religious Relics.* Chapel Hill: University of North Carolina Press.
Dever, W. G.
  1997   Biblical Archaeology. Pp. 315–19 in vol. 1 of *The Oxford Encyclopedia of Archaeology in the Near East,* ed. E. M. Meyers. 5 vols. New York: Oxford University Press.
Gibson, S.
  2004   *The Cave of John the Baptist: The Stunning Archaeological Discovery That Has Redefined Christian History.* New York: Doubleday.
Jacobovici, S.
  2004   *James, Brother of Jesus.* DVD. New York: Wellspring Media.
  2007   *The Lost Tomb of Jesus.* DVD. Port Washington, NY: Koch Vision.
Jacobovici, S., and Pellegrino, C.
  2007   *The Jesus Family Tomb: The Evidence Behind the Discovery No One Wanted to Find.* New York: HarperOne.
Kane, J. P.
  1971   By No Means "The Earliest Records of Christianity." *Palestine Exploration Quarterly* 103: 103–8.
Kraeling, C. H.
  1946   Christian Burial Urns? *Biblical Archaeologist* 9: 16–18.

Lemaire, A.
  2002   Burial Box of James, the Brother of Jesus: Earliest Archaeological Evidence of Jesus Found in Jerusalem. *Biblical Archaeology Review* 28: 24–33.
Murphy, F. J.
  2005   Circumstantial Evidence. Review of Gibson 2004. *America* 192: 19–20.
Scham, S.
  2004   St. John's Cave? Review of Gibson 2004. *Archaeology* 57: 52.
Shanks, H., and Witherington, B., III
  2003   *The Brother of Jesus: The Dramatic Story and Meaning of the First Archaeological Link to Jesus and His Family.* San Francisco: HarperSanFrancisco.
Silberman, N. A., and Goren, Y.
  2003   Faking Biblical History. *Archaeology* 56: 10–20.
Sukenik, E. L.
  1947a A Hoard of Coins of John Hyrcanus. *Jewish Quarterly Review* 37: 281–84.
  1947b Some Unpublished Coins of Aelia Capitolina. *Jewish Quarterly Review* 37: 157–60.
  1947c The Earliest Records of Christianity. *American Journal of Archaeology* 51: 351–65.
Taylor, J. E.
  2005   Review of Gibson 2004. *Palestine Exploration Quarterly* 137: 175–81.
Willoughby, H. K.
  1949   Review of *The Earliest Records of Christianity*, by E. L. Sukenik. *Journal of Biblical Literature* 68: 61–65.

The Future of the Historical Documentary
Scholarly Responses to "History Channel Meets CSI"

MILTON MORELAND

While books, journals, and magazines about the Bible and archaeology reach thousands of interested readers annually, in recent years some form of a biblical archaeology documentary is watched by millions of television and internet viewers each month. For example, by my personal count, no fewer than 14 new documentaries on the setting of the historical Jesus—with reference to recent archaeological excavations—appeared on English language television programs between 2004 and 2009. Most of the major media outlets have been involved in the proliferation of the film genre (especially the A&E network, the Discovery Channel, *Frontline* for PBS, the History Channel, the ABC network, and the BBC). By the late 20th century, the biblical archaeology documentary film virtually replaced the book as the medium through which most of the public received information about archaeology. While one might approve of the fact that information about biblical archaeology is so widely available through the mass marketed television networks (and increasingly, over the internet), as the venue for information has shifted, archaeologists have less and less control over the medium through which the interested public receives archaeological information. In the past two decades, archaeologists have rapidly become actors and talking heads for filmmakers who edit and transport their research to the public.

The purpose of this essay is not to lament the growth of the documentary film genre as a primary medium for public dissemination of scholarly knowledge about archaeology. Scholars legitimately can complain about both their lack of editorial control in this medium and the overly simplistic content and argumentation of many documentary films. But a proactive approach will serve the academy better than disinterested castigation of this popular medium. After a brief autobiographical reflection on what I have designated the "ossuary phenomena" of 2002–3,

109

this essay turns to an examination of the film genre and recent documentary films and concludes with an appraisal of future prospects for scholars who desire to be involved with documentary films that provide information about archaeology and the Bible. Archaeologists should not discount the potential of a visually appealing film as a means of reconstructing the past in a format that is both credible and accessible. Although the genre has its pitfalls, scholars must attune themselves selves to its potential and become involved in producing documentaries that present current scholarship.

A Wake-Up Call: The Ossuary Phenomena

In 2002, when I attended the public and scholarly events in Toronto related to the so-called James Ossuary, I was amazed to see that the fields of biblical studies and archaeology could so easily become part of a media circus. Highly respected scholars, including archaeologists, epigraphers, and Biblicists, were compelled to respond to unsubstantiated claims that a recently revealed inscription on an ancient ossuary, which was purchased on the black market, might be the "first archaeological link to Jesus and his family" (Shanks and Witherington 2003). As is now a typical practice in the media age, a few months after the glorified press release and media events in Toronto, Simcha Jacobovici's documentary film about the ossuary (*James, Brother of Jesus*) was broadcast on the Discovery Channel. Following those memorable Toronto meetings and the release of the Jacobovici's film, I met with three of my colleagues at Rhodes College and developed a plan to study the media attention and public responses to what we began calling "the ossuary phenomena." Thus, our group—the archaeologist, epigraphist, church historian, and scholar of American religions and tourism—embarked on what became a five-year project involving undergraduate students and aimed at better understanding the interplay between media and artifacts.

I used to think that documentary films were insignificant and not worth mentioning in scholarly discourse. Occasionally, I found them entertaining and informative enough to show to a class of undergraduate students. But through the process of examining the ossuary phenomena, I went from thinking that documentary films were mostly insignificant to thinking that biblical scholars and archaeologists need to take these films very seriously.

Our team of researchers visited the Royal Ontario Museum in Toronto, where the ossuary was on display for one month at the end of 2002. We talked with dozens of people who either heard about the ossuary through some media outlet or who had been part of the group of approximately 100,000 visitors who saw the ossuary when it was on display at the Royal Ontario Museum. The team interviewed dozens of scholars, religious leaders, and museum officials, asking them what they thought was significant about the ossuary and about why and how it was displayed (Bremer 2009). Through this process, it became clear to our team of researchers that a documentary that was written, directed, and produced by a professional filmmaker, rather than scholars' publications, had provided the storyline about the ossuary that was best known to the interested public (Moreland 2009). In many respects, the public's opinion of the ossuary was manufactured and manipulated by carefully planned press releases and a well-choreographed and well-timed documentary film that made the claim (on the DVD jacket), "that after nearly 2,000 years, historical evidence for the existence of Jesus has come to light, literally written in stone."

The ossuary phenomena of 2002 and 2003 were both fascinating and disturbing. I found them fascinating because they signaled a rapid development in the relationship between scholars and the public imagination as informed by mass media. On the other hand, these events were troubling because, in this case, the process of information dissemination thwarted reliable channels of correspondence and reasonable scholarly practices; and the result was hyperbole, power struggles, and legal wrangling. The ossuary phenomena caused me to reflect on the evolving connections between scholars and the media. I began to ask, what should be the public role of scholars in documentary film productions related to the fields of biblical studies and Near Eastern archaeology? Should scholars be actors and talking heads in the commercially driven enterprise that we know as the documentary film industry? If so, how can scholars play a more significant role in the production of documentary films in order to provide a beneficial outcome?

The short answer to the question of whether scholars should be involved in the documentary film genre is unequivocally affirmative. Despite the typical lack of editorial control, reasonable and thoughtful scholars must participate in this genre. Notwithstanding the fact that academic training does not usually prepare scholars for this type of enterprise, rational archaeologists who are not touting conspiracy theories or overembellished theses must continue to seek ways to participate in documentaries—as talking-head experts, consultants, and members of production companies. And despite the fact that the documentary genre has itself suffered from embarrassing cases of highly dubious workmanship, scholars must find ways to use this medium to present the interested public with accurate data and reasoned analysis.

One of the first revelations I had as I began to review documentary films is that I knew very little about the genre itself. I realized that, before I began to criticize the films, I needed to know something more about the genre. What are the expectations of filmmakers? What are the general goals and professional values of film producers? How do filmmakers identify topics and write storylines? How do documentarists speak about their craft? Scholars are extremely well trained in identifying the fine nuances and literary conventions of written material. They know the many different intentions and functions of books and must apply similar critical acumen to film. The next section thus provides some insights into the history of the genre in order to identify and illustrate some of the benefits and pitfalls of presenting scholarship in this format.

Assessing The Documentary Film Genre

In comparison to fictional materials that claim to be only imitations of reality or "melodramatic spectacle," documentary films allegedly provide less-filtered or untampered representations of our past and present worlds (Nichols 2010: xii). However, the ideal of authenticity has always been combined with poetic license ever since the beginning of documentary film production. While not identical to "news" programming, documentaries, as the name implies, were intended to document the world in film. Because of the desire to combine artistry and esthetics with reporting, documentarists are typically quick to point out the differences between purely instructional films and documentary films. Many of the issues surrounding the production of documentaries—authenticity, artistic freedom, marketing and audience appeal—have been present since the nascent stages of the genre.

While it would be naive to think documentaries provide an authentic picture of the past, film producers and promoters often can rely on their viewers' belief that the film will be "true" simply because it is labeled a documentary. Since its inception, the genre has been widely accepted as a trustworthy medium. In his history of documentaries, Barnouw observes how the earliest filmmakers set the stage for current documentarists. Already by 1910, they functioned as reporters, explorers, propagandists, promoters, popular educators, war correspondents, and advertisers (Barnouw 1993: 29). As explorers, filmmakers gained large followings by producing short documentaries of "native" groups in distant lands that, in retrospect, "gave western audiences a reassuring feeling about the colonial system" (Barnouw 1993: 23). Besides ethnographic and local interest topics, filmmakers quickly became regular producers of state propaganda. In the early 20th century, American presidents and British royalty were particularly adept at exploiting the new film genre for their political gain. Clearly, by World War II, the use of the documentary for political goals was well established on both sides of the Atlantic.

The birth of the genre occurred at the same time that newsreel footage was first being broadcast to the masses in movie theaters. Newsreel footage was, in some respects, a type of short documentary that focused on the major events of the day. With the increasing popularity of film as a medium for presenting accurate news stories, there was an easy correlation between news reporting and documentary film. Many viewers of both newsreels and documentaries subscribed to the idea that the "camera does not lie." Not unlike many of the current documentarists who frame their work as "investigative reporting," the thin line between news and documentary has existed since the beginning of cinema. Arguably, this coexistence has had a significant impact on the public acceptance of documentaries as trustworthy sources of information.

After the new commercial enterprise of documentary filmmaking was established, the demand for film footage expanded as competition grew for more film productions. Theater owners and audiences began to demand access to more filmed presentations of events from around the world. Thus, the early success of the genre led to another tendency that has consistently been a part of the filmic venture: "Along with colonialist tendencies, documentary film was infected with increasing fakery" (Barnouw 1993: 24). If the necessary film footage was unavailable, filmmakers lacked no imagination in creating scenes that were presented as "real" events. Staged events and misrepresentations were integral to the film genre from the beginning. Despite embarrassing revelations of faked and staged scenes, the power of the moving image, in combination with the connection to "news" reporting, led audiences from the beginning to accept the genre as authentic.

Long-standing viewer expectation of legitimacy in documentary films can be related to several other factors. Regarding the basic film medium, Nichols suggests that "Documentaries offer the sensuous experience of sounds and images organized to move us: they activate feelings and emotions; they tap into values and beliefs, and, in doing so, possess an expressive power that equals or exceeds the printed word" (Nichols 2010: 100). The idea that documentaries "move us" may help explain a component of the persuasiveness of the film genre in comparison to print publications, but it is only part of the story. In their history of the genre, Ellis and McLane (2005) explore the intentional ways that documentary film producers have attempted to persuade their audiences of the veracity of their medium. Early documentary filmmakers such as Robert Flaherty and John Grierson claimed that their films creatively presented the real lives of their typically exotic subjects, though necessarily through a poetic lens. In comparison to studio productions, Grierson argued, "the original (or native) actor, and the original (or native) scene, are better guides to a screen interpretation of the modern world. . . . They give it power of interpretation over more complex and astonishing happenings in the real world than the studio mind can conjure up" (1966: 147). Grierson, as a primary representative of the genre in its first 50-year period (he is often called "the father of documentary film"), was highlighting the fact that documentaries were "screen interpretations"; and he never underestimated the role of these films in presenting "the real world." His famous definition of the genre, "the creative treatment of actuality," still holds sway in many documentary circles (Grierson 1933: 7; see the discussion in Kerrigan and McIntyre 2010).

The documentary film genre, from its earliest roots, has relied on the good faith of the audience to support both the poetic license of the filmmaker and the idea that films of this type will essentially be factually dependable. When compared to fiction films, Nichols observes, "The conventions and constraints, codes and expectations may function somewhat differently, but both fiction and documentary set out to make something from the historical evidence they incorporate. Matters of institutional discourse, textual structure, and viewer expectation constitute the heart of the difference" (Nichols 1991: 116). Developing persuasive hypotheses from historical evidence always has pitfalls. Archaeologists and historians well know the ease with which dominant historical discourses can obscure rather than illuminate the past. Because of "viewer expectation," the documentary film genre provides an important opportunity for scholars to teach the public about their disciplines; but it also allows for significant misrepresentation and misinformation to be easily disseminated. Documentary, more than written nonfiction, "produces the referential illusion and in fact derives its prestige from that production" (Guynn 1990: 223). Visual "evidence" is more persuasive than written material. As Renov has argued, "every documentary claims for itself an anchorage in history; the referent of the nonfiction sign is meant to be a piece of the world (albeit a privileged because a visible and/or audible one) and, thus, was once available to experience in the everyday" (Renov 1993: 31).

For the most part, the first half-century of documentary production featured films on contemporary cultural topics and social journalism, not on archaeological and historical issues. Interest in historical topics increased in the second half of the 20th century as documentaries increasingly found support in state funded television programming on the BBC and PBS and as other British and American TV networks initiated documentary series for mass appeal (that is, *Project XX* and *The Twentieth Century*; see Ellis and McLane 2005: 189–93). Thanks to the public release of archival film footage from World War II, the historical documentary grew in popularity throughout the 1970s. *The World at War* (1975) is often noted as a precursor to recent historical documentaries: "Using archive film, photographic and other still images, and interviews with eyewitnesses, it broke up historical events into smaller, accessible story lines. These are occasionally supplemented by the use of location shooting to establish atmosphere and to fill a gap where archive footage did not exist" (Ellis and McLane 2005: 253).

The increase in instructional documentaries on historical topics through the 1970s was augmented by technical advances in film production and new types of recording and editing equipment. The real boom came in the mid-1980s when *Frontline* began as a documentary series on WBGH in Boston (1983). Within a year (in 1984), the first major network that focused primarily on documentaries—A&E, the Arts and Entertainment Network—made its debut. The Discovery Channel began shortly thereafter in 1985. Three more channels were launched in the 1990s: A&E began two other channels that focus on documentary broadcasts—the History Channel in 1995 and the Biography Channel in 1999; and the National Geographic Channel became available in markets around the world between 1997 and 2001.

Since 1983, *Frontline* has developed one of the most trusted brands of documentary film. *Frontline* productions must follow more than 80 strict journalistic guidelines that contain tough statements about accuracy, truthfulness, impartiality, and fairness to all participants and that also cover issues related to funding, conflicts of interest, and editing techniques.[1] In *Frontline*'s first two decades, Ken Burns became the most famous producer and cinematographer for the series. With more than 20 films and series, and with significant corporate sponsorships, Burns nearly perfected the art of historical documentary production. Though occasionally criticized for taking too much artistic license on historical topics (e.g., Toplin 1996; Blight 1997; Rose and Corley 2003), he is often praised for the care he takes in presenting historical topics in a manner that strongly appeals to the viewing public.

Burns is probably most famous in cinematography for his use of still images. As filmmakers like Burns took up more topics about the past, viewers were treated to resourceful techniques related to the use of archival photos. To make the past come alive on film, Burns used framing techniques and camera movements that accentuated specific aspects of an image. In an essay about Burns's series, *The Civil War*, Lancioni discusses the ways that his reframing innovations provide a new perspective on the antebellum African-American experience. By focusing on background images in photos of the Civil War, Burns recreated and illustrated little known aspects of the lives of enslaved people. "Ultimately, reframing visually advances the argument that history is not a product, an absolute truth enshrined in libraries and archives, but rather an on-going critical encounter between the past and present. That encounter, moreover, is not passive or accidental; it is rhetorical" (Lancioni 1996: 398). While working with archival materials, Burns created a new visual perspective on the past. In combination with alluring video from battlefields, period music, actors providing reenactments and reading Civil War–era letters and diaries, and a running interpretation from historians such as Shelby Foote, Burns drew in millions of viewers and opened a floodgate of renewed interest in historical documentaries. In many respects, his work provided a model for filmmakers who were interested in biblical archaeology.

Using voice-of-God narration, talking head experts, archival photos, ancient texts, artwork, period music, and reenactments of historical scenes, historical documentaries have created an objectified "memory" of past events and people for many television viewers. Following Burns, filmmakers have attempted to construct history for the modern viewer

---

1. WGBH Educational Foundation, "Journalistic Guidelines," 2012. On-line: http://www.pbs.org/wgbh/pages/frontline/us/guidelines.html.

through documentaries. Unfortunately, most of the films on the Bible and archaeology fail to meet the Frontline production guidelines. While there are several terrific success stories in which scholars and documentarists have teamed up to produce high quality films, many filmmakers have relied on the popular reputation of the genre's authenticity and have taken liberties with their materials. Some films that have little or no objective scholarly content can be explained by appealing to the long tradition of documentary poetic license. In other cases, it is clear that budgetary constraints, poor editing, and inferior workmanship contribute to a film's meager or misinformed content. In what follows, I turn to several specific examples of documentary films on archaeology and the Bible in order to show how the genre has affected these disciplines and to suggest how scholars can use the film genre to inform the public better about their field.

Learning from Past Documentaries

That's Entertainment: Documentary as Spectacle

When critiquing documentary films, we do well to remember that filmmakers are explicitly trained to activate the viewer's "aesthetic awareness" (Nichols 2010: 104). The history of the genre and my discussions with documentarists make it clear that documentarists do not usually intend to produce instructional or training films, nor do they often think of their craft as news reporting. Rather, documentary films aim to persuade the audience of a particular point of view through well-ordered visual stimulation, supplemented by a sound track that interprets (through the role of the talking head and voice-of-God narrative) and arouses the viewer's interest (through music). In many cases, a well-argued and defensible thesis is not a top priority. Esthetically pleasing presentations outweigh the emphasis on scholarly content, for documentaries rarely have the luxury of slowing down to clarify argumentation or provide well-developed theses lest they lose their audience and disturb the flow of the storyline.

Two projects quickly come to mind as examples of films that placed a high priority on visual stimulation. Jacobovici's 2006 film, *The Exodus Decoded*, is a prime instance of a film that attempts to captivate the audience with visual stimulation. This high-budget film, which was produced by James Cameron, was packed with digitally enhanced scenes and eye-catching computer animations (created by Gravity Visual Effects). In the past decade, I have experimented with a variety of documentary films in a range of undergraduate college courses (traditional age, adult degree completion, in-person and on-line instruction). This film never fails to generate a lot of discussion. Students are amazed at the visual effects. Although many are impressed with the esthetics, even before we evaluate in detail the historical and archaeological arguments, few students find the film to be convincing. After I ask them to read scholarly reviews of the film, I have found that fewer than five percent of my students think the thesis is even plausible. In fact, so many of them find the argument so implausible that they wonder why the film was made. In terms of documentary filmmaking, this is a case of high visual impact and low scholarly content.

The second film project that well illustrates this type of documentary style was produced by National Geographic. The 2005–2006 series *Science of the Bible* combined a large number of reenactments with scientific investigation and useful scholarly insights. Although the "science" was often well conceived and the scholarly interpretations were generally of high quality, the desire to provide the viewer with a constant stream of visual stimulation through reenactments demonstrated the producer's goal of attracting a large audience. The reenactments capture the viewer's attention, and so the audience is (implicitly) directed to historicize the biblical stories. Despite the scholarly voices of reason that can often be heard playing on the soundtrack, the visual force of the documentary series has a bigger impact than the aural scholarship. As I have argued elsewhere, documentaries of this type can contribute to the regrettable idea that archaeological artifacts should be understood as objects that can either prove or disprove a person's faith (Moreland 2009).

The Role of the Talking-Head Scholar

Documentary films are stories. In many cases, they are also commercial enterprises. Films present a story that can sell. Scholars, therefore, are often narrators and actors in films that are intended to make a profit for the production company. Many documentarists appear to be primarily interested in producing esthetically pleasing storytelling that will captivate an audience. But images and music are only a part of the rhetorical force. In most types of documentary film, the role of the talking-head scholar (or archaeologist in the field), who usually appears with credentials labeled on the screen, is a significant factor in the measure of the film's reliability. In many historical documentaries, scholars provide the core interpretation of the images and data; they move the discourse forward through their carefully edited appearances on the screen and in the soundtrack.

In spite of the fact that scholars have long provided key elements in the persuasiveness of historical documentaries, one of the most common observations about documentaries that I hear from fellow scholars and students in my classes is that the editing of scholarly comments typically does not do justice to the complexity of the scholar's ideas. A scholar's comments become part of a filmmaker's edited storyline, often without full consideration of the thesis that the scholar was espousing. As already noted, visual evidence is more compelling than scholarly voiceovers. Few documentary films allow the participating scholars the time to interrogate the visual presentation thooughly, let alone fully describe the complexities of a scholarly thesis.

In my study of Jacobovici's *James, Brother of Jesus*, I noted that 23 scholars were used in the film. Their total word count is about one-third of the narrative: about 2,312 words out of about 6,157 words in the film (Moreland 2009: 93). Although this appears to be a considerable portion of the audio content, the scholars' voices are edited together to support the writer's thesis, often masking or distorting the scholars' views. The film attempts to show the genuineness of the ossuary inscription, and there is little indication that many of the scholars who appeared in the film did not think that the inscription was authentic. When filmmakers desire to tell a particular story, they will find a way to do it, regardless of scholarly input. Convincing filmmakers to tell stories that accurately reflect current scholarship and the opinions of individual scholars must be a necessary step in the collaborative process of documentary production.

Questioning Documentary Authenticity

When considering documentaries that cover Near Eastern archaeology and the Bible, viewer expectation of historical reliability is, in my experience, still quite high. But viewer confidence in the authenticity of the material will not last forever. Each year, I observe more students who are not willing simply to trust the content of documentaries because they are generically labeled as such. Winston notes that, "Like journalists, documentarists too are in the entertainment business, if only in their need to gain and hold the attention of their audiences. Documentaries, like journalism, have an elevated need to tell the truth if they are to maintain their integrity; but, far more than journalism, they are also vehicles for personal self-expression" (Winston 2000: 128). As observed previously, the poetic license or self expression of filmmakers has always been a priority in this genre. Nevertheless, even well-meaning film producers can easily lose sight of scholarly theses when more appealing or profitable storylines are competing for their attention.

Add to this the explosion of on-line documentary access, and the problem multiples. Dozens of groups with fringe, outdated, political, and radical ideas about the Bible and archaeology are producing videos for mass, on-line distribution. A simple internet search for videos on "biblical archaeology" reveals thousands of documentary-style film productions espousing almost every imaginable idea about the interpretation of archaeological material in relation to biblical stories. Because most of the interested public probably cannot identify a plausible scholarly approach to the use of archaeology in relation to the Bible, the wide proliferation of documentaries that claim to represent the truth about the historicity and meaning of the Bible and archaeology will have a long-term impact. In the world of on-line documentaries, mainstream scholarly ideas appear to make up only a small percentage of the material presented. Most of these documentaries promote the idea that archaeologists are discovering materials that prove the truth of biblical stories—such as Noah's Ark, the Red Sea crossing, and the resurrection of Jesus. These on-line films clearly appeal to religiously conservative audiences. While many scholars and archaeologists choose to ignore this proliferation of on-line material, their silence increasingly provides room for this simplistic and often misleading use of archaeology.

Archaeologists Solve Biblical Mysteries

Popular acceptance of this genre's reliability also suffers when film-makers put a high priority on garnering larger audiences through advertising that a particular film or TV series will solve the "mysteries" of the Bible. In the past two decades, several major documentary series and dozens of individual films have promoted the idea that there are biblical mysteries that can be solved by archaeological evidence. Although there is not space in this essay to explore each film or series in detail, a brief reflection on the rhetoric of these mystery films is warranted. The general idea behind documentary projects such as A&E's *The Mysteries of the Bible* is that modern science, including archaeology, can illuminate dark spaces of the biblical past. This 45-part series, which originally aired from 1994 until 1998, is similar to the aforementioned *Science of the Bible* (National Geographic) and the BBC's *Ancient Evidence* series, which covered the "mysteries" of the Old Testament, Jesus, and the Apostles (10 episodes aired on BBC and the Discovery Channel in 2003).

In each case, archaeology is viewed as "evidence" that can explain a biblically related problem. Archaeologists regularly appear as experts in the programs, though much of the filmed footage also contains scenes from the modern Israeli landscape, and dramatic reenactments that were often filmed in Turkey or the United States. While many of the individual films provide helpful, scholarly information, the basic idea that archaeologists intend to solve biblical mysteries returns us to the past era of biblical archaeology, when archaeologists were trying to "prove" the Bible; an idea that most modern scholars eschew. While one might argue that archaeology has solved some biblical problems, the basic premise of these films obscures the fact that archaeology of the ancient Near East is often unconcerned with matters directly related to biblical stories; and even when archaeologists touch on topics related to the Bible, their discoveries tend to complicate further rather than solve the problems.

Conspiracy Theories: Archaeologists Keep Secrets

Documentary film makers have increasingly taken on the role of the seemingly righteous crusader who faces danger and ridicule to discover what scholars have hidden. Conspiracies strike a nerve with documentary viewers because our knowledge of human nature suggests the hazy possibility that our received traditions are rooted in lies (Goldberg 2001).

Conspiracy theories stimulate the popular imagination and lead some people to believe that the world's chaos is the byproduct of concealed truths and that recovering these secrets will set things right. They can be powerfully seductive because they validate our suspicion that not all is right in the world. The seductive allure of stories about forgotten manuscripts and artifacts grows out of the popular idea that covert forces have concealed truths that need to be brought to light by the reporter or film maker (Fenster 1999).

A recent example that received a significant amount of media attention was Jacobovici's film, *The Lost Tomb of Jesus*. In the film, Jacobovici acts out the role of the investigative reporter as he seeks to uncover the Jesus family tomb, which, in his estimation, was hidden from the public for several decades after it was accidentally discovered in 1980. In the film, Jacobovici's basic assumption is that archaeologists discovered this tomb and then did nothing to reveal its faith-shaking importance to the interested public. When the tomb was discovered, it actually did receive significant media attention and a thorough assessment in the scholarly community. Of course, for the purposes of the film, it is much more exciting to think that archaeologists found a faith-shattering discovery and kept it hidden from the public. In reaction to this type of filmed argument, archaeologists should be involved in a wide variety of popular media that will help displace the idea that there are certain powerful entities in the scholarly world that are attempting to keep religious truths from the public.

Conclusion: Scholarly Responsibility in the Public Arena

In light of this historical trajectory in the documentary genre, what are the prospects for the future of scholarly collaboration with documentarists and what can be learned from the first few decades of scholars' participating in these films? First, it must be stated that the documentary genre is not uniformly problematic. Several excellent documentaries have recently presented scholarly information about the Bible and archaeology in an effective way. Notable examples are Gary Glassman's NOVA production, *The Bible's Buried Secrets: Beyond Fact or Fiction*, and Isy Moregensztern and Thierry Ragobert's Icarus Films production, *The Bible Unearthed*. Even the Discovery Channel attempted to redeem itself with a three-part series entitled *Who Was Jesus?* These films have all had significant input from scholars, and it shows. How can scholars keep this positive momentum going?

I would encourage scholars to avoid sensationalized film productions that are clearly driving at an unsubstantiated thesis. When joining a film project, we need to research the producers and find out as much as possible about the goals and thesis of the production. We need to maintain the same due diligence that we have with published materials in print formats. When the *Washington Post*'s television critic, Lonnae

O'Neal Parker, reviewed Jacobovici's *James Brother of Jesus*, she declared that the film was "History Channel meets *CSI*." As a television critic reviewing a show for a wide public audience, she concludes that the documentary was "a fascinating mystery that will most especially appeal to those who require the help of science to walk by faith" (Parker 2003). Reputable scholars need to be savvy enough to avoid participating in dramatic documentaries that seek to prove a radical idea through means that are reminiscent of television crime dramas.

Documentary films are no doubt problematic, but as scholars who work with tested methods of historical research, we will do ourselves a great disservice if we avoid presenting our ideas in this popular medium. There are many people who are willing to appear in documentaries in order to promote specific theological constructs and improbable historical reconstructions. As scholars who are interested in the academic integrity of the fields of archaeology and biblical studies, we need to continue to invite film makers to tell interesting stories that derive from well-tested historical inquiry. Admittedly, the genre will never be ideal as a venue for conveying the complexities of scholarly argumentation. We must remain forever vigilant about who is making the film and to what end our comments and ideas might be used. Yet we must team up with responsible filmmakers in order to remain engaged as archaeologists and public scholars with a genre that can have an important impact on social, political, and religious issues that touch and sometimes invade our field of study.

References

Barnouw, E.
1993   *Documentary: A History of the Non-Fiction Film.* 2nd ed. Oxford: Oxford University Press.
Blight, D. W.
1997   Homer with a Camera, Our Iliad without the Aftermath: Ken Burns's Dialogue with Historians. *Reviews in American History* 25: 351–59.
Bremer, T.
2009   The Brother of Jesus in Toronto. Pp. 31–58 in *Resurrecting the Brother of Jesus: The James Ossuary Controversy and the Quest for Religious Relics*, ed. R. Byrne and B. McNary-Zak. Chapel Hill: University of North Carolina Press.
Ellis, J. C., and McLane, B. A.
2005   *A New History of Documentary Film.* New York: Continuum.
Fenster, M.
1999   *Conspiracy Theories: Secrecy and Power in American Culture.* Minneapolis: University of Minnesota Press.
Goldberg, R. A.
2001   *Enemies Within: The Culture of Conspiracy in Modern America.* New Haven, CT: Yale University Press.

Grierson, J.
  1933   The Documentary Producer. *Cinema Quarterly* 2: 7–9.
  1966   First Principles of Documentary. Pp. 145–56 in *Grierson on Documentary*, ed. F. Hardy. Berkeley: University of California Press.
Guynn, W.
  1990   *A Cinema of Nonfiction*. Madison, NJ: Farleigh Dickinson University Press.
Kerrigan, S., and McIntyre, P.
  2010   The "Creative Treatment of Actuality": Rationalizing and Reconceptualizing the Notion of Creativity for Documentary Practice. *Journal of Media Practice* 11: 111–30.
Lancioni, J.
  1996   The Rhetoric of the Frame: Revisioning Archival Photographs in *The Civil War*. *Western Journal of Communication* 60: 397-414.
Moreland, M.
  2009   Christian Artifacts in Documentary Film: The Case of the James Ossuary. Pp. 73–135 in *Resurrecting the Brother of Jesus: The James Ossuary Controversy and the Quest for Religious Relics*, ed. R. Byrne and B. McNary-Zak. Chapel Hill: University of North Carolina Press.
Nichols, B.
  1991   *Representing Reality: Issues and Concepts in Documentary*. Bloomington: Indiana University Press.
  2010   *Introduction to Documentary*. 2nd ed. Bloomington: Indiana University Press.
Parker, L. O.
  2003   Resurrecting Interest in Jesus's Brother. *Washington Post*, April 19.
Renov, M.
  1993   Toward a Poetics of Documentary. Pp. 12–36 in *Theorizing Documentary*, ed. M. Renov. New York: Routledge.
Rose, V. E., and Corley, J.
  2003   A Trademark Approach to the Past: Ken Burns, the Historical Profession, and Assessing Popular Presentations of the Past. *The Public Historian* 25: 49–59.
Shanks, H., and Witherington, B., III
  2003   *The Brother of Jesus: The Dramatic Story and Meaning of the First Archaeological Link to Jesus and His Family*. New York: HarperCollins.
Toplin, R. B., ed.
  1996   *Ken Burns's* The Civil War: *Historians Respond*. New York: Oxford University Press.
Winston, B.
  2000   *Lies, Damn Lies and Documentaries*. London: British Film Institute.

An Ancient Medium in the Modern Media
Sagas of Semitic Inscriptions

CHRISTOPHER A. ROLLSTON

Introduction

Prima facie, the arcana of the field of Northwest Semitic epigraphy would not seem to be an auspicious source of fodder for sensationalizing by the modern semi-popular media. After all, the standard fare for a Northwest Semitic epigrapher is the deciphering of ancient scripts and languages, the parsing of the verbiage, the enumeration of relevant comparative Semitic data, discussions of palaeography, orthography, and phonology, and attempts at understanding the semantic domains of a text and its basic Sitz im Leben. Nevertheless, the history of Northwest Semitic studies is punctuated by periodic "penumbras." The factors that precipitate the problematic assumptions and assertions are normally varied, and often there is a mélange of contributing secondary and tertiary factors. In this article, I shall focus on some of the typical difficulties for attempts to navigate between the rock of Scylla and the whirlpool of Charybdis, that is, between the world of the scholar and that of the media. Ultimately, I believe scholars can, and must, do better.

The Media at Sea Sans Compass: Sensationalizing Dilettantes

Sometimes, the culpable protagonist is a dilettante from the popular media, a *bête noire* who propounds some bemusing edifice of chaff but manages to delude nonspecialists because of the artistry of the sophistry. Such dilettantes are often able to find a scholar who is willing to embrace (or has already embraced) the sensational position, and this serves to provide the sensational proposal with the sort of legitimacy

Author's note: I am grateful to Eric and Carol Meyers for the invitation to present at the Duke Symposium and for their invitation to include this article in the symposium volume. I am also grateful to Erin Darby for her kind assistance during the course of the conference. My research assistants, Stephen Paul and Travis Weeks, were helpful with some of the bibliographic materials referenced in this article. Moreover, I would like to thank J. Maxwell Miller and Gerald Mattingly for discussing the subject of this article during the preliminary stages of its writing.

123

that causes some (for example, nonspecialists and gullible specialists) to believe that the proposal has merit. After all, it has the aura of veracity if a professor from a respected institution supports the media's claim.

Simcha Jacobovici is a paradigmatic pundit of this ilk (Jacobovici and Pellegrino: 2007), with his sensational assertion that the tomb complex and burial boxes (ossuaries) of Jesus of Nazareth, his wife, and his son had been found. The saga began in the most mundane of manners, that is, with Yosef Gat conducting a 1980 salvage excavation for the Israel Antiquities Authority at a tomb in the Jerusalem neighborhood of East Talpiyot. The contents of the tomb included 10 ossuaries and were described in some detail by Amos Kloner (1996), who reported that 6 of the ossuaries were inscribed. The other 4 were not inscribed, and one of them was quite damaged. Based on all the finds in the tomb, Kloner dated the tomb to the late Second Temple period. He also estimated that the bones of ca. 35 people were interred there. L. Y. Rahmani (1994: 222–24) reported on the personal names inscribed on the ossuaries as follows: (1) Mariamênou {ê} Mara ("Mariamne who is also called Mara"), (2) Yhwdh br Yšwʿ ("Yehudah bar Yeshuaʿ"), (3) Mtyh ("Mattiyah"), (4) Yšwʿ br Yhwsp ("Yeshuaʿ bar Yehosep"), (5) Ywsh ("Yoseh"), (6) Mryh ("Maryah"). Stephen Pfann (2006) has since corrected Rahmani's reading of Mariamênou {ê} Mara with "Mariame kai Mara" (that is, Miriam and Mara). The names are not remarkable, certainly not sensational.

The scholarly expertise of Kloner, Rahmani, and Pfann not withstanding, Jacobovici and Pellegrino (2007) argue that the ossuaries of the Talpiyot Tomb were those of Jesus of Nazareth and various members of his family. To be precise, they claim that the ossuary inscribed "Yeshuaʿ bar Yehosep" is that of Jesus of Nazareth; the one inscribed "Maryah" is that of Jesus' mother; the one inscribed "Mariam(n)e" (according to their reading, following Rahmani) is that of Mary Magdalene of the Gospels; the one inscribed "Yoseh" is that of Jesus' brother Jose; the one inscribed "Yehudah bar Yeshua" is that of a son born to Jesus and Mary Magdalene; and the ossuary inscribed "Mattiyah" is that of another relative of Jesus of Nazareth. Jacobovici and Pellegrino also assert that the persons buried in the ossuary inscribed "Yeshuaʿ bar Yehosep" and the one inscribed "Mariam(n)e {ê} Mara" (according to their reading) were married. Finally, it has even been argued in the media that the ossuary with the inscription "Yaʿakov bar Yehosep ʾahui d Yeshua" (that is, the "James Ossuary") was stolen from the Talpiyot Tomb decades ago (and it is assumed that the entire inscription is ancient).[1]

---

1. For the suggestion that the Yaʿakov bar Yehosep Ossuary originally hailed from the Talpiyot Tomb, see the official *Jesus Family Tomb* Web site: www .jesusfamilytomb.com. Many media reports also assume that the entire inscription is ancient. See the other discussion of that ossuary in this volume, including Jodi Magness, "Confessions of an Archaeologist: Lessons I Learned from the Talpiyot Tomb Fiasco and Other Media Encounters," pp. 89–95; Byron R. McCane, "Scholars

However, the problems with this proposal are legion. Note that, for these six inscribed ossuaries from the Talpiyot Tomb, there are just two personal names with patronymics: (1) "Yehuda bar Yeshuaᶜ'" and (2) "Yeshuaᶜ bar Yehosep." Also, there are no matronymics, no references to marital status, and no references to fraternal or sororal relationships, and the term *Magdala* (a geographicon) does not occur on the ossuary that is said to be hers. Moreover, of the two names with patronymics, the name Yehuda bar Yeshuaᶜ does not fit the historical record. That is, there is no ancient historical source that refers to Jesus of Nazareth as having a son named Yehuda. The names Yehosep, Yoseh, Yeshuaᶜ, Yehudah, Mattiyah, Maryah, Mariame, Miryam, and Martha (or the variants thereof) all have multiple attestations in the multilingual corpus of ossuaries, and some are very common. Decades ago, Sukenik (1931) published an ossuary inscribed "Yeshuaᶜ son of Yehosep." The names Yeshuaᶜ and Yehosep recur in the family of Babatha's first husband (note also: her husband was named Yeshuaᶜ, and their son was named Yeshuaᶜ as well), and her first husband's father was "Yeshuaᶜ bar Yehosep" (Lewis 1989: 35–40). That is, even with the small corpus of epigraphic attestations of personal names, the Talpiyot Tomb appearance of "Yeshuaᶜ bar Yehosep" is not unique in the epigraphic record.

These are critical lacunae, because without them it is not possible for someone today to ascertain the precise kinship relationships of antiquity. First-century tombs may have been "family tombs," but it is problematic to assume that a given tomb represents a nuclear family and that one can discern without empirical evidence the nature of the relationships within that family. The standards for cogent prosopographic constructs are high. The proposal of Jacobovici and Pellegrino fails to meet the minimal standards for cogency, and it even fails to meet the minimal standards for plausibility. Of course, the statistical and putative DNA evidence propounded is also riddled with serious methodological problems (Rollston 2006; Meyers 2006). Scholars have a responsibility to marshal empirical evidence demonstrating the problems with proposals such as this; and in the case of this Talpiyot Tomb, that has in fact happened. Nevertheless, I still meet people who accept the tenuous, sensational proposal of Jacobovici and Pellegrino. The damage, it seems, had been done.

All Trained, Restrained Hands on Deck:
The Sagacity of Methodological Doubt, Personal Restraint,
and Field Expertise

Sometimes a sensationalistic construct about an inscription hails directly from a trained scholar, often someone with modest amounts

---

Behaving Badly: Sensationalism and Archaeology in the Media," pp. 101–108, and Mark Goodacre, "The 'Jesus Tomb' and the Blogosphere," pp. 56–68.

of formal training in epigraphy itself. There are multiple possible reasons for this phenomenon; however, the most common may be that the scholar has simply jettisoned (to varying degrees) the requisite levels of a "hermeneutic of suspicion." Perhaps the scholar desperately wishes for something to be true (for example, for religious, political, ideological, or personal reasons), and so the necessary scholarly restraint is subverted by the earnest desire for a cherished assumption to be fortified and vindicated. A good example is an unprovenanced seal that surfaced on the antiquities market, that is assumed to be ancient (though I am not convinced of this), and that is asserted to bear the name of Queen Jezebel of Israel.

Here are the relevant details. Several decades ago, Nahman Avigad published a seal inscribed with the letters *yzbl* (Avigad 1964; cf. Avigad and Sass 1997: 275 [#740] = IAA 65–321). However, he was disinclined to posit that it belonged to Queen Jezebel (biblical Hebrew: *ʾyzbl*) of the 9th century B.C.E., the notorious Phoenician princess who became the wife of Ahab, King of Israel (1 Kgs 16:31). Avigad stated that "there is, of course, no basis for identifying the owner of our seal with this famous lady," although he also stated that "they may have been contemporaries, and the seal seems worthy of a queen" (Avigad 1964: 275; also Mykytiuk 2004: 216). However, Marjo Korpel has recently argued at length that this seal is that of Queen Jezebel (2006a; 2006b; 2008).

This is a most precarious of proposals. After all, the root *zbl* is reasonably well attested in Northwest Semitic as part of personal names and divine epithets. It appears in the second-millennium B.C.E. corpus of Ugaritic texts, often as an epithet for the god Baʿal (Del Olmo Lete and Sanmartin 2004: 998). In addition, the root is arguably attested in Mari Akkadian (Huffmon 1965: 186). It is also attested in Iron Age Phoenician, for example, in the personal names Bʿlzbl and Šmzbl (Hoftijzer and Jongeling 1995: 303; Benz 1972: 304). It appears in the Hebrew Bible multiple times (for example, 1 Kgs 8:13; Hab 3:11; 2 Chr 6:2) and is the basis for the personal name Zebul (Judg 9:28) and also for the name of the eponymous founder of the Israelite tribe of Zebulun (for example, Gen 30:20). Thus, this root is not particularly rare in Northwest Semitic, and it is used for multiple personal names. Nevertheless, Korpel claims that "actually *zbl* is not an element of Hebrew personal names, whereas it is attested in Canaanite names" (Korpel 2006a: 362). She also states that the "foreignness of the owner's name points to the conclusion that it is indeed the seal of Jezebel" (Korpel 2006a: 362). However, as noted, this root *does* occur in Israelite personal names. Simply put, Korpel is factually wrong. Furthermore, she also assumes that the name on the seal must be feminine, even though the Avigad-Sass corpus of seals and bullae correctly notes that the "owner's gender [is] uncertain" (Avigad and Sass 1997: 275). There are even more problems. Korpel restores two letters in the broken area at the top of the seal in order to produce the name Jezebel. To restore a *lamed* is acceptable, as this is a dominant feature of seals (*lamed* = "belonging to"). However, she also restores an *ʾalep*. This is convenient for her proposal; but the fact is that something else, or nothing at all, might be restored. Restorations are tenuous bases for prosopography. Even more problematic is the fact that the seal contains no patronymic (that is, no "daughter of Ethbaʿal") and no title (such as "queen" or "wife of Ahab"). Titles and patronymics are critical for prosopography, but this seal has neither.

Yet another difficulty is Korpel's assumption that the seal dates to the 9th century. Amihai Mazar (personal communication) has stated that "to the best of my knowledge there are no inscribed seals dated to the ninth century found in any reliable archaeological context in Israel." Similarly, Helene Sader has said (personal communication) that she is not aware of any epigraphic Phoenician seals or bullae dating to the 10th or 9th centuries that have been found at the renewed excavations in Beirut, Sidon, Tyre, or Burak; and she has also noted that no provenanced epigraphic seals from the 10th or 9th centuries are in the collection of the Department of Antiquities of Lebanon. Furthermore, Alan Millard (personal communication) agrees with me that the earliest provenanced epigraphic Aramaic seals and bullae are from the 8th century (see Avigad and Sass 1997: 285 [#760], 288 [#768]).

Korpel argues that the size of the seal and various aspects of its iconography reflect its status as a royal seal. However, because seals come in different sizes, there is no evidence that large seals are always royal. Furthermore, because the iconography of seals is diverse, no aspect of iconography is diagnostic of royalty. Yet, among the most stunning statements Korpel makes is that the lotus flower on the seal was a symbol of vanity; she then states that Jezebel was "a vain lady" and so the lotus would be fitting for her (Korpel 2006a: 359–60; Korpel 2006b: 383–96). The lotus happens to be a very common feature on seals, and to associate it with the vanity of the owner is ridiculous. Ultimately, I consider Korpel's proposal to be tenuous at best. It falls into the category of sheer speculation, and in its speculation it is particularly weak (Rollston 2009). Part of the problem here is that Korpel does not work within the field of epigraphy—she is a biblical scholar, not an epigrapher. Korpel clearly wants this to be the seal of Jezebel. This is, of course, consistently a most problematic *Tendenz*, whereas the most cogent scholarship should be disinterested scholarship.

I wish that I could suggest that Korpel's proposal is of a rare sort, but variants of it are fairly common. Consider the case of the Tell es-Safi inscription. A distinguished archaeologist, Aren Maeir, has been directing excavations at this site since 1997. During the 2005 season, a potsherd with a crude, archaic, incised inscription bearing two names, *ʾlwt* and *wlt*[ ], was discovered (Maeir et al. 2008). Maeir was cited in the popular media as suggesting that this name might be "the equivalent of the name Goliath."[2] True, he also said that "the Goliath of the inscription from Gath is not the biblical Goliath." But note that the rationale for his statement was that "most scholars regard the Goliath story as legend rather than history." Nevertheless, Maeir is cited as stating that "the inscription does, however, give a real-life context to the story, and it demonstrates that the name Goliath was probably in circulation in Gath about a century or so after the legendary battle between David and Goliath" (Shanks 2006: 16). During subsequent statements to the press, Maeir continued to be cited as referring to the inscription as the "Goliath Inscription" (Shanks 2007: 12), a sensationalistic flourish that sustained the flawed identification of the names in the inscription. The problem, of course, is that there is no *gimel* in the name on the ostracon. No *gimel*, no Goliath. Case closed. No discussion. The *editio princeps* of this inscription (Maeir et al. 2008) is certainly much more cautious, perhaps because of the high caliber of the epigraphic work of his co-authors, but the damage had already been done. Part of the difficulty here may be that Maeir is a very good archaeologist, but not an epigrapher or a philologist. Ultimately, I suppose the lesson is that the field is best served when scholars publish and lecture (and speak to the press) about subjects that fall within their fields of expertise.

Here is another example: the *Jerusalem Post* carried a story in January 2008 about Eilat Mazar's claim that a seal she discovered was to be read "Temeḥ" and that it might be associated with the family of Temech mentioned in the book of Nehemiah (Neh 7:55).[3] This sensational find received worldwide attention because of the supposed biblical name on this "astounding" seal. The problem, though, was that she had read the seal from right to left. This might seem to be a sane move, but it was not. Seals are written in mirror image so that the impression has the letters in the correct orientation. After photos began to circulate, some suggested that the seal *might* be read in mirror image; but they vacillated. I immediately noted on various blogs and lists that it *must* be read in mirror image because of the stance of the *mem*.[4] There could be no doubt. It is now recognized that the seal is indeed written in mirror image and that the name is Shulamit, not Temeḥ. Eilat Mazar's mistake was going immediately to the press before consulting epigraphers. Joseph Naveh or Shmuel Aḥituv could have rapidly provided her with the correct reading, but she assumed that she could read it herself. To be sure, she could read the letters, but she committed the error of reading them in reverse order. Again, because epigraphy is not her field, she propagated a blatantly false reading.

2. An Associated Press (2005) story about this discovery was widely cited.
3. See Lefkovits 2008.
4. For example, ANE-2@yahoogroups.com on January 17, 2008.

The "Cave of John the Baptist" illustrates another aspect of the problem. The cave is located near Jerusalem, at Kibbutz Tzuba. Shimon Gibson began excavating there in 2000 with the assistance of James Tabor
and several years later published a book about the cave entitled *The
Cave of John the Baptist: The Stunning Archaeological Discovery That
Has Redefined Christian History* (Gibson 2004). This is a sensationalist title, of course, and garnered much attention—the very thing it was
intended to do. The Associated Press printed a story about this "Cave
of John the Baptist" on August 16, 2004, and the story became an international interest.[5]

Some 20 steps were found descending into the cave and terminating at
a pool of sorts. During the course of the excavation, some crude images
drawn on the walls of the cave became visible. Because of the length of
the hair on an image of a human, Gibson and Tabor declared, according
to the Associated Press release, that there was "no real doubt that this
was John the Baptist." After all, they asserted, John was a member of the
Nazarites, for whom the shearing of hair was forbidden. Also of import,
they argued, is that a carving of a face appears in the same part of the
cave. Because John the Baptist was beheaded, they concluded that this
"face" must be a depiction of his severed head. Moreover, many pot-
sherds from small jars were found at the cave site, and Gibson suggested
that these jars were used for purification rituals by pilgrims visiting this
site because of its association with John the Baptist. The entire scenario
was scintillating for the general public.

Certain data should have given Gibson and Tabor some pause. For
example, the carvings in the tomb are Byzantine, not from the era of the
historical John the Baptist (that is, not from the early 1st century c.e.).
Moreover, there were no epigraphic remains—certainly not an inscription naming John the Baptist—that could be used to substantiate the
claim that the cave was that of John the Baptist. Of course, even more
rudimentary problems plague this proposal: it would be risible to argue
that John the Baptist was the sole Nazarite of the region and era, or that
the presence of some sort of *miqveh* (ritual bath) must be considered
that of John the Baptist. After all, *miqva'ot* are hardly rare in the late
Second Temple period. Again, some methodological restraint was in order, but was not exercised. Again, the damage was done.

Another example comes from the excavations at Khirbet Qeiyafa,
where an Iron Age ostracon was discovered in 2008. Haggai Misgav was
the site epigrapher, and the inscription was published in an expeditious
and commendable manner (Misgav, Garfinkel, and Ganor 2009). The
ostracon, dated to the 10th century b.c.e., is ca. 15 cm by 16.5 cm, and
consists of 5 lines of text with 15–20 graphemes (often rather faded)
per line. The writing in ink is on the concave side of the ostracon. The

---

5. For text of the original article, see Associated Press 2004.

authors of the *editio princeps* did a fine job even though the inscription is difficult to read. Indeed, other experts provided readings and interpretations that differed (sometimes in substantive ways) from that of the *editio princeps*, attesting to the difficulties that reading this inscription entailed (Aḥituv 2009; Demsky 2009; and Yardeni 2009).

Despite the responsible scholarship in the reading of the Qeiyafa ostracon, some rather astounding claims were ultimately made. For example, the University of Haifa released a press statement claiming that "Gershon Galil of the Department of Biblical Studies at the University of Haifa has deciphered" the Qeiyafa Ostracon.[6] Furthermore, this press release argued that this inscription was the "earliest known Hebrew writing." Moreover, it was claimed that "the significance of this breakthrough relates to the fact that at least some of the biblical scriptures were composed hundreds of years before the dates presented today in research and that the Kingdom of Israel already existed at that time." Galil, according to this press release from his university, believed that this ostracon demonstrated that "it can now be maintained that it was highly reasonable that during the tenth century B.C.E., during the reign of King David, there were scribes in Israel who were able to write literary texts and complex historiographies such as the books of Judges and Samuel." The same basic sentiments are present in Galil's published article on this inscription (Galil 2009).

These are striking assertions and conclusions. And there are problems. On the basis of the content of this inscription (even if one accepts all of Galil's readings, and I do not) it is an absolute *non sequitur* to assume with any certitude that "during the reign of King David, there were scribes in Israel who were able to write literary texts and complex historiographies such as the books of Judges and Samuel." That is, Galil is arguing that the books of Judges and Samuel can be dated to the reign of a particular king (David) *because a five-line inscription was found at an archaeological site!* Such logic is strained past the breaking point. After all, the inscription is brief and contains no reference to David or to Judah. Moreover, the precise date of it is not certain—I would date it earlier than the 10th century. In addition, the script is definitely not Old Hebrew; the language of the inscription is difficult to determine with certitude because of the general dearth of evidence for this period, and it lacks definitive linguistic isoglosses. To be sure, some words have been touted as isoglosses, but the presence of these words (including ʿbd) in various Semitic languages renders such touting specious at best. Some have even suggested that the presence of the common Semitic roots *mlk* and *špṭ* can be used as evidence that the inscription is Hebrew;

---

6. The press release, dated January 7, 2010, was made on the University of Haifa's official Web site. See the text of the release on the "Communications and Media Relations" page of that Web site: http://newmedia-eng.haifa.ac.il/?p=2043.

but this is an indefensible position, for these roots occur in a number of different ancient Semitic languages. The sole phrase that might be considered demonstrative of Hebrew as the language is /ʾl tʿs/; however, because the root ʿśh ("to do," "to make") is present in languages such as Ugaritic, Moabite, and even Old South Arabic (demonstrating its presence across much of the landscape of Semitic languages), I would be disinclined to claim that this root be considered a definitive isogloss for Hebrew. Moreover, the negative /ʾl/ is found in Ugaritic, Phoenician, Old Aramaic, Imperial Aramaic, and even Old South Arabic. Obviously, this negative cannot be considered something that is demonstrative of Old Hebrew. That is, Galil's startling claims about the Bible, made on the basis of this inscription, simply do not follow (see also Rollston 2011). Yet his proposal received international attention. The public was led to believe what he said. Again, the damage was done.

Basically, the point is this: archaeologists and epigraphers must strive to be disinterested. To be sure, none of us can claim to be disinterested in an absolute sense, but we must strive to be more circumspect. Furthermore, scholars should check their interpretations, before communicating with the press, with colleagues and students who are capable of expert analysis of the data and who, if need be, can be brutal, trenchant, and honest in their advice. There is already a superabundance of drivel in popular culture; scholars must avoid adding more.

Recalibrating the Ship's Rudder:
A Case Study in a Necessary Retraction

Sometimes a good scholar will accept premature and tenuous conclusions as fact. No one is perfect. No one's constructs of the evidence are always correct. Even very fine scholars may make mistakes. If so, a scholar should be willing to admit the mistake—that would be the right thing to do. The Ebla tablets are instructive in this regard. During the mid-1970s, thousands of cuneiform tablets were discovered by Italian excavators at Tell Mardikh, or ancient Ebla, in Syria. Some of the tablets were written in Sumerian, but many were written in a language that reflected Semitic features: a language that came to be known as Eblaite. Giovanni Pettinato, who was the site epigrapher, began to read the tablets and soon declared that among the place-names mentioned in a large economic tablet were Sodom, Gomorrah, Admah, Zeboiim, and Bela. These cities are also mentioned in Genesis 14, and Pettinato was quoted as stating that the ordering of the cities at Ebla was the same as that of Genesis (Pettinato 1976; Freedman 1978).

David Noel Freedman of the University of Michigan tried to be cautious but found it difficult because of the dramatic implications of Pettinato's readings. Debates at that time about the historicity of the Genesis narratives led Freedman to claim that the Ebla data meant that some of the material in Genesis preserved accurate historical data from the third millennium B.C.E., that is, that some of the material in Genesis was very ancient and also historically reliable. Therefore, he wrote that "it is now my belief that the story in Genesis 14 not only corresponds in content to the Ebla (economic) tablet, but that the Genesis account derives from the same period" (Freedman 1978: 151–52). On the basis of these putative data, Freedman concluded that the "editors" of Genesis were "seriously concerned to get the story straight" and that "they had access to authentic historical records, either written or oral or both, but in any case reliable" (Freedman 1978: 155). Freedman's position was based primarily on the Ebla reference to five cities also found in Genesis 14.

Other voices were more cautious. Robert Biggs of the University of Chicago and Thorkild Jacobsen of Harvard University had urged restraint. Freedman, however, was concerned about the effects of restraint. He noted that "so far stupendous claims have been few and muted . . . while a chorus of voices . . . have been raised warning us against undue expectations, especially in relation to the Bible" (Freedman 1978: 147). He added that "in this situation, the danger may lie in the opposite direction: in the general stampede to look wise and be discreet, a really significant piece of information may be overlooked, and there will be silence when circumstances call for boldness and loudness, even showmanship" (Freedman 1978).

Nevertheless, the readings of Pettinato soon became subject to correction, just as Freedman's article on the Ebla tablets was in press. Freedman was able to augment (correct) his article with an addendum: "After this article was already in press, I received a letter from Mitchell Dahood, who is working on the tablets with Pettinato. The information which Dahood passed on may cause a complete reevaluation of the earlier material upon which I based my presentation." Then Freedman cited Dahood's letter itself:

> Giovanni [Pettinato] tells me that he considers the reading of the first two names, Sodom and Gomorrah, quite certain, but that he is no longer ready to defend the next two city names because of his improvement in the reading of the signs, improvement that could only come with greater experience in reading the tablets. In any case, the cities three and four of the Genesis 14 list do not occur in the same tablet, so the argument in favor of the antiquity of the Genesis list is weakened. I had not known that they were not in the same tablet. (Freedman 1978: 143)

Alfonso Archi, who soon replaced Giovanni Pettinato as the site epigrapher, argued that the place name Pettinato had read as Gomorrah was actually to be read i-ma-ar, that is, Emar (in modern Syria). Moreover, he argued that the site referred to at Ebla as Si-dam-mu was not biblical Sodom of the Dead Sea region but rather a city named Sidamu in northern Syria (Archi 1979; cf. Shanks 1980). Pettinato's readings had been sensational but proved to be problematic. Freedman was a superb scholar, with many contributions to the field that will stand the test of time; but with regard to the Ebla tablets, his initial, published assumptions were misplaced, and his castigation of cautious scholars was ill founded. To his credit, Freedman was among the first to admit he had been wrong. That he was willing to do so leaves a laudable legacy.

Navigating for Placid Waters: Desiderata of Providing the Media with Reliable Scholarship

I would like to suggest that all of the problems I have described revolve around sensationalism by the media, rogue scholars, or both. Sometimes the media will misconstrue the sober statements of cautious scholars.[7] Nevertheless, mainstream scholars can also be culpable of propagating tenuous constructs of the evidence and uttering problematic and sensationalizing statements to media.

However, the professionalism of the field requires that the bar be set high(er). Here are some final musings: (1) Scholars that interface with the media must always strive to be circumspect and intentional. They must confer with colleagues and students, searching for critiques of conclusions rather than collegial confirmation. (2) Scholars must always remember that epigraphic finds are rarely as "dramatically important," "sensational," or "stunning" as they might seem at first blush. (3) "Gale-force winds" often develop when inscriptions are discovered, and the media typically want rapid and decisive comment, especially if the find putatively connects with something that is important biblically, religiously, or politically. Scholars should remind the media that the best constructs of the data are usually the result of a slow, methodical, scholarly process (presentations at guild meetings, publications in refereed journals). Immediately after a find, when they are often in the "eye of the storm," scholars should avoid making definitive statements and instead caution the media against printing definitive statements. (4) I should like to conclude with one final, sober reflection. Just as a mislabeling of a site on a biblical map (Miller 1987) becomes virtually impossible to excise (because maps have a long shelf life, are readily copied, and few people are capable of discovering and eradicating an error on a map), so too a tenuous or risible construct about an inscription can be very difficult to purge from both scholarly and popular circles. For this reason, the twin pillars of methodological caution and methodological rigor are imperative desiderata.

---

7. Note: because of this problem, I now always send the media member that contacts me a written synopsis of my views of the subject, thus making it harder for them to misunderstand something I said orally during an interview.

References

Ahituv, S.
  2009   The Khirbet Qeiyafa Inscription—Response C. Pp. 130–32 in Amit,
        Stiegel, and Peleg-Barkat, eds.

Amit, D.; Stiebel, G. D.; and Peleg-Barkat, O., eds.
  2009   *New Studies in the Archaeology of Jerusalem and Its Region.* Jerusa-
        lem: Israel Antiquities Authority and the Hebrew University of Jerusa-
        lem [Hebrew].

Archi, A.
  1979   The Epigraphic Evidence from Ebla and the Old Testament. *Biblica* 60:
        556–66.

Associated Press
  2004   The Cave of John the Baptist? Archaeologists Say Cave in Israel Was
        Where John Baptized Disciples. *CBS News World*, August 16. On-line:
        http://www.cbsnews.com/stories/2004/08/16/world/main636394
        .shtml.
  2005   Finding Said to Boost Proof of Goliath. *USA Today*, November 10.
        On-line: http://www.usatoday.com/news/world/2005-11-10-goliath_x
        .htm.

Avigad, N.
  1964   The Seal of Jezebel. *Israel Exploration Journal* 14: 274–76.

Avigad, N., and Sass, B.
  1997   *Corpus of West Semitic Stamp Seals.* Jerusalem: Israel Exploration
        Society.

Benz, F. L.
  1972   *Personal Names in the Phoenician and Punic Inscriptions.* Studia Pohl
        8. Rome: Pontifical Biblical Institute.

Del Olmo Lete, G., and Sanmartin, J.
  2004   *A Dictionary of the Ugaritic Language in the Alphabetic Tradition.*
        2nd ed. Leiden: Brill.

Demsky, A.
  2009   The Enigmatic Inscription from Khirbet Qeiyafa—Response B. Pp. 126–
        29 in Amit, Stiegel, and Peleg-Barkat, eds.

Freedman, D. N.
  1978   The Real Story of the Ebla Tablets: Ebla and the Cities of the Plain.
        Biblical Archeologist 41: 143–64.

Galil, G.
  2009   The Hebrew Inscription from Khirbet Qeiyafa/Netaʿim. *Ugarit-Forsc-*
        hungen 41: 193–242.

Gibson, S.
  2004   *The Cave of John the Baptist: The Stunning Archaeological Discovery*
        That Has Redefined Christian History. New York: Doubleday.

Hoftijzer, J., and Jongeling, K.
  1995   *Dictionary of the North-West Semitic Inscriptions.* Leiden: Brill.

Huffmon, H. B.
  1965   *Amorite Personal Names in the Mari Texts.* Baltimore: Johns Hopkins
        University Press.

Jacobovici, S., and Pellegrino, C.
  2007   *The Jesus Family Tomb: The Discovery, the Investigation, and the Ev-*
        idence That Could Change History. New York: HarperOne.

Kloner, A.
1996   A Tomb with Inscribed Ossuaries in East Talpiyot, Jerusalem. *'Atiqot* 29: 15–22.

Korpel, M. C. A.
2006a   Seals of Jezebel and Other Women in Authority. *Journal for Semitics* 15: 349–71.
2006b   Queen Jezebel's Seal. *Ugarit-Forschungen* 38: 379–98.
2008   Fit for a Queen: Jezebel's Royal Seal. *Biblical Archaeology Review* 34: 32–37, 80.

Lefkovits, E.
2008   First Temple Seal Found in Jerusalem. *Jerusalem Post*, January 17. Online: http://www.jpost.com/home/article.aspx?id=89079.

Lewis, N., ed.
1989   *The Documents from the Bar Kokhba Period in the Cave of Letters: Greek Papyri*. Jerusalem: Israel Exploration Society.

Maeir, A.; Wimmer, S. J.; Zuckerman, A.; and Demsky, A.
2008   A Late Iron Age I/Early Iron Age II Old Canaanite Inscription from Tell es-Safi/Gath, Israel: Palaeography, Dating, and Historical-Cultural Significance. *Bulletin of the American Schools of Oriental Research* 351: 39–71.

Meyers, E. M.
2006   The Jesus Tomb Controversy: An Overview. *Near Eastern Archaeology* 69: 116–18.

Miller. J. M.
1987   Biblical Maps: How Reliable Are They? *Bible Review* 3: 32–41.

Misgav, H.; Garfinkel, Y.; and Ganor, S.
2009   The Khirbet Qeiyafa Ostracon. Pp. 111–23 in Amit, Stiegel, and Peleg-Barkat, eds. 2009.

Mykytiuk, L. J.
2004   *Identifying Biblical Persons in Northwest Semitic Inscriptions of 1200–539 B.C.E.* Society of Biblical Literature Archaeology and Biblical Studies 12. Atlanta: Society of Biblical Literature.

Pettinato, G.
1976   The Royal Archives of Tell Mardikh-Ebla. *Biblical Archaeologist* 39: 44–52.

Pfann, S. J.
2006   Mary Magdalene Has Left the Room: A Suggested New Reading of Ossuary CJO 701. *Near Eastern Archaeology* 69: 130–36.

Rahmani, L. Y.
1994   *A Catalogue of Jewish Ossuaries in the Collections of the State of Israel*. Jerusalem: Israel Antiquities Authority.

Rollston, C. A.
2006   Inscribed Ossuries: Personal Names, Statistics, and Laboratory Tests. *Near Eastern Archaeology* 69: 125–229.
2009   Prosopography and the *Yzbl* Seal. *Israel Exploration Journal* 59: 86–91.
2011   The Khirbet Qeiyafa Ostracon: Methodological Musings and Caveats. *Tel Aviv* 38: 68–83.

Shanks, H.
1980   New Ebla Epigrapher Attacks Conclusion of Ousted Ebla Scholar. *Biblical Archaeology Review* 6: 55–56.

2006 New Finds: Gath Inscription Evidences Philistine Assimilation. *Biblical Archaeology Review* 32: 16.

2007 Whither Goliath? *Biblical Archaeology Review* 33: 12.

Sukenik, E. L.

1931 Nochmals: Die Ossuarien in Palätina. *Monatsschrift für Geschichte und Wissenschaft des Judentums* 75: 462–63.

Yardeni, A.

2009 The Khirbet Qeiyafa Inscription—Response A. Pp. 124–25 in Amit, Stiegel, and Peleg-Barkat, eds.

PART 3

Archaeology, Politics, and Local Communities

Walk about Jerusalem
Protestant Pilgrims
and the Holy Land

TONY W. CARTLEDGE

As the sun slides slowly behind the city of Jerusalem, a Palestinian driver brings his bus to a smooth stop in a busy parking lot atop the Mount of Olives. Weary and subdued, a diverse collection of Protestant pastors spills onto the warm asphalt as their Israeli guide shepherds them into formation before the wonderland of shapes and shadows, steeples and spires, minarets and mosques that make up their first glimpse of the Holy City. He distributes flatbread and salt, offers a prayer in Hebrew, and asks his charges to think about loved ones who have not yet seen Jerusalem. Sweeping his arm toward the golden gleam of the Temple Mount, the guide reverently intones, "Welcome home."[1]

So it is that two score more of American evangelicals are added to the rolls of those who have fallen in love with Israel, to profound effect.

In this paper, I will explore several questions relative to those Protestant pastors and the laypeople they will bring with them on their next trip. Do travelers such as these really count as pilgrims, or are they mere religious tourists? How do their motivations and experiences relate to those of pilgrims from other branches of the Christian vine? Is there anything particularly distinctive about what Protestants bring to or take away from their Holy Land experience? Finally, I will venture some suggestions about the role of archaeology as it relates to Protestants' appreciation of the land.

Pilgrimage and Tourism

The past several decades have birthed a burgeoning literature in which sociologists, anthropologists, and ethnographers have sought to

---

1. Adapted from an experience related by Steve Bolton, pastor of Oxford Baptist Church in Oxford, NC, while participating in a "familiarization" tour in 1999 with guide Ezra Eini. Personal communication.

define and defend varying approaches to understanding pilgrimage and tourism.

Victor Turner's seminal studies of the 1970s set the playing field and remained dominant for some time (Turner 1973; Turner and Turner 1978). Turner envisions pilgrimage as a departure from quotidian routines, a "liminal" experience in which pilgrims experience a transcendence of space and time as they journey toward the sacred center of their faith. In the process, caught "betwixt and between" different worlds, fellow pilgrims experience an unaccustomed sense of community that Turner calls *communitas*.[2]

John Eade and Michael Sallnow (1991a) take a different view, suggesting in their introduction to a collection of essays that Turner's concept of *communitas* is not a universal experience. Pilgrims are just as likely to encounter conflict with other pilgrims who jostle for the same space or who interpret sites differently, they argue, as well as with local residents who live and do business near sacred places. The essays, in a variety of ways, deconstruct "pilgrimage" into smaller categories of meaningful behavior (Eade and Sallnow 1991b).

In *Sacred Journeys: The Anthropology of Pilgrimage*, editor Alan Morinis (1992) and other writers express greater confidence that pilgrimage remains a useful concept. "Pilgrimage is born of desire and belief," writes Morinis (1992: 1), and can be defined as "a journey undertaken by a person in quest of a place or a state that he or she believes to embody a valued ideal" (1992: 4). Morinis identifies six types of sacred journeys, with his "devotional" category most descriptive of Protestant pilgrimage.[3]

Writing in the same volume, Erik Cohen (1992: 47–61) undertakes a structuralist approach to contrast the roles of pilgrims, whom he describes as being drawn centripetally on a journey to the center of their world, and tourists, who follow centrifugal forces that take them from the center to the periphery, the world of the "Other." Cohen observes that some writers speak of a convergence through which contemporary travel may stand in as a substitute for religion, with popular tourist attractions acting as "the shrines of modernity," while others see a clear divergence between the two, with tourism consisting of little more than shallow traveling for pleasure (Cohen 1992: 48–49). He concludes that

---

2. Turner also observes that pilgrimages tend to bloom during periods of destruction or rapid social change, notes that these journeys could be voluntary, obligatory, or serve as rites of passage, and acknowledges that pilgrimage may have commercial aspects.

3. Morinis's typology of pilgrimage (1992: 10–14) includes "devotional" (which seeks to encounter or honor divinity), "instrumental" (for example, seeking healing), "normative" (part of a ritual cycle in some cultures), "obligatory" (the Islamic *hajj* or Catholic penitential requirements), "wandering" (hoping to be guided to a place of satisfaction), and "initiatory" (a rite of passage seeking a transformation of self).

tourism has become "a modern metamorphosis of both pilgrimage and travel" in which deep structures of "symbolic significance and mystical power" have been diminished by secularization: "Pilgrimage then often becomes indistinguishable from tourism, so that the analytical distinction between pilgrim-tourists, who travel toward the religious, political, or cultural centers of their cultural world, and traveler-tourists, who travel away from them into the periphery of that world, tends to become empirically blurred" (1992: 57–58).

David Brown (1996), in writing about Cohen's distinctions between tourists and pilgrims, concludes that each may readily shift from one role to the other. "The structure of tourism is basically identical to that of all ritual behavior," he writes: "it first translates the tourist into a sacred world, then transforms/renews him, and finally returns him to normality. This other world is sacred because it is out of space and out of time. The normal rules are in abeyance (if not actually reversed), and replaced by Turner's close and egalitarian '*communitas*'" (Brown 1996: 35).[4]

Simon Coleman's critique (2002) of earlier studies calls for an awareness that ethnographers who study pilgrimage "are always performing a definitional balancing act" and cautions against confining their work to a "pilgrimage ghetto" that ignores related studies. "Sacred travel frequently overlaps with tourism, trade, migration, expressions of nationalism, creations of diasporas, imagining communities," he observes (Coleman 2002: 363).

Ellen Badone (2004) points to a similar crossing of boundaries as she compares ethnography, pilgrimage, and tourism:

> All three processes construct a "there" where "goods" not available "here" are perceived to be accessible: knowledge, self-transformation, or leisure and recreation. While at the abstract level, the quest for one of these goods may predominate in a particular type of journeying— knowledge in ethnography, self-transformation in pilgrimage, leisure and recreation in tourism—in practice, all three goods contribute in varying degrees to the experience of each type of travel. Recreation implies the re-creation of the self, just as knowledge leads to self-transformation, and both pilgrims and ethnographers, like tourists, engage in leisure activities. As a result, the boundaries separating pilgrimage, touristic travel, and ethnography are indeed blurred (Badone 2004: 182).

---

4. Brown (1996: 41) speaks of pilgrims and tourists who are both fake and genuine. "Genuine pilgrims are also fake tourists and quite readily turn into genuine tourists. They have only to be 'ripped off' once too often to rediscover their Centre back home and, in sudden reversal, come out with all the old discredited cultural stereotypes. Likewise, genuine tourists are fake pilgrims who can turn into the genuine article; to walk out altogether on their fellow tourists, for instance, it only needs the jollity to be forced on them once too often."

In the introduction to the volume in which her essay appears, Badone and fellow editor Shirley Roseman suggest that "rigid dichotomies between pilgrimage and tourism, or pilgrims and tourists, no longer seem tenable in the shifting world of postmodern travel" (Badone and Roseman, 2004: 2).[5]

If the boundaries between pilgrimage and tourism are blurred, where do Protestants fit into the fuzzy picture? Valene Smith notes that in the first centuries after the Protestant Reformation, it was commonly thought that while Catholics might go on pilgrimages, "the Protestant rejection of 'images' (saints, relics and most sculptures) converted their faithful to religious tourism" (Smith 1992: 8). She observes, however, that "the terms *pilgrimage* and *tourism* both define cultural constructs" that can change through time. In contemporary culture, Smith envisions the pilgrim-tourist path to be "two parallel, interchangeable lanes, one of which is the secular knowledge based route of Western science; the other, the sacred road of faith and belief." Travelers along either lane can switch between them "depending on personal need or motivation, and as appropriate to time, place, and cultural circumstances" (Smith 1992: 15).

There is little question that a single journey can incorporate multiple paths of meaning, but all persons who journey to sacred sites with spiritual intent may fall under the rubric of "pilgrim," Protestants no less than anyone else. Protestant pilgrims may hope for a renewed encounter with Jesus as they seek baptism in the Jordan River or sit by the Sea of Galilee and contemplate its watery witness to the Teacher's lingering presence. On the other hand, they may also relax in the spa at their hotel or float in the Dead Sea. Tour groups may shift quickly from meditating in the grotto of the Church of the Nativity to the new experience of eating falafel and the familiar routine of shopping for souvenirs.

Shopping, I suggest, offers a helpful illustration of the dichotomy engrained in the experience: while Protestant visitors may buy cheap postcards and bookmarks, souvenir mugs or khaffiyehs, the items they favor most are made of olive wood or other materials they suppose to be of local origin; carved into nativity sets, crosses, or camels, the items serve as markers of memory and constitute an effort to bring home a piece of the Holy Land.[6] Protestant visitors do not think of souvenirs as sacramental relics, as did early pilgrims, and their purchases are typi-

---

5. They recall, however, that Victor and Edith Turner had earlier expressed similar thoughts: "A tourist is half a pilgrim, if a pilgrim is half a tourist" (Turner and Turner 1978: 20, cited by Badone and Roseman 2004: 2).

6. Hahn (1990) points to the significance of souvenirs for both pilgrims and tourists. "They are like the modern souvenir postcard in that they point to an authentic experience; however, also like the postcard, the image does not represent the experience alone. Instead, it indicates a location where that experience took place. Rather than being full of significance, the location is instrumental for the pleasures of the tourist or the salvation of the pilgrim" (Hahn 1990: 93).

cally unlike the burial shrouds and plastic bottles of lamp oil or holy water favored by the Orthodox. Protestant pilgrims may not believe the tokens they buy are imbued with the divine presence, but the items are nonetheless invested with significant memories. Souvenir carvings or ceramics may not be as indigenous as vendors routinely claim, but pilgrims identify them with the Holy Land.

Protestants and Pilgrimage

If Protestants can indeed act as pilgrims, we should note ways in which they approach pilgrimage differently from their Orthodox and Roman Catholic cousins. (Pilgrim practices of Jews, Muslims, Hindus, and other faith groups are also of interest but beyond the scope of this essay.)

Orthodox Pilgrimage

In a study of Greek Orthodox pilgrims, Glenn Bowman (1991) notes that lay Orthodox give comparably little attention to spiritual purity while they are young; but after their children are married, they enter "a phase during which one sheds social and familial responsibilities and turns one's attention to sacred things in preparation for ascension after death into Paradise" (1991: 103). That turn toward the sacred often involves a pilgrimage to Israel, typically in old age, where "Greek Orthodox pilgrims envision their pilgrimage to the holy places as a sloughing off of impurities consequent on the Fall in preparation for death and resurrection" (1991: 108). The cleansing nature of the pilgrimage begins with a confession of sins before departure and continues at the point of arrival, where monks of the Brotherhood of the Holy Sepulchre meet Orthodox pilgrims and wash their feet.

Once in the land, the Orthodox undertake several predictable activities. As they visit various sites, Bowman writes, they focus on the Orthodox churches that have been built to commemorate specific biblical events. Giving little attention to historical and biblical orientations provided by their guide, they prefer to rush into each shrine to touch or kiss all icons within reach without lingering over any except those of Christ, the Virgin Mary, perhaps the saints after which they were named (Bowman 1991: 110).[7]

While Protestants may think of such behavior as borderline idolatry, Charles Lock explains that for the Orthodox, the veneration of statues and icons is "another way of seeing, a way that depends not on distance but on proximity, one that involves a recognition of that which is

---

7. For the Orthodox, Bowman says, "The interiors of the churches prefigured Paradise, and, since all the saints in Paradise were present through their icons within the churches, there was no reason why a pilgrim should grant any of them, except perhaps the Lord and his mother who had effected their *metastoicheiosis*, or transelementation, any more attention than any other" (Bowman 1991: 110).

depicted. Recognition, that dramatic moment of *anagnorisis* that precipitates *proskinesis*, the act of veneration, the bowing down, the kiss: recognition is the end and aim of pilgrimage. The rest is sightseeing" (2003: 131).

While in the Holy Land, Orthodox pilgrims typically arrange to be baptized in the Jordan. Wearing funeral shrouds they have purchased in Jerusalem, and dipping similar garments obtained for others who were unable to make the journey, they seek rebirth in the Jordan's waters before carefully putting away the shrouds, in which they will be buried (Bowman 1991: 109).

Travel to sacred sites may be desirable for the Orthodox, Bowman says, but "what the pilgrimage to the Holy Land is about, at heart, is being present in Jerusalem during the Holy Feasts" (1991: 111). Holy Week is the most preferred, and to a lesser extent feasts honoring the Assumption of the Virgin and the Exaltation of the Cross.

Orthodox pilgrimages characteristically conclude with a special ceremony in the Church of the Holy Sepulchre with a "Ceremony of the Holy Fire." There, Bowman writes "the experience of *communitas* reaches a peak as thousands of pilgrims, crammed to the point of immobility into the confines of the Anastasis, pass the Holy Fire—announcing the imminence of the resurrection—from hand to hand until the whole church is bright with the flames of thousands of 'resurrection candles'" (1991: 112).

For the Orthodox, then, tradition, ritual, and sacred space combine to inspire pilgrims to a holy life for the remainder of their days and to prepare them for a good death beyond.

Catholic Pilgrimage

For most Roman Catholics, except for the rare case in which one's journey has been assigned as an act of penance, the purpose of pilgrimage is more devotional or inspirational. While the Orthodox focus on preparing for Paradise by becoming separate from the world, the Latin church focuses on sending people back into the world for service and right living (Bowman 1991: 105, 112).

Catholic pilgrims also focus much of their attention on church buildings that have been constructed over biblical sites, but generally as a way of incorporating the ancient event into their shared memory. As Bowman traveled with a group of Catholics touring the Holy Land, he observed that they incorporated Bible readings and appreciation for artwork in the churches in an effort to reimagine the biblical events: "the places serve primarily as *loci* where the pilgrims are better able to body forth the subjects of their meditations in their imaginations" (1991: 114).

While Catholics may also venerate statues or shrines in a way that seems alien or mystical to Protestants, the objects are employed primarily as aids to memory and imagination. In a study of Maltese Catholics, Jon Mitchell observes that crucifixes and sacred art "stand as physical inscriptions of the remembered moments" and are thus invested with sacred meaning (1997: 89–90).

Like the Orthodox, Catholics find special meaning in liturgical ceremonies, especially the celebration of mass. Bowman noted that several participants who showed little emotion while visiting biblical sites wept through mass, even when it was offered in a modest monastery chapel that reeked of boiling cabbage from the monks' downstairs kitchen (1991: 115).

Protestant Pilgrimage

Protestant pilgrims inevitably incorporate times of worship into their Holy Land experience but do so most meaningfully in the open air: on the traditional Mount of Beatitudes, beside the Sea of Galilee, or just uphill from the Garden Tomb. For the most part, it is the land that Protestants come to see. They have imagined the craggy cliffs and steep valleys of southern Judah, the rolling hills and rolling Sea of Galilee. They want to see, smell, and touch the land of their shared biblical memory. They want to walk where Jesus walked, to weep where Jesus wept, to sleep in some proximity to where Jesus slept.

Instead of admiring the massive churches that cover sacred sites, they often resent them. This has been true from the first florescence of Protestant pilgrimage in the 19th century. William Jowett, who was not so much a pilgrim as an advance scout for the Christian Missionary Alliance, visited the area in 1825 and found the demonstrative piety and elaborate rituals in the Church of the Holy Sepulchre to be "vain in the sight of God, and detrimental to the simplicity of the Gospel" (fig. 1). Indeed, he said, "It would be difficult for me to rise in this place to the spirit of devotion. The fulsome pageantry of the scene must be first removed: the ground of Mount Calvary, now encumbered with convents, churches, and houses and disguised by splendid altars, gaudy pictures, and questionable reliques, must be cleared."[8]

The Protestant love of landscape grows from a bibliocentric and iconoclastic mentality that gives little credence to the visions of Saint Helena and the monuments she inspired but wants to get as close to

---

8. Lock (2003: 116), citing R. Hummel and T. Hummel (1995: 22). The liberal Protestant minister Harry Emerson Fosdick expressed similar disappointment, finding in the Church of the Holy Sepulchre "garish, gawdy decorations, the competing din of five simultaneous services, the hideous, dissonant gongs, the very lamps which hang in multitudes from the roof, their differences advertising their five-fold sectarianism—all this represents a type of religion that Jesus disliked and represents nothing that he pleaded for and for which he died" (Fosdick 1927: 244). See also Greenberg's "Protestant Pilgrims: Disjunction between Expectation and Reality," a review of famed 19th-century authors who found disappointment in Israel (1994: 87–112).

Figure 1. An Orthodox woman leans forward to kiss an icon of Jesus beneath the elaborate altar at "Mt. Calvary" inside the Church of the Holy Sepulchre."

the land of the Bible as possible. Protestants love the Sea of Galilee because they know Jesus was there, and no one has contrived to cover its stormy waves with a stony church. They love the Garden Tomb and Gordon's Calvary because those sites fit their biblically inspired imaginations much better than the sooty stone and oily marble in the Church of the Holy Sepulchre (fig. 2). They love Capernaum because it still has the look of a simple village where Jesus visited the home of his friend Simon Peter.[9]

In these landscapes, Protestant pilgrims "can imagine Jesus, not as Christ, one of the Holy Trinity, but as a man, Himself a lone seeker after the sublime" (Lock 2003: 123). Knowing this, savvy tour guides portray Jesus as a fellow pilgrim when leading Protestant groups. In describing the speech he typically makes to Protestants as they stand on the Mount of Olives and overlook Jerusalem for the first time, former tour guide Jackie Feldman explains that his monologue "frames Jesus, in accordance with longstanding Protestant practice in viewing the land, not as a divine aspect of the Trinity but as the first and chief among fellow pilgrims to Jerusalem" (Feldman 2007: 362).

For this reason, Protestant tours to the Holy Land typically try to cram as many biblical sites as possible into the time allowed; and they give priority to landscapes or archaeological digs, tending to visit churches mainly when they are built on top of a site and thus unavoidable. As a rule, Protestants—particularly those who are not trained or conversant in Catholic or Orthodox traditions—want to see the pristine land of the Bible, not the profligate overgrowth of the church.

Thus, skilled guides assist these visitors in connecting the Bible of their imagination with the land that lies before them. "For Protestant pilgrims," Feldman writes, "Holy Land landscape is a projection of sacred text onto the contours of the land, and the public reading of a biblical text is often the primary act of orientation. Because pilgrims' desire to experience biblical events in their original landscape is strong, whereas their knowledge of the history and geography of the land is usually poor, the acts of naming, framing, and elevation, important in all tourist productions, become essential" (Feldman 2007: 355).

The Israeli government puts special emphasis on these activities during the two-year course required of licensed tour guides. This effort pays off in two ways. Not only do Protestants make up the majority of tour groups coming into Israel, but their upright posture and love of high vistas constitutes both "Protestant and Zionist ways of looking" that are strengthened through the exercise: "As the pilgrims listen to

---

9. For the same reason, Holy Land-themed tourist attractions that have sprung up in America tend to focus on recreating the landscape, rustic structures, and feel of the Holy Land, not its commemorative churches. For a review of such sites, see Long 2003, especially the chapter entitled "Starred and Striped Holy Lands," pp. 43–87.

Figure 2. Garden Tomb. Protestant visitors reverently wait their turn to enter the Garden Tomb, which matches their biblical imagination more closely than the Church of the Holy Sepulchre as the place of Jesus' burial.

scripture, view the site from above, point and photograph, the scene itself becomes engraved in their minds and bodies, so that it . . . can be easily triggered when they later hear the passages read in church or in Bible study back home" (Feldman 2007: 362).

The benefit for the State of Israel is that the pilgrims' warm feelings of biblical memory become intertwined with the Zionist view that modern Israel is the legitimate heir of the land that God promised to Abraham and his descendants.

Protestants and the State of Israel

Idinopulos has argued that pilgrimage can never be separated completely from issues of power: "in the Holy Land, ancient and modern, there was no pilgrimage without political, national, imperial, and even revolutionary significance" (1996: 10).

The convergence of pilgrimage and power, of course, is not a new concept. As long as political and religious systems have existed, political leaders have sought ways to bend religious sentiment to their own purposes. In Israel, Idinopulos argues, the practice goes at least as far back as King David, whose political genius led him to make Jerusalem a central pilgrimage shrine for all Israel. In so doing, he contrived to centralize Hebrew worship and consolidate control over the disparate and contentious Israelite tribes. "And what David first saw, Byzantine Emperors and Umayyad Caliphs themselves also saw. Pilgrims, pilgrimage sites, and the pilgrimages themselves are means to express, deepen, and extend power" (Idinopulos 1996: 16).

"It matters little whether we call Holy Land pilgrimage a sacralization of political power or a politicization of the sacred journey," Idinopulos continues. "The important point is that piety and power, religion and politics are comfortably in bed together in Jewish, Christian and Muslim pilgrimage" (1996: 16). In Israel, the biggest share of the bed is occupied by Christian Protestants, many of them from the conservative evangelical branch of the family tree.

As a point of clarification, I note that the term *evangelical* is often misused. By definition, it describes one who believes the gospel of Christ is life-changing and should be shared, thus awakening an evangelistic and missionary impulse. Believers all along the liberal to conservative spectrum can take seriously Jesus' "Great Commission" (Matt 28:19–20) to "go and teach all nations," and a variety of Christian groups self-identify as evangelicals. In popular usage of recent years, however, the term "evangelical" has come to be used almost exclusively as a label for fundamentalist Protestants[10] who are not only biblical literalists

---

10. For example, Christian pollster George Barna's criteria for identifying survey respondents as "evangelicals" requires that they meet nine criteria. In addition to meeting two characteristics associated with being "born again," evan-

but political conservatives. Many evangelicals who fall into those categories also hold a premillennial, dispensationalist interpretation of Scripture, in which the role of Israel is key to their prophetic forecasts relative to the end times.

Protestants as Roots Pilgrims

My observation, based on personal experience as a pilgrim and tour leader, as well as on conversations with tour guides and other tour leaders and participants, is that mainline Protestants and moderate evangelicals see their time in Israel as a sort of "roots" pilgrimage. They do not seek connections with their genealogical ancestors, as do African-Americans who frequent former "slave castles" on the south coast of Ghana or the countries from which their ancestors were taken. Rather, they come to the Holy Land in search of their spiritual roots.[11] Few take the extremist path of Landmark Baptists, who believe the Baptist faith runs in an unbroken line from John and Jesus; but many still regard centuries of Roman Catholic and Eastern Orthodox traditions as unrelated to their own heritage, which they sense most readily on the holy ground of the Holy Land (fig. 3).

As the Hebrew verb *yada'* suggests, "knowing by experience," Protestants want the concrete engagement that comes with treading the dusty paths and verdant valleys that Jesus knew. Like the psalmist, they want to walk about Zion and count its towers (Ps 48:12). Like Job, they want to move from imagination to experience and say "Before, I had heard of you with the hearing of the ear, but now my eye sees you" (Job 42:5).

While all travelers may harbor mixed motives, Protestants whose primary purpose is pilgrimage hope for a renewed experience with Christ and other biblical heroes who inhabit the shared memory of their spiritual imagination. They come to the Holy Land looking backward in time, hoping to enrich their present lives through gaining a sense of what life might have been like for Abraham and Sarah, Hosea and Gomer, Joseph and Mary. Their goal is to return home as better people, rejuvenated in faith and better equipped for Christian service. While they may also depart Ben Gurion airport with warmer feelings for the

---

gelicals must also meet seven other standards: "Those include saying their faith is very important in their life today; believing they have a personal responsibility to share their religious beliefs about Christ with non-Christians; believing that Satan exists; believing that eternal salvation is possible only through grace, not works; believing that Jesus Christ lived a sinless life on earth; asserting that the Bible is accurate in all that it teaches; and describing God as the all-knowing, all-powerful, perfect deity who created the universe and still rules it today." The definition appears at the end of relevant surveys on the Barna.org Web site, as here: http://www.barna.org/barna-update/article/12-faithspirituality/211-survey -describes-the-spiritual-gifts-that-christians-say-they-have.

11. See also Badone and Roseman 2004: 7.

State of Israel—or with renewed concern for the Palestinians who live beneath Israeli restrictions—their primary agenda is personal rather than political.

Protestants as Prophecy Pilgrims

Fundamentalist and dispensationalist pilgrims, on the other hand, look both ways. They share with their more liberal kindred a desire to walk where Jesus walked and encounter the biblical world; but they also look forward, to the prophetic future they believe will unfold on the hallowed landscape of the Holy Land.

A comparison of promotional materials for Holy Land tours is illustrative: while brochures from educational or moderate evangelical groups tend to highlight the layered archaeological richness of Megiddo, for example,[12] flyers produced for more conservative groups tout the same site as the place where prophecy will be fulfilled in the world-ending battle of Armageddon. For example, stock brochures produced by Templeton Tours typically proclaim: "Prophecy will come alive at Megiddo as we look over the Valley of Armageddon, site of the final world war!"[13]

Brochures for mainline or moderate sponsored tours often emphasize devotional elements of visiting sites in and around the city of Jerusalem. While dispensationalist-fundamentalist brochures also speak to the devotional aspects, they also stress prophetic elements and a Zionist agenda.[14]

---

12. Brochures for tours packaged by Educational Opportunities emphasize the archaeological heritage of Megiddo: "Travel the ancient caravan route to Tel Megiddo where 20 different cities lie superimposed upon each other." The brochure cited describes the "Holy Land Classic 2009" tour, downloaded from the Educational Opportunities Tours official Web site: http://www.eo.travelwithus.com/find_trip/results. aspx?c=6. The published brochure for a July 2009 tour sponsored by the Campbell University Divinity School speaks of Tel Megiddo as a place "where many layers of civilization can be seen."

13. From brochures for an April 2009 tour hosted by author Gary Chapman and a November 2009 tour hosted by pastor Don Wilton, both conservative Southern Baptists. A brochure promoting a November 2009 tour hosted by evangelist Ralph Sexton proclaims "From the Tel-Megiddo, we will explore the plain of Armageddon and see the prophetic scriptures come alive! Powerful services and Bible studies will touch your heart to be faithful in these last days!" All three brochures downloaded from the Templeton Tours official Web site: http://www.templetontours.com/HolyLand/ index.shtml.

14. Both Chapman's and Wilton's brochures (see previous note) promise that, after touring the Western Wall area, "We'll also visit the Museum of the Temple Treasures to see many of the recreated elements for the proposed new temple." The "Temple Treasures" museum is part of the "Temple Institute," an ultra-Orthodox group whose statement of principles declares "Our long-term goal is to do all in our limited power to bring about the building of the Holy Temple in our time." See the "About the

Figure 3. Lithostratos. Protestant students take time to ponder the pavement thought to have been part of the Antonia, where Jesus may have been held following his arrest.

Dispensationalists see the preservation of the Jews and the re-establishment of the State of Israel as miraculous pointers to the existence of God and the surety of prophecies pointing to the end of the world. Israel, in their view, is destined to be both center stage and the source of leading actors in an eschatological drama that begins with a "rapture" of Christian believers and a time of intense tribulation in which Jews will suffer greatly and most will die; but a "remnant" of 144,000 will convert to Christianity and launch an impressive wave of evangelism prior to the climactic conflagration at Armageddon, leading to the final act in which Jesus will return and set up a 1,000-year rule from his throne in the newly cleansed Jerusalem.[15]

The dispensationalists' fascination with Israel is two-sided: in their minds, "Jewish chosenness and Jewish suffering are two sides of the same coin. . . . The ingathering of Jews in the land of Zion is only a prelude to Armageddon, where the majority of the Jewish people will perish. . . . In a very literal sense, the Israel which dispensationalists regard as a fulfillment of prophecy is born to die" (Haynes 1995: 161).

Israel has played an important role in the thinking of various American sectarian groups from the 17th century onward (Greenberg 1994), but its significance mushroomed in tandem with the populist dissemination of dispensationalist thought in the 20th century: countless Christians who could not define the words *fundamentalist* or *dispensationalist* have had their beliefs shaped by precisely these views.[16] Tens of millions, especially in America, have adopted premillennial dispensationalism through the teaching of televangelists such as Oral Roberts, Rex Humbard, Jimmy Swaggart, Jerry Falwell, Benny Hinn, and their assorted kin. As the popularity of televangelism grew, Timothy Weber notes, "New media enterprises such as Paul Crouch's Trinity Broadcasting Network (TBN) and Pat Robertson's Christian Broadcasting Network (CBN) featured premillennialist teaching morning, noon, and night" (Weber 2004: 191–92).

Temple Institute" link on the Temple Institute official Web site: http://www.templeinstitute.org/about.htm.

Pentecostal televangelist Benny Hinn hosts multiple tours each year. His brochure for a special tour to celebrate Israel's 60th anniversary touts a chance to "Be inspired by Pastor Benny's prophetic teaching on the Mount of Scopus, where our Lord Jesus will someday soon return in glory and power." Hinn's trips are organized by Gil Travel Group. See the "North America Brochure" at http://www.giltravel.com/benny-hinn/registration.html.

15. Stephen Haynes offers a convenient summary of the rise of dispensational premillenialism (1995: 141–70).

16. As Timothy Weber notes in *On the Road to Armageddon: How Evangelicals Became Israel's Best Friend*, "Since the mid-1990s, tens of millions of people who have never seen a prophetic chart or listened to a sermon on the second coming have read one or more novels in the Left Behind series, which has become the most effective disseminator of dispensationalist ideas ever" (2004: 15).

But television is not the only medium spreading the premillennialist gospel. Legions of followers have read Hal Lindsey's end-time forecasts in *The Late Great Planet Earth* (1970), and subsequent books on a similar theme, some explaining why earlier predictions of the end failed to materialize. Together, Lindsey's books have sold upwards of 40 million copies (Weber 2004: 188–91).[17] Lindsey's books, however, were a mere warm-up for the record-breaking "Left Behind" series that was envisioned by Tim LaHaye and written by Jerry Jenkins. From the debut of *Left Behind* in 1996, the 12-volume series (along with offshoots such as children's versions and graphic novels) had sold more than 63 million books by 2008, made its authors exceedingly rich, and sparked a number of copycats and spinoffs (Weber 2004: 192–96; Monahan 2008: 817).

As they approach the Holy Land, dispensationalists view Israel through a literalist lens of biblical apocalyptic. When they stand and scan the Holy Land, they see Israel as the interpretive key to prophecy, the site of history-ending conflict, and the locus of Christ's millennial reign. Gazing across the Kidron Valley at the Dome of the Rock, they do not see an impressive Islamic shrine but envision a third temple standing in its place, a temple in which Christ sits enthroned and all nations come to worship at his feet.

Protestants as Propagandists

The fundamentalist-dispensationalist fascination with the State of Israel, especially after the expansion brought by the Six Day War in 1967, made its adherents ripe for exploitation by the Israeli government, who saw in them a gold mine of good will and activist support for Israel.

While mainline-moderate Protestants are generally supportive of Israel, they are also inclined to sympathize with the Palestinian plight and to appreciate the multilayered history of the region that makes any hope of lasting peace so tenuous and complicated.

Lasting peace for Israel, however, is not on the fundamentalist-dispensationalist agenda. Not only do dispensationalists fully expect Israel to be the site of world-ending war, but some of them actively seek to bring it about through supporting right-wing Zionist groups in Israel who want to destroy the Dome of the Rock and the Al Aqsa Mosque so they can "cleanse" the Temple Mount with the ashes of a sacrificial red heifer (Num 19:1–10) bred with the aid of dispensationalist cattle ranchers from Texas.[18] Afterwards, the groups hope to build a third temple on the Temple Mount and restore the Old Testament system of sacrifices.[19]

---

17. Lindsey currently produces a television program, *The Hal Lindsey Report*, that claims to be "politically incorrect, prophetically correct." He promotes the program and posts "prophetic" commentaries at the *Hal Lindsey Report* official Web site: http://www.hallindsey.com/.

18. See Dreher 2002.

19. See Weber 2004: 249–68; and the official Web site of the Temple Institute: http://www.templeinstitute.org.

Fundamentalist-dispensationalists do this not because they support the agenda of ultra-Orthodox Jews who want to restore temple worship for its own sake but because they believe the fulfillment of prophecy requires the presence of a temple in Jerusalem. They are doing their part to hasten Armageddon.

In the meantime, American fundamentalist-dispensationalists are Israel's closest allies. They insist that God's promise to bless those who bless Abraham and curse those who curse him (Gen 12:1–3) remains an interpretive explanation for any nation's prosperity or lack of it. Jerry Falwell, founder of an Independent Baptist empire, often expressed such a view. "I firmly believe God has blessed America because America has blessed the Jew," he wrote in *Listen, America!*" a book that helped launch the Religious Right. "If this nation wants her fields to remain white with grain, her scientific achievements to remain notable, and her freedom to remain intact, America must continue to stand with Israel" (Falwell 1980: 98). Other prominent televangelists have made similar pronouncements.[20]

Such firm support for Israel encouraged a flowering of Christian Zionism and a partnership with Israeli officials that gave rise to what Weber calls "tour bus diplomacy."

During the 1980s, Israel's Ministry of Tourism invited evangelical pastors to visit Israel on free "familiarization tours" that were carefully designed to inculcate both spiritual bonds with the Holy Land and political support for the State of Israel. The goal was for pastors, inspired and experienced through their Holy Land travel, to recruit parishioners and other pastors to climb aboard an El Al Airlines flight and see the Holy Land with a trained Israeli guide. In the process, Weber observes, the Israelis were "building a solid corps of non-Jewish supporters for Israel in the United States by bringing large numbers of evangelicals to hear and see Israel's story for themselves" (2004: 214).

Political parties within Israel sometimes competed for evangelical attention. In an eye-opening span of a few pages, Weber shows how the Likud party and the Israeli government courted Falwell just as he was pulling his "Moral Majority" together, going so far as to provide a Windstream jet to facilitate his travel (2004: 218–20). Falwell used his connections to lead or sponsor tours for other evangelical leaders. He brought 3,000 first-year undergraduates from Liberty University to Israel for what amounted to propagandistic endorsements of Israel's right to the land, portraying Palestinians as obstacles to God's purposes.

---

20. Pentecostal preacher Jimmy Swaggart put it even more bluntly (and graphically) in Mike Evans' *Israel: America's Key to Survival*: "I feel that America is tied with the spiritual umbilical cord to Israel. The ties go back to long before the founding of the United States of America. The Judeao-Christian concept goes all the way back to Abraham and God's promise to Abraham which I believe also included America" (Evans 1981, cited in Dehmer 1986: 7 and Pieterse 1991: 75).

Participants in Falwell's tours were often treated to meetings with high government officials, and Falwell hosted banquets to honor Israeli leaders during the tours (Weber 2004: 219, citing Halsell 1986).

Prophecy pilgrims are also encouraged by nongovernmental groups such as the "International Christian Embassy for Jerusalem," which sponsors large celebrations during the Festival of Succoth, leading upwards of 5,000 conservative Christians on marches through the streets of Jerusalem. The sponsoring organization has no government standing but has succeeded in recruiting top officials, including prime ministers Benjamin Netanyahu in 1998 and Ariel Sharon in 2002, to speak to the pilgrims and thank them for their support of Israel (Weber 2004: 215–18).

Through cultivating clergymen for political purposes—especially fundamentalist-dispensationalists who have a strong media presence—the Israeli government has won many friends through what could safely be called "propaganda pilgrimage."

Protestants and Archaeology

Before closing, I venture a few observations relative to Protestants and archaeology. I do not wish to suggest that Orthodox and Roman Catholic academics or clergy have no interest in archaeology, but the previous discussion suggests that lay pilgrims from those traditions are generally more interested in churches and shrines built to commemorate a biblical event than in the land surrounding it. Likewise, Orthodox and Catholic pilgrims show greater fascination with the crucifixes, altars, icons and artwork located above the ground than with archaeological remains that lie beneath the soil.[21]

In contrast, most Protestant pilgrims prefer the bare landscape, and the barer, the better (fig. 4). While resentful or indifferent to the presence of Islamic mosques or Christian shrines that blanket holy ground with granite and marble, they admire archaeology because it strips the earth to the same surface that their spiritual ancestors may have walked and to the same foundations that may have supported the palace of David or the synagogue Jesus would have visited in Capernaum.

Protestants are also enamored with archaeology because, despite constant reminders that archaeological evidence can be interpreted differently, it remains, after all, evidence. While Catholics and the Orthodox may revere a site based on longstanding church traditions, Protestants look for something more tangible and find it in the work of archaeologists. One can doubt the accuracy of a saint's vision, and the saint is no longer around to plead his or her case—but the ashlars and foundation stones of ancient cities are still there. Broken pottery and charred bones and carbonized seeds are still there. Coins and bullae and the occasional

---

21. Personal communication from veteran Israeli guide Doron Heiliger, March 9, 2009.

seal or inscription are still there. For many Protestants, archaeology is *real* in a way that church tradition is not. In his study of the way Israeli guides lead Protestant tour groups, Feldman spoke of how Protestant pilgrims see "archaeology as 'proof' of truths" (2007: 365).

That is not to say, however, that all Protestants approach truth claims in the same way. Mainline or moderate pilgrims are not as interested in proving that "Jacob slept here" as in gaining proximity to the biblical world, an experience that illuminates the age-old story in which they also claim a place as the latest chapter. Archaeology brings them closer to that world, and because they hold to neither an inerrant Bible nor an inerrant Church, they remain open to new discoveries, even those that challenge biblical claims about Joshua's conquests or Solomon's building projects.

Fundamentalist-dispensationalists look at archaeology in a more selective fashion. They happily cite finds that appear to offer external proof of Bible truths but quickly part company when the archaeologist suggests that Jericho had no walls when the Hebrews came through.[22] As it relates to the past, fundamentalist-dispensationalists favor sites and interpretations that reinforce their religious beliefs and support the State of Israel's claim as legitimate heir to the promised land. As suggested above, however, the most conservative branch of evangelicalism is more interested in the future fulfillment of prophecy than in understanding and appreciating the past: the primary role of archaeology is to "prove the Bible" or identify sites important to their eschatological and prophetic passions.

Conclusions

Christian pilgrims of various sorts constitute a major element in Israeli tourism, about a third of 2.8 million visitors that were expected in 2008, with more than half a million of them coming from America.[23] Israel wants that number to grow and continues to target American evangelical travelers with significant funding and innovative methods such as a promotional music video produced by the Ministry of Tourism and posted on YouTube.[24]

No doubt, Protestants of all stripes will continue to comprise a large segment of those pilgrims. I would suggest that both the State of Israel

---

22. Consider periodic letters to *Biblical Archaeology Review*, for example, in which conservative readers write to cancel their subscriptions after reading an article that questions the historical veracity of a biblical tradition.

23. R. Gee, "Israel Tourism Booming, Thanks to Tight Security, Christian Visitors," *Cox News*, June 15, 2008. http://www.coxwashington.com/hp/content/reporters/stories/2008/06/15/2008/07/15/ISRAEL_TOURISM_TX15_COX.html. (site no longer exists).

24. See "Go Israel—You Will Never Be the Same!" on YouTube: http://www.youtube.com/watch?v=fhTdYqFF_1o&feature=related.

Figure 4. Israeli guide Doron Heiliger (foreground left) takes Protestant pilgrims to the high ground of Mt. Precipice, across from Nazareth, so they can contemplate the hills and valleys where Jesus grew up.

and the cause of archaeology could be well served by reaching out to those Protestants who can appreciate both the land and its archaeological heritage for their own sakes rather than as keys to prophecy alone. If courting Protestant pilgrims continues to be a part of Israel's economic and political strategy, it would seem prudent to pursue those pilgrims who are more concerned with the preservation of the Holy Land than with its ultimate demise.

References

Badone, E.
  2004   Crossing Boundaries: Exploring the Borderlands of Ethnography, Tourism, and Pilgrimage. Pp. 180–89 in *Intersecting Journeys*, ed. E. Badone and S. Roseman. Chicago: University of Illinois.
Badone, E., and Roseman, S.
  2004   Approaches to the Anthropology of Pilgrimage and Tourism. Pp. 1–23 in *Intersecting Journeys*, ed. E. Badone and S. Roseman. Chicago: University of Illinois.
Bowman, G.
  1991   Christian Ideology and the Image of a Holy Land: The Place of Jerusalem Pilgrimage in the Various Christianities. Pp. 98–121 in *Contesting the Sacred: The Anthropology of Christian Pilgrimage*, ed. J. Eade and M. Sallnow. New York: Routledge.

Brown, D.
1996 Genuine Fakes. Pp. 33–47 in *The Tourist Image: Myths and Myth Making in Tourism*, ed. T. Selwyn. Chichester: Wiley.
Campbell University Divinity School
2009 Israel: Bible Lands Study Tour. Privately printed brochure.
Cohen, E.
1992 Pilgrimage and Tourism: Convergence and Divergence. Pp. 47–61 in *Sacred Journeys: The Anthropology of Pilgrimage*, ed. A. Morinis. Westport, CT: Greenwood.
Coleman, S.
2002 Do You Believe in Pilgrimage? *Communitas*, Contestation and Beyond. *Anthropological Theory* 2: 355–68.
Dehmer, A.
1986 *Unholy Alliance: Christian Fundamentalism and the Israeli State.* Washington, DC: American-Arab Antidiscrimination Committee.
Dreher, R.
2002 Red Heifer Days: Religion Takes the Lead. *National Review Online*, April 11. On-line: http://old.nationalreview.com/dreher/dreher 041102.asp.
Eade, J., and Sallnow, M., eds.
1991a Introduction. Pp. 1–29 in *Contesting the Sacred: The Anthropology of Christian Pilgrimage*, ed. J. Eade and M. Sallnow. New York: Routledge.
1991b *Contesting the Sacred: The Anthropology of Christian Pilgrimage.* New York: Routledge.
Evans, M.
1981 *Israel: America's Key to Survival.* Plainfield, NJ: Logos International.
Falwell, J.
1980 *Listen, America!* New York: Doubleday.
Feldman, J.
2007 Constructing a Shared Bible Land: Jewish Israeli Guiding Performances for Protestant Pilgrims. *American Ethnologist* 34: 351–74.
Fosdick, H. E.
1927 *A Pilgrimage to Palestine.* New York: MacMillan.
Greenberg, G.
1994 *The Holy Land in American Religious Thought, 1620–1948: The Symbiosis of American Religious Approaches to Scripture's Sacred Territory.* Lanham, MD: University Press of America.
Hahn, C.
1990 Loca Sancta Souvenirs: Sealing the Pilgrim's Experience. Pp. 85–96 in *The Blessings of Pilgrimage*, ed. R. Ousterhout. Chicago: University of Illinois Press.
Halsell, G.
1986 *Prophecy and Politics: Militant Evangelists on the Road to Nuclear War.* Westport, CT: Lawrence Hill.
Haynes, S.
1995 Dispensational Premillennialism: The Jew as Key to the Kingdom. Pp. 141–70 in *Reluctant Witnesses: Jews and the Christian Imagination*, ed. S. Haynes. Louisville: Westminster John Knox.

Hummel, R., and Hummel, T.
  1995   *Patterns of the Sacred: English Protestant and Russian Orthodox Pilgrims of the Nineteenth Century.* London: Scorpion Cavendish.
Idinopulos, T.
  1996   Sacred Space and Profane Power: Victor Turner and the Perspective of Holy Land Pilgrimage. Pp. 9–19 in *Pilgrims and Travelers to the Holy Land,* ed. B. le Beau and M. Mor. Omaha: Creighton University Press.
LaHaye, T., and Jenkins, J.
  1996   *Left Behind: A Novel of the Earth's Last Days.* Wheaton, IL: Tyndale.
Lindsey, H.
  1970   *The Late Great Planet Earth.* Grand Rapids: Zondervan.
Lock, C.
  2003   Bowing Down to Wood and Stone: One Way to Be a Pilgrim. Pp. 110–32 in *Pilgrim Voices: Narrative and Authorship in Christian Pilgrimage,* ed. S. Coleman and J. Elsner. New York: Berghahn Books.
Long, B.
  2003   Starred and Striped Holy Lands. Pp. 43–87 in *Imagining the Holy Land: Maps, Models, and Fantasy Travels,* ed. B. Long. Bloomington: Indiana University Press.
Mitchell, J.
  1997   A Moment with Christ: The Importance of Feelings in the Analysis of Belief. *The Journal of the Royal Anthropological Institute* 3: 79–94.
Monahan, T.
  2008   Marketing the Beast: *Left Behind* and the Apocalypse Industry. *Media, Culture, & Society* 30: 813–30.
Morinis, A.
  1992   Introduction: The Territory of the Anthropology of Pilgrimage. Pp. 1–28 in *Sacred Journeys: The Anthropology of Pilgrimage,* ed. A. Morinis. Westport, CT: Greenwood.
Pieterse, J.
  1991   The History of a Metaphor: Christian Zionism and the Politics of Apocalypse. *Archives de Sciences Sociales des Religions* 75: 75–104.
Smith, V.
  1992   Pilgrimage and Tourism: The Quest in Guest. *Annals of Tourism Research* 19: 1–17.
Turner, V.
  1973   The Center Out There: The Pilgrim's Goal. *History of Religions* 12: 191–230.
Turner, V., and Turner, E.
  1978   *Image and Pilgrimage in Christian Culture: Anthropological Perspectives.* Oxford: Blackwell.
Weber, T.
  2004   *On the Road to Armageddon: How Evangelicals Became Israel's Best Friend.* Grand Rapids: Baker Academic.

Community and Antiquities at Umm el-Jimal and Silwan

A Comparison

BERT DE VRIES

This essay compares the relationship between archaeology and community at Umm el-Jimal, Jordan, and Silwan, Jerusalem. Umm el-Jimal and Silwan are both substantial modern communities (6,000 and 40,000 residents, respectively) with significant archaeological sites at their geographic cores. The goal is to examine these two situations in the light of traditional and shifting standards and practices in order to reach better understanding of the ways to build improved, just relationships between living communities and the archaeological sites in their midst.

Archaeology and Community: General Comments

Traditional Patterns and Habits

From its inception, archaeology has been perceived in the purview of enlightenment-based expert practitioners of the scientific method. The history of disjuncture between archaeological site research and local community development springs from the myths of Western scientific, superior knowledge and concomitant local ignorance (McAlister 2005:14). From this, early archaeologists presupposed a disconnection between the people of past cultures and the people living on the land. While they imagined the people of ancient and classical cultures as fellow travelers whose great achievements in monuments and literature inspired or matched those of the scholar, the modern, local residents were seen as uncultured peasants, the inheritors and therefore mismanagers of the decayed and collapsed remnants of the glorious past. At best, they were exotic others, like the colorful characters forever doing nothing in the foregrounds of David Roberts's paintings of Palestine or the performers of Cretan folk dances reenacting Arthur Evans's "labyrinth dance" at Knossos (Gere 2009: 82–84). This "postcolonial" critique of the history of archaeology in Jordan has been well presented by Irene Maffi (2009).

Local communities were not systematically consulted or surveyed for their views of the significance and meaning of the antiquities in their midst. Worse, they sometimes found themselves disposed and even removed from ancient landscapes they considered their ancestral homes (Brand 2001; see Tarawneh 2000 for Jordanian examples). Conversely, local communities were mystified by archaeologists' interest in their landscape. This mystification led quite logically to the myth of archaeologists as treasure hunters. A common result was alienation of locals from what they had once considered their own. Not surprisingly, this alienation is sometimes manifest in their illicit excavation for ancient "treasures" (cf. Burleigh 2008). A key issue, therefore, has been radically reduced access of local communities to the antiquities landscape and the resulting loss of potential income from site and tourism development investments.

New Directions

In the past two decades, Western archaeologists have been giving up their monopoly on the interpretation of archaeological landscapes. This change has occurred as local education brought greater culture awareness, local academic institutions developed professional archaeology programs, and national authorities matured in power and expertise. Moreover, postprocessual theory allowed for alternative voices in recognition of the possibility of the coexistence of multiple interpretations of the same landscapes. In both of these ways, local communities have gained greater prominence as power groups and alternative voices deserving inclusion with benefits and access; they also have received a better hearing on questions of the meaning of their cultural heritage (Shankland 2000: 167–76).

At the same time, local cultures have been increasingly recognized as the last stratum in the occupation histories of sites. Local residents have been given a voice in the interpretation of their heritage and have also found themselves included in that picture. In the Middle East, this has necessitated the extension of archaeological interests to the Islamic periods so that the heritage of modern communities can be linked to past cultures. For most (Muslim) Jordanians and Palestinians, this has meant not only a new respectability for their own Islamic past but also a greater recognition of the role of pre-Islamic cultures in their formative histories. For Palestinians in particular, this was achieved through the examination of relatively recent village material cultures through the innovative work of Albert Glock and his students (Ziadeh-Seely 2000: 326–45; de Vries 2010: 109–10). For Israelis—and others whose identities are shaped by a mythic golden age in the distant past—it has meant the recognition of the numerous archaeological strata down to the formation of the modern state (de Vries 2010: 107–8).

The goal of this essay is to study these new directions, using two

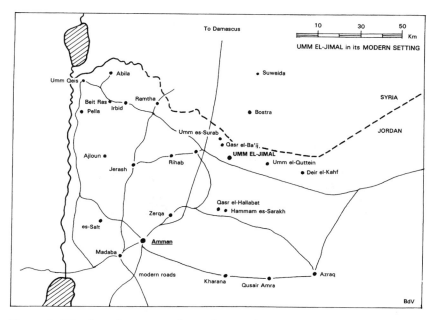

Figure 1. Map locating Umm el-Jimal in Jordan's network of modern roads.

case studies, in order to find ways to overcome traditional problems. The case of Umm el-Jimal involves the relationship of a fairly uniform single community's relation to its antiquities. This simpler case can therefore serve both as an illustration of the problems and a model for solutions. Silwan is more difficult, and it is hoped that discussing it in conjunction with Umm el-Jimal will provide a glimmer of clarity. The goal is not simply intellectual comprehension but the creation of conditions of peace, in which competing communities can find mutuality in a properly interpreted, shared material heritage (Greenberg 2009).

Umm el-Jimal

Archaeological History of the Site

Umm el-Jimal is located in the basalt plain of northern Jordan, 15 km east of modern Mafraq between two wadis supplying it with winter run-off water, on the western edge of the Bādiya (figs. 1–2). Earliest occupation left a Paleolithic flint scatter on the banks of the eastern wadi. Millennia later, local people, Arab nomads, settled under the umbrella of Nabataean influence from Bostra, initially established the village of Umm el-Jimal in the 1st century c.e. with an estimated population of 2,000–3,000 people. This Nabataean stratum became Umm el-Jimal's

Figure 2. View of Umm el-Jimal looking south from an ancient house inside the protected ruins; Byzantine Barracks are on the left, and a modern mosque and three cell-phone towers are in the background on the right.

signature story, overshadowing all the other occupation phases in the popular imagination.

The Romans incorporated Umm el-Jimal into the Province of Arabia between the 2nd and 4th centuries c.e. The settlement included a Nabataean/Roman community with an adjacent local village, and the site served as a military station during the 4th century. This in turn gave way gradually to a civilian town as Roman imperial power began to diminish. From the 5th to 8th centuries, Umm el-Jimal continued as a prosperous rural farming and trading community of 6,000–8,000 people living in sturdy basalt houses and worshiping in 15 Christian churches during the late 5th and 6th centuries. The town continued in diminished numbers during the Umayyad and early Abbasid periods until its total desertion in the 9th century (de Vries and 1998).

Remarkably preserved after 1,100 years of only sporadic occupation, the site was reoccupied by Druze migrating from the Syrian Jebel Druze and the Lebanese Shouf Mountains in the early 20th century. During that time, many buildings were reconstructed to render the site habitable. Because the rebuilders used ancient techniques, the result looked more like a restoration, so that casual visitors have tended to see this work as Nabataean or Roman (Brown 2009). After the Druze abandonment, the Arab Msa'eid tribe, which had served the Druze as herders, pitched their tents in and around the antiquities and used the stone structures for stables and storage. For a while, their children were educated in schoolrooms in adapted Byzantine structures. After the government prohibited this use of antiquities in 1972 and fenced off the ruins in 1975, the Msa'eid constructed the modern village that now surrounds the fenced site. This village has continued to grow since the 1950s and is now a community of 6,000 people with its own well-run municipal government and services (de Vries et al. 2009).

Since 1972, the Department of Antiquities has managed the standing Byzantine-Islamic ruins inside a fenced enclosure and also has a guard assigned to al-Herri, the ruins of the adjacent Roman-era local village. Extensive cemeteries, ancient regional roads, and agricultural hinterlands remain in private hands, much of it under the homesteads of the modern village or on the deep-well irrigated farm tracts that now cover much of the countryside.

History of Archaeology at Umm el-Jimal

Umm el-Jimal was systematically surveyed by a Princeton University Expedition in 1905 and 1909, on the eve of the Druze reoccupation (de Vries 1998: 27–36). Most of the modern research, from 1972 to 1998, has been done through the Umm el-Jimal Project (UJP), a New Archaeology field study that I directed, based at Calvin College.[1] Since 1998, the Department of Antiquities of Jordan has been engaged in clearing key structures and in the remodeling of an Umayyad farmstead for its adaptation of a site museum.

During the last three years a partnership between UJP and Open Hand Studios (OHS)[2] has focused site development work, which involves both creating a virtual museum[3] and preserving and developing the site as a museum-on-the-ground. Two site-documentation seasons in January 2009 (de Vries et al. 2009) and 2010 included applying methods to enfold the Umm el-Jimal community into this project, described as follows.

Antiquities and Community at Umm el-Jimal: Current Shape of the Fieldwork

Multifaceted Documentation and the Building of Long-Term Relationships

The main objectives were the use of up-to-date technology and presentation techniques, the implementation of linked virtual and real presentations of the site, and the overt partnering with communities, organizations, and individuals with relationships to the site. The field staff was organized into five teams recruited for specific expertise. Two of these, the Virtual Reconstruction Team and the Virtual Museum and Site Development Team, worked directly on the antiquities site and its presentation on the internet. The Video Production Team split its

1. See www.ummeljimal.org/fieldwork.html
2. See www.openhandstudios.org.
3. The open-information Web site www.ummeljimal.org.

efforts between visual documentation of the antiquities and filming interviews with community members. The Modern Cultural Heritage team documented the tent and house occupation of the ancient site during the past century, interviewed numerous members of the community about their remembered heritage, and negotiated the planning and installation of a Cultural Heritage Center outside the antiquities to be operated by the residents for the benefit of both local/regional inhabitants and tourists. The Educational Curriculum Team developed a multidisciplinary strategy for the teaching of archaeology to Jordanians in the primary and secondary schools in partnership with the Ministry of Education to be adopted for use in Jordan's public and private schools and adapted for international use (fig. 3).

The Practice of Inclusive Archaeology

A key element of this work is the building of relationships with various communities with interest in the site. This starts with the traditional choices: (1) the academic community, expressed through affiliation with the American Schools of Oriental Research, publication of research results, and site conservation with grant assistance from the Archaeological Institute of America (2010–11); and (2) the Department of Antiquities of Jordan in its role as a partner in site museum construction and installation, site tour development, and building consolidation. The educational component is carried out as a partnership with the Curriculum Department of the Jordanian Ministry of Education. For this aspect, the most significant partnership is with the Umm el-Jimal community. The people of Umm el-Jimal are represented by a citizens' committee, and the municipality of Umm el-Jimal is represented by the mayor and his staff. The occupation history of the living community at Umm el-Jimal is thus being treated as the final level in its occupation history from the Paleolithic to the present, and a just relationship between community and antiquities is being defined.

Antiquities and Community at Umm el-Jimal: An Assessment

Personal Relationships

The Umm el-Jimal Project has employed local men and boys over a succession of the decades, and Sally de Vries and I were the only constants in this personnel process. Our efforts to be fair and kind paid off in excellent community relations for more than one generation. In the 90s, high school boys would say things like, "Twenty years ago my grandfather worked for you!"[4] Some community members have been

---

4. One young man, who had become especially fond of us, later named his first daughter "Sally" after my wife; we now have familial status as adopted grandparents.

Figure 3. Schoolboys in al-Herri, the ruins of the local Roman-era village on the edge of which they live.

intrigued by the antiquities from playing in them as youngsters. Muaffaq Hazza is an example. As a child he learned the distinct features of every ruin and became familiar with the numerous architectural forms and inscriptions; and from helping the scholars who came to study the texts, he learned to read some of them, especially the Greek ones. Eventually, he became an invaluable member of the UJP Team and is currently a member of its core staff.

In 1998, Muaffaq teamed up with anthropologist Melissa Cheyney, a veteran of three seasons of excavating burials in the village, to conduct a survey of the community's own sense of the significance of the antiquities. They found that, like the archaeologists, the residents valued the antiquities but in different ways. First, they remember fondly where and how their families lived in the ruins before 1970; second, they saw the reuse of architectural pieces in their homes, and especially in the house of Sheik Hail es-Serour, as a source of individual and communal status; and third, they saw the ruins as a useful source of building materials. Ironically, they found this utility to be more innocent and less destructive than the archaeologists' disturbance of the masonry in the course of their excavation (Cheyney 2009: 361–63).

Community, Antiquities, and Heritage at Umm el-Jimal

Conventional archaeological wisdom would have it that the modern residents lack a real connection to the archaeological heritage of the site. After all, the ancient residents, Arabs in Nabataean to early Islamic contexts, left the site unpopulated 1,100 years ago. Moreover, when Howard Butler began his famous documentation in 1905, the site was still uninhabited, although he did observe the very beginning of Druze and Msa'eid transhumance visits from the Jebel Hauran in southern Syria. It would seem that the modern residents had no apparent historical or cultural link with the ancient residents whose ruined structures they began to reoccupy.

However, our recent investigations led us to a different conclusion. First, as we studied the history of the Druze (Brown 2009) and Msa'eid (Cheyney 2009; our 2009 and 2010 field seasons) at Umm el-Jimal, our awareness of their relationship to the antiquities was dramatically enhanced by documentation of the material evidence of their sojourn in the ruins. This documentation has included systematic recording of the Druze/Msa'eid remodeling of the standing Byzantine structures (begun in de Vries 1998: 99–109), mapping of the numerous Msa'eid summer tent sites among the Byzantine ruins, and recording the Druze and Msa'eid family names on lintels and doorposts of the houses they used. These physical connections became poignantly real in some of the interviews conducted in 2009 and 2010. For example, the current sheikh, Abdullah es-Serour, has argued rather powerfully that when the Msa'eid lived in the ruins, they maintained and protected them but that now that they've been moved out, the buildings stand vacant and are collapsing.

In short, it became clear that the current community is to be counted as a still-living archaeological stratum of the site and thus must be included in the list of those who claim it in their cultural heritage. As such, they have the right to speak as interpreters of the meaning of the material remains, as heirs of the site's heritage, and as decision-making participants in these ventures. Because Umm el-Jimal's Byzantine antiquities are so well preserved, they form a critical mass, visible from every house, school, office and business in the modern village. Therefore, for anyone growing up and living in the village, the antiquities by their very monumentality inevitably become a mark of identity. This identity process is nurtured through lessons in the school curriculum, but even without overt intellectual awareness there is an inevitable subconscious identification with these ruins.

Economic Potential and the Hierarchy of Communities

On a pleasant Friday in late January 2010 we witnessed a bucolic annual ritual. Apparently enjoying the weekend holiday, numerous villager families were strolling through the ruins, with children's voices chiming the pleasures of a family outing. On closer inspection, we saw that these visitors were mostly women and children and were not merely on a stroll to enjoy the ruins. No, this was the annual *khubeizeh* harvest. *Khubeizeh* is a wild spinach-like vegetable prominent in the Jordanian cuisine; along with stinging nettles, it grows abundantly in the ruins after the December-January rains. When I asked how she was enjoying herself, a lady answered, "Not very much, the *khubeizeh* is very little this year." On this weekend day, the ruins of ancient Umm el-Jimal were a food source for the kitchens of modern Umm el-Jimal. While their children cavorted and their husbands strolled, the women harvested.

Otherwise, after the site was fenced and its buildings were no longer usable for school or animal shelter, there has been little to no local economic advantage from the existence of spectacular world-renowned antiquities in the middle of the village. There have been the sporadic employment opportunities for day laborers during the Umm el-Jimal Project's field seasons and the more regular site clearance and construction, which have employed roughly a dozen workers full time over the past decade. However, the current flow of tourists involves one- to three-hour visits through a single entrance, which is accessible without entry into the village. Facilities for tourists are limited to one simple bathroom in the tourism office; there is no kiosk for the purchase of food or a place to reside for a more extended stay. From an economic point of view, the village feels excluded and by-passed.

To rectify this, the Department of Antiquities of Jordan is currently completing a site museum-visitor center, which will include small artifact displays, a tourist shop, a small indoor-outdoor café, and restrooms. This development promises to accommodate a greater flow of visitors and encourage longer stays. However, because the facility is on-site, its financial operation and management will most likely be controlled from Amman, as is the case in other sites, such as the rest house at Um Qeis, which has become an upscale restaurant operated and staffed by an Amman restaurateur (Brand 2001). As at Um Qeis, the new visitors center will likely channel nearly all the income away from the community and will be too costly to serve local customers.

Planning the Umm el-Jimal Heritage Center

With little hope for direct economic benefit from the operation of the museum-visitor center and site tours for outside visitors, the project partners have devised an additional scheme to satisfy the community's economic interests and to raise awareness of the connection between the antiquities and the community: the establishment of the Cultural Heritage Center in the village at a point of intersection between the village business sector and the archaeological site. This center is designed to present the culture of the living community as the last phase in the archaeological history of Umm el-Jimal. The Center's program design,

planning, and operation will be overseen by a committee of citizens in
partnership with Umm el-Jimal's municipality offices. The Center will
serve as a museum displaying the recent history and culture of the community, a lecture and video-presentation hall, a regional craft center,
an archaeological and cultural education center for school children and
adults, a hostel for archaeologists and backpackers, and a community
center for wedding receptions and other public gatherings. Two crucial
elements for the sustainability of this heritage center are: (1) linking
the heritage of the modern community to the cultural history of the
archaeological site, and (2) providing income generation and thus financial benefit for the community.

In short, the Umm el-Jimal Heritage Center will play a key role in
restoring the former integral connection between community and antiquities, giving the residents a sense of inclusion and the feeling that
justice has been done and bringing the antiquities back to their prideful
place as a monument in and of the community.

Silwan Compared to Umm el-Jimal
Touring the City of David: Mythified History

Location of the Site in the Community (Figure 4)

While the antiquities of Umm el-Jimal require over an hour's journey
into rural northern Jordan, Silwan[5] and its antiquities are reached by a
short stroll from the Dung Gate of Jerusalem's Old City. The community of about 40,000 is built on the slopes of the River Kidron / Wadi
en-Nār and its western tributary, the Wadi Hilweh. With respect to its
antiquities, the so-called City of David and its related water installa-
tions have become Silwan's signature "story," the telling of which has
left the material history of its other strata unknown. These excavated
remains are located on the spur between the two wadis, sloping down
from the south wall of the Temple Mount (Haram esh-Sharif) to the
Siloam Pool, where the wadis join. Unlike Umm el-Jimal, where the
Byzantine ruins form a dramatic skyline, the antiquities here were not
visible before excavation; and even now, after nearly a century of excavations, they remain mostly hidden from view among the densely built
neighborhoods of modern Silwan, especially if one approaches on foot

---

5. I thank Raphael Greenberg of Emek Shaveh, Hamed Salem of Birzeit University, and Ray Dolphin of the United Nations East Jerusalem Office for the Coordination of Humanitarian Affairs for their help with the Silwan portion of this chapter. I,
not they, am responsible for any errors in what follows. For an up-to-date and compre-
hensive summary of both the excavations and the relations between the community
and the power groups, see Mizrachi 2010, a booklet available in print or on the Web
(www.alt-arch.org/docs/booklet_english.pdf).

Figure 4. The core townscape of Silwan. The community is built on the steep slopes of the Wadi Nār (Kidron Valley) and Wadi Hilweh. The spur in the center of the photo sloping down toward the intersection of the two wadis is the City of David / Wadi el-Hilweh neighborhood.

from the Old City. A visitor needs help even to find the antiquities, and lots more to fathom their meaning.

Viewed abstractly, this mixture of archaeological remains and residences should offer the local community a natural role in the presentation of its antiquities to visitors. But, as has been pointed out so often, this is not the case. The greatest shock for me as an uninformed visitor coming to the City of David in Silwan for the first time was the total exclusion of the local Palestinian Arab residents from the site presentation process. Forty thousand people are denied the right and privilege of the communal hospitality that they could exercise in introducing visitors to the archaeological remnants among which they reside; and there is no immediate prospect for the salvaging of a healthy, inclusive relationship between community and antiquities, unless the observance of the principles laid out in the introduction of this essay could be the means of a dramatic reversal. The example of Umm el-Jimal, I believe, is the main reason why the organizers in the conference at Duke University ("Archaeology, Politics and the Media") saw the value of having the Umm el-Jimal Project presented as a model of what can be done.

The Signage at the Entry

Walking from the Dung Gate toward Silwan, one passes a construction fence decorated with kitschy scenes of archaeology volunteers operating sieves and of happy tourists (from America?) on an open bus, labeled "Jerusalem Safari," of the type used in sub-Saharan game preserves. A slit in this fence allows a glimpse of the deep and massive excavation trench known as the "Givati Parking Lot" site (Mizrachi 2010: 44–64). Opposite the fence, in the Wadi Hilweh street, stand several Israeli soldiers with machine guns preventing a young mother wearing *hijab* and her child from leaving their Silwan neighborhood for the Old City. Behind them is what they are guarding, the entrance to the "City of David." The gate is flanked by a huge bronze sculpture, the replica of a harp, next to which large brass letters on a new limestone wall spells ʿĪr Dawīd in Hebrew (fig. 5). I have arrived at the entrance to the tourism complex called "City of David," owned and operated by Elʿad, the privately funded Jewish settler organization in charge of the excavations and the tour operation in the City of David National Park.[6]

Inside, a courtyard with olive trees perpetuates the drama of King David. Alcoves with open arches contain identical 12-branched bronze sculptures symbolizing the Twelve Tribes of Israel, below which, on two of them, inscribed in bronze Hebrew and English letters are verses from David's Psalm 122, a song of ascents. Facing another alcove, a man wearing a scull cap prays (fig. 6). Throughout this visitors center and all along the associated archaeological tour are elaborate signs in Hebrew and English. In the midst of a community of 40,000 speakers of Arabic, there is not one word written in Arabic; and, obviously, no persons of Arab background are in the crowd milling about the booth selling tickets for tours in English or Hebrew. (To be fair, the older directional signs along the walking paths also include Arabic.) All the words and symbols are unwelcoming except to those who revere the majestic sacredness of David, the poet king of ancient Israel. The local community is not welcomed.

The Tour: How the City of David Is Packaged

The tour begins with a 3-D film, narrated by Amos, whose words and visuals spin the myth of the City of David further. We will get the history of the City of David, he asserts, "With help of a shovel and the Bible." And, "Three thousand years after King David we have returned to the Hill where it all began."

Rather than antiquities themselves, the film pans a three-dimensional mockup of an imagined City of David. Soaring like eagles (with 3-D lenses) over the houses of a residential urban complex, moving from south to north, we enter the monumental gates of the "palace of David," a monumental fortified complex. Accompanied by biblical pas-

---

6. See www.cityofdavid.org.il.

Figure 5. View of the City of David Visitors Center entrance; the houses in the top half of the photo are east across the Kidron Valley (Wadi en-Nār).

sages, Amos guides us through time from David to the construction of the First (Solomonic) Temple, which appears in all its 3-D glory, to Hezekiah's siege preparations for the Assyrian assault, portrayed as the dramatic cutting through of the famous Hezekiah's Tunnel, to the Babylonian destruction, the construction of the Second Temple, and its destruction by the Romans in 70 C.E. The film then leaps over 2,000 years to its glorious climax in the present. With triumphal music amplified to a rousing crescendo Amos exclaims: "Neighborhood by neighborhood Jerusalem was restored as the eternal capital of the State of Israel!"

Thus, the myth is presented by a cinematic rendering in place of real archaeology and by biblical verses in place of stratigraphy, all climaxing in the modern political climate of settlers and annexations. The "neighborhood" of Silwan was annexed to the municipality of Jerusalem in 1967; but for the film's audience Silwan, physically only some meters beyond the walls of our little theater, has been rendered invisible, obliterated in the glorious restoration of the City of David. What was serious archaeological study before 1990 has been subverted into the service of the sacred nationalist agenda of Elʿad.[7]

---

7. For an excellent summary of the other archaeological work in Silwan, see Greenberg 2009 and the pieces, including Mizrachi 2010, posted on Emek Shaveh's Web site (*Archaeology in Jerusalem Past and Present,* www.alt-arch.org). Emek

Figure 6. Visitor praying before one of the alcoves with the 12-branched brass sculptures.

On the live tour, Adaya, who also spoke in the film, begins her more restrained site presentation at the lookout post on top of the theater. She gives a geographic orientation stressing the strategic location of the site (fig. 7). The bluff on which the lookout post stands is made to appear high because the lookout is constructed on the precipice overlooking the Kidron Valley (Wadi en-Nār); this blunts the fact that the spur of the City

Shaveh is a nonprofit organization established in 2008 to address the politicization of archaeological sites in Jerusalem, especially those in Silwan. It asserts that archaeology can connect rather than divide the peoples of the region.

of David is dwarfed by the much higher terrain surrounding the site. She rightly explains that this location was necessary because of the famous Gihon Spring at its base. She points out the cave-tomb openings across the way, just above the refuse strewn on the lower slopes. "See the garbage? Look just above it." Modern Silwan, which looms across the wadi, is absent from her talk and from the signage. She concludes the overview by saying, "Our best guide here today in the City of David is the Bible." Like Amos in the film, she produces a copy of the Bible to have ready for pertinent quotations as we tour the excavations.

We descend under the floor of the Visitors Center to visit what remains here from the excavations conducted by Eilat Mazar. Adaya points out the two remnants of the massive foundations, and gives Mazar's interpretation that these must be for the fort-palace of David (Mazar 2009). She briefly mentions the dispute over this but avers that "you can make up your own mind." This is a reference to serious criticism by reputable archaeologists challenging Mazar's interpretation. In the main, they say that her jumping to the "David"-conclusion is improper archaeological use of written sources; that is, there is no evidence of a specific person named David in the material remains (Greenberg 2009). Others challenge Mazar's interpretation of the architecture, arguing that the hodge-podge of foundation walls does not add up a single large structure and that the dates for these remnants are a century too late for David (Finkelstein et al. 2007). I agree with these critiques and am especially astounded at the contrast between this basement-level evidence and the architectural rendering of the complete palace in the film we had just seen. There is a fine line between honest site presentation based on real material evidence and "creative" reconstruction based on Bible stories. Elʿad has crossed this line to suit its religioethnic rationale for restoring Jerusalem. It becomes clear that the meaning of the phrase "being restored neighborhood by neighborhood" is not restoration in the archaeological sense but dispossession in the sociopolitical sense. Thus, I can see that the residents of Silwan are not merely discouraged from entry by the Israeli soldiers at the gate but are irate that the very information presented on the tour can be understood as a rationale for the dispossession process outlined in municipal plans being implemented by Jerusalem's mayor (UNOCHA 2009: 4–9).

From here, we take the stairway and concrete path to Area G, which consists of the visually most spectacular part of the whole archaeological site, the famous "stepped-stone structure," the 10th century B.C.E. stone reinforcements of the slope below the hilltop foundations we just left. Well excavated by Yigal Shiloh's team from 1978 to 1983 (Shiloh 1984: 15–21; figs. 16–29; plates 26–36), this structure is now celebrated as a key element of the City of David. After describing it briefly, Adaya turns to the houses built up against this revetment in the time of Hezekiah (8th century B.C.E.) and destroyed in the 6th. I'm not convinced

Figure 7. Tour guide Adaya giving her geographic orientation on the observation platform above the projection room. Behind her are the Silwan
houses she ignored.

that the masonry or the artifacts found (clay seals with Hebrew names,
a purported stone toilet seat) are indicative of the opulent "luxury" she
enthusiastically attributes to the residents of pre-Babylonian Jerusalem
(fig. 8). Her "proof" of the biblical character of these residents comes
from a seal inscribed with the name Germaryahu son of Shaphan, whom
she claimed was Gemariah, the son of Shaphan who was a military officer of King Jehoiakin, mentioned in Jeremiah (36:10).

I agree with her that these houses and the houses farther south in
Area E (Shiloh 1984: 14) are interesting. Archaeologically, they are the
most interesting aspect of the entire site because they give us a slice
of the life of ordinary residents going about their daily business. But it
strikes me that she has missed an opportunity for discussing intercon-
nections between ancient Jerusalemites with Hebrew names and others
in their multiethnic environment. She does not mention that the finds
in the destruction debris of these houses also included some ostraca
with "south Arabian names in the South Arabian script" (Shiloh 1983:
19). Instead, she singles out Israelite uses of material remains from the
10th century B.C.E. to the Herodian period in the 1st century B.C.E. She
ends by commenting, "You can see Jerusalem being rebuilt layer upon

Figure 8. Adaya describing the late Assyrian houses of Area G built into the earlier "stepped stone structure." The toilet is the stone with the round hole lying in the collapse debris behind her and to her left.

layer, and today you can see the latest layer"; for this last she points to the Jewish Quarter of the Old City, barely visible above us to the north-west. The houses of Silwan, so near behind our backs, do not count as a "layer." The historic tour de force in the isolation of these ancient Hebrew-named Israelites and their direct identification with modern Israeli nationalists boggles my mind.

From here, I leave the group to wade through the gushing waters of Hezekiah's Tunnel, tour the lawns of Area E, and stand at the edge of the famous Pool of Siloam. I've done all that before, and my purpose is not to reconstruct the archaeology—others have done that much better than I can—but to compare the relationship of archaeology and community here to that at Umm el-Jimal.

Reflections on the Tour: El'ad's "Required Past"

The overwhelming impression is that the City of David is presented in total isolation from the community, Silwan, in which it is situated. The focus is on Israelite ethnicity, flowing from the heroic myth of David and concentrated in the very feel of the stones one can touch. This ancient Israelite ethnicity is linked directly, without intervening history, to modern Israeli national identity, sacralized with biblical quotations. Though I saw one man praying in the entry court, the tour is not particularly religious. In fact, a group of Israeli soldiers did a site tour while we did ours, and I understand this to be a regular drill (Rapoport 2009: 28–30). One gets the feeling the City of David is being groomed as a place of national sacrament, a new Masada; and the slogan "This is where it all began" targets the origin of the nation. The tour's biblical references are to monarchic triumph, not to priestly expiation or prophetic justice. At the tunnels system called the Warren Shaft, one is told to imagine oneself standing where David, Bathsheba, and a succeeding string of biblical royal figures once stood.

Clearly, others in my tour group had bought into this sacramental aura in advance; but I, a Dutch-Canadian Calvinist skeptic academic, felt clearly excluded. Imagine, then, what this tour would be like for any of the 40,000 Palestinian Arab residents who, even more than I, cannot share this myth of national outcome in which their own historic identity is ignored and threatened. On the safe assumption that my group is representative, one pictures a stream of over 350,000 visitors annually (Rapoport 2009: 28), whose interests totally exclude and whose money completely bypasses the local community. From the point of view of the residents, this stream is an invasive amplification of occupation, which includes soldiers with machine guns to restrict, confine, and threaten.

More than at Umm el-Jimal, where the noninvolvement of the community is more a matter of arbitrary sociopolitical structure, the particular way in which a site history is presented at Silwan is determinative of its relationship to the living community. A pre-Elʿad stratigraphic chart reveals that there were 21 strata of material remains, from the Chalcolithic to the modern (Shiloh 1984: 3; Mizrachi 2010: 42–43). However, the tour in essence presents only 10 of these (Adaya's "layer by layer"), a particular 1000-year slice of more than 3,000 years of history, and then presents this slice as exclusively Hebrew-Judaic in a mythic limbo that ignores the agency of many others.

As many have pointed out, this is an abuse of archaeology, an embarrassment to the many serious professional archaeologists, especially Israeli colleagues, who see their discipline turned into pseudoscience. Elʿad members do not have to say to the Palestinian neighbors, "You do not belong here; we plan to expel and replace you"; their rendition of the archaeology is delivering this message for them. In a fine article on the manipulation of history and archaeology in Palestinian-Israeli diplomacy, Sandra Scham uses the concept of "desired past," essentially the re-creation of the past with use of "ubiquitous symbols and slogans" without regard to perceived evidence in order to reinforce arguments for claiming coveted territory and control in the present (Scham 2009: 164–67). Such a process of distortion fits the City of David presentation of the perceived past exactly, but the use of the "desired past" is applied with such unrestrained sledgehammer force that I would strengthen the phrase to "required past" in this instance.

At Umm el-Jimal and many other sites with which I'm familiar, archaeology has been practiced with too great a measure of indifference to the interests of the local community and has in some instances even been used as a pretext for its displacement. But as we have seen, there has been a move in the last 20 years to incorporate the local community because of its rights as a current stratum in site occupation and as a participant in site development. Ironically, at the very time that this change has been happening elsewhere, archaeology at Silwan/City of David has been turned into a weapon for invasion and displacement of the community.

Antiquities and Community at Silwan

The current status of the difficult standoff has been well presented in both academic and popular media and need not be repeated here (see Eric Meyers's chapter in this volume, pp. 202–215). Especially important is the work of Raphael Greenberg and his many contributions to the materials presented on the Emek Shaveh Web site. Greenberg's article, "Toward an Inclusive Archaeology in Jerusalem: the Case of Silwan/The City of David" (2009), is republished on the Web site; a plea for using archaeology at Silwan as a tool for reconciliation rather than exclusion, it is essential reading. Emek Shaveh's Web site gives the best overall coverage, providing archaeology, maps, municipal development plans, and an up-to-date bibliography of current articles covering the crisis. Their booklet (2010), mentioned in n. 1, is the most current and informed presentation of facts; see also Rapoport 2009.

It is clear in these numerous publications that a growing number of Israelis, including serious archaeologists and civil rights activists, are focusing on the City of David–Silwan situation. Ironically, this comes at the very time that the hand of El‛ad appears stronger than ever as its private ventures receive staunch backing from the Jerusalem municipality and Israeli government and ongoing licensing from the Israel Antiquities Authority. This last factor enables archaeologists such as Eilat Mazar and Ronny Reich to continue excavating, apparently oblivious to El‛ad's tendentious archaeological presentations, which have been critiqued by some of their colleagues.

The presentation of the City of David archaeology fits into a larger package of strategies to advance the dislocation of the Silwan community. El‛ad is also using typical settler tactics to occupy houses owned by Palestinians and spaces created by bulldozing existing houses. The Jerusalem municipality has used its prerogatives, claimed in the post-1967 annexation of occupied East Jerusalem, essentially to gut sections of the Silwan community by reserving large portions, including the antiquities and much of the town center on the valley floor, for inclusion in a zone entitled the "Holy Basin" or the "Historical Basin."[8] This historic area stretches around the Old City from Silwan in the south to the Mount of Olives in the East up to Sheikh Jarrah in the north and is planned to be under the auspices of the Israel Nature and Parks Authority. The Holy Basin is part of the 22 percent of annexed East Jerusalem set aside for green space, in addition to which 35 percent has been designated for exclusive Israeli settlement, so that space for Arab use has been reduced to 43 percent (UNOCHA 2009). A key element here is the municipal plan to annex the Silwan neighborhood of al-Bustan, where some 80 houses are to be destroyed in order to create green space, parking lots, and a large public building to serve as a center for Holy Basin tourists, not for Silwan residents. The invented archaeological rationale for this gutting—a figment of "required past"—is that the al-Bustan neighborhood is supposed to have been King David and Solomon's Garden.[9] Unlike the people of Umm el-Jimal, they and the other residents of Silwan are overpowered by a collusion of agencies and have difficulty exercising the few rights they have at the municipal level.

Constructive Comparisons between Umm el-Jimal and Silwan

Site Names and Identity

It is, in a way, fortunate that ancient names for Umm el-Jimal are not known (de Vries 1998: 36–38). Consequently, both the ancient site and the modern community are known by its modern name, "Umm el-Jimal." The ancient site is a piece of cultural real estate within the boundaries of the municipality of Umm el-Jimal. The community and antiquities can be called "Modern Umm el-Jimal," whereas the Roman-period remains are properly called "Roman-period Umm el-Jimal." I use "Roman-period" deliberately, because the site was settled not by Romans but mainly by local people of Arab culture living under Roman occupation.

The same convention should be adopted for Silwan. "Silwan" is historically more rooted than "Umm el-Jimal," because it comes from the Roman-period name "Siloam," which is in turn derived from Hebrew "Shiloah." Like Umm el-Jimal, Silwan serves as a neutral geographic term, in this case designating the area as a neighborhood of modern East Jerusalem. As with Umm el-Jimal, it would be appropriate to call an earlier archaeological stratum here "Persian-era Silwan," or "Iron Age Silwan." Though it may sound awkward, those terms would be neutral and would acknowledge that there are stratified remains from numerous cultural eras in Silwan.

---

8. The latter term is preferred by many as being more neutral and also reflecting the fact that not all the areas within it have holy sites (Lapidoth and Ramon 2006: 16).

9. For a descriptive list of all the parties involved in this conflict, and mostly arrayed against the Silwan community, see Mizrachi 2010: 44–46.

In this perspective, designating the archaeological remains of Silwan by the biblical term City of David (Hebrew, *ʿIr Dawīd*) is not appropriate because this nomenclature singles out one specific set of ancient strata at the expense of all others, including the Umayyad remains in the area, from the Chalcolithic to the present. Most modern residents of Silwan do not identify the City of David remains as precious to their heritage. That designation is therefore not neutral but exclusive, and it provides a symbolic separation of the antiquities from the community in which they are located.

The adoption of the name City of David is representative of the way the larger landscape was renamed in terms of biblical geography in the process of Israeli nationalization after 1948. This renaming meant the erasure of the Arab identity embedded in the historic landscape (Abu el-Haj 2001: 85–98). When actual sites could not be identified with biblical place names, the renaming committee satisfied itself with approximations and guesses. The main task was the creation of a new national-sacred geography which made Jewish immigrants feel readily at home but estranged the residents of Palestinian towns and villages (Benvenisti 2002: 11–54). Thus, the land was sacralized in terms of the religious myths of a specific group, at the expense of others. W. J. T. Mitchell shows that such a "Holy Landscape" does not exist in the geographic sense as a place of material substance (as in the term *landscape archaeology*) but rather as a mythic, iconic, idol-like representation, a landscape of the mind. This conception is not neutral, acceptable to all associated with the place. As Mitchell says, "One has to ask: Whose myths? Whose memories? What was erased, rendered invisible, that this landscape might present the face it does? How does this face betray the signs of contestation and struggle between rival myths, disparate memories?" (Mitchell 2000: 196).

Those questions are relevant to the naming of the archaeological landscape of Silwan by the term *City of David*. This designation precedes archaeology in biblical texts (e.g., 2 Sam 5:7; 2 Chr 32:30) and supersedes archaeology in the literalist mythology of the settler group Elʿad, which has taken control of the excavations and has created and operates the City of David park. The City of David now appears on all maps as though it is a place just north of Silwan, rather than *in* Silwan; and it is referred to as part of another construct of mythic geography, the Holy Basin. Following Benvenisti (2002: 52–54), a compromise symbolizing coexistence would be to accept Silwan as the common name for the entire community and give the double name *ʿIr Dawīd* (Hebrew) and *Wadi Hilweh* (Arabic) to the subdistrict with the archaeological remains.

Partnerships and Inclusive Archaeology

A key element in the process of inclusion at Umm el-Jimal is the use of partnerships. Including the local community in the planning and

authorization of archaeological work and related development has not
only created an aura of goodwill around the project but has also improved its theoretical content and published results. Particularly, giving
voice to the ideas, value judgments, and desires of the community has
broadened the question of meaning of the antiquities far beyond the narrow professional goals of traditional academics like me.

Such a model of formal cooperation could be implemented at Silwan
in two ways, if the will to do so were there: (1) the inclusion of the residents of Silwan in the site development process and (2) participation by
Palestinian professional archaeologists in the research strategies, field
work, and publications. The community is ready for this as shown by
its organization of an alternative touring and lecture program (in addition to the alternative tours organized by Emek Shaveh) based at the
Wadi Hilweh Information Center and the Lecture/Protest Tent set up
in al-Bustan neighborhood (fig. 9; see http://silwanic.net). These community efforts are bolstered by assistance from Israeli and Palestinian
professional archaeologists.[10]

As a professional looking in from east of the Jordan, I can list more
than 20 qualified Palestinian professional archaeologists, active in the
Palestinian Department of Antiquities, the various universities of Gaza
and the West Bank, and in private agencies. The possibility of cooperation between Palestinian and Israeli archaeologists has been positively
explored by Sandra Scham and Adel Yahya, results of which they published in "Heritage and Reconciliation" (2003). One might object that
this suggestion for cooperation is just a pipedream, but I see it as one
structural application of Greenberg's eloquent plea (2009) for inclusive
archaeology as an instrument for making peace instead of following the
existing alternative—the constant and intensifying conflict embedded
in the archaeology of exclusion and dispossession.

Final Comments

We archaeologists like to think that crude and cruel attitudes toward the "natives"—caricatured, for example, in Cormac McCarthy's
portrayal of the scalp-hunting "scientist" Judge Holden in *Blood Meridian*—are passé.[11] However, archaeology in both old- and new-world
settings has only slowly shed its past of colonial/imperial treatment of

---

10. Emek Shaveh organizes and publishes these tours on its Web site. At least
one alternative plan for the creation of an archaeological park that would not require
the demolition of any houses in Silwan, drawn up by architect Yosef Jabareen, was
rejected by Jerusalem Mayor Mir Barkat (http://apjp.org/letter-to-mayor-of-jerusalem;
Jabareen 2010).

11. McCarthy's Judge Nobel, in the tradition of Kurtz in *Heart of Darkness*, exposes the man of superior knowledge and science as the culture rapist, whose display
of all-knowing power combines avid specimen and artifact collection with unremit-
ting bloodletting and savaging of native Americans (McCarthy 2001).

Figure 9. "We will not leave." A poster in the Silwan community protest/ lecture tent in al-Bustan. The tent also serves as the orientation center for alternative tours led by volunteers.

local inhabitants. At Umm el-Jimal, that traditional approach became ensconced in the bureaucratic structure the Jordanian government inherited from the British Mandate. This meant that little special formal consideration was given to those living on and around archaeological sites. Control of sites became a matter of national rather than local responsibility. Hopefully, this neglect is now being corrected through the joint initiatives of government agencies, citizens groups and archaeologists. In a sense, a similar history of inheritance of rules of relationship from the British Mandate (and Ottoman precedents) prevails for Silwan. However, the unresolved occupation and the special privilege given to newcomers, El'ad's settlers, have enabled a return to colonial-era treatment that is no longer acceptable.

Cormac McCarthy used Judge Noble's utter disdain for the "savagery" of the native Americans he murdered and scalped to portray the fabricated rationale for their destruction in the colonization of the American West. Ironically, while he disdained the living, he lovingly recorded the material remains of their ancestors, in tribute to a more sophisticated past. In Middle East archaeology too, orientalist stereotyping portrayed the culture of modern "natives" as a decayed and corrupted figment of a sophisticated past.[12] That dismissal of contemporary native cultures was never legitimate, and it certainly cannot be a pretext for Umm el-Jimal and Silwan today. The population of Umm el-Jimal, though rural and tribal in cultural tradition, is today amazingly well educated and counts a substantial number of postgraduate degree holders, including Ph.D.s, and even a member of the national parliament among its residents. From the few acquaintances I have in Silwan, my impression is that a similar level of sophistication prevails among some of its Palestinian residents. Members of both communities have the right of inclusion simply by virtue of their humanity. In addition, both communities are fully qualified for partnership in the development of the archaeology in their midst.

---

12. For the imaging of the American West and the Middle East as parallel frontiers, see Mitchell 2000: 200–205.

References

Abu el-Haj, N.
  2001   *Facts on the Ground: Archaeological Practice and Territorial Self-Fashioning in Israeli Society.* Chicago: University of Chicago Press.
Benvenisti, M.
  2002   *Sacred Landscape: The Buried History of the Holy Land Since 1948.* Berkeley: University of California Press.
Brand, L. A.
  2001   Displacement for Development. *World Development* 29: 961–76.
Burleigh, N.
  2008   *Unholy Business: A True Tale of Faith, Greed and Forgery in the Holy Land.* New York: HarperCollins.

Brown, R. M.
　2009　The Druze Experience at Umm el-Jimal: Remarks on the History and Archaeology of the Early 20th Century Settlement. Pp. 377–89 in *Studies in the History and Archaeology of Jordan X: Crossing Jordan*, ed. F. al-Khraisheh. Amman: Department of Antiquities of Jordan.

Cheyney, M.
　2009　Archaeological Development and the Economy of Housing at Umm el-Jimal: Some Preliminary Findings. *Annual of the Department of Antiquities of Jordan* 53: 361–63

de Vries, B. de
　1971　His Land and History. *The Reformed Journal* 21: 6–11.
　1998　*Umm el-Jimal: A Frontier Town and Its Landscape in Northern Jordan.* Journal of Roman Archaeology Supplement 26. Portsmouth, RI: Journal of Roman Archaeology.
　2010　Archaeology. Pp 104–112 in *Encyclopedia of the Israeli-Palestinian Conflict*, ed. C. A. Rubenberg. Vol. 1. Boulder: Lynne Rienner.

de Vries, B.; de Vries, S.; Koning, L.; Oord, S.; Roukema, D.; Workman, M.; Christians, P.; DeKock, J.; Mulder, C.; al-Hunaiti, T.; al-Fayez, M.; Lücke, B.; and Hazza, M.
　2009　Site Presentation in Jordan: Concept Design and the January 2009 Documentation Season at Umm el-Jimal. *Annual of the Department of Antiquities of Jordan* 53: 364–70.

Finkelstein, I.; Herzog, Z.; Singer-Avitz, L.; and Ussishkin, D.
　2007　Has King David's Palace in Jerusalem Been Found? *Tel Aviv* 31: 142–64.

Gere, C.
　2009　*Knossos and the Prophets of Modernism.* Chicago: University of Chicago.

Greenberg, R.
　2009　Toward an Inclusive Archaeology in Jerusalem: the Case of Silwan/the City of David. *Public Archaeology* 8: 35–50.

Jabareen, Y.
　2010　The Politics of State Planning in Achieving Geopolitical Ends: The Case of the Recent Master Plan of Jerusalem. *International Development Planning Review* 32: 27–43.

Lapidoth, R., and Ramon, A.
　2006　*The Historical Basin of Jerusalem: The Status Quo and Alternatives for Agreement.* Jerusalem Institute for Israel Studies Series. Jerusalem: Jerusalem Institute for Israel Studies. On-line: http://www.jiis.org/.upload/publications/Historical_Basin.pdf.

Maffi, I.
　2009　The Emergence of Cultural Heritage in Jordan: The Itinerary of a Colonial Invention. *Journal of Social Archaeology* 9: 5–34.

Mazar, E.
　2009　*The Palace of King David: Excavations at the Summit of the City of David. Preliminary Report of Seasons 2005–2007.* Jerusalem: Shoham Academic Research and Publication.

McAlister, M.
　2005　*Epic Encounters, Culture, Media, and U.S. Interests in the Middle East Since 1945.* Berkeley: University of California Press.

McCarthy, C.
2001   *Blood Meridian*. New York: Modern Library.
Meyers, E. M.
2009   Archaeology and National Parks in Jerusalem: Who Owns the Past? On-line: http://www.bibleinterp.com/articles/silwan.shtml.
Mitchell, W. J. T.
2000   Holy Landscapes: Israel, Palestine, and the American Wilderness. *Critical Inquiry* 26: 193–223.
Mizrachi, Y.
2010   *Archaeology in the Shadow of the Conflict: The Mound of Ancient Jerusalem (City of David) in Silwan*. Jerusalem: Emek Shaveh. On-line: www.alt-arch.org/docs/booklet_english.pdf.
Rapoport, M.
2009   *Shady Dealings in Silwan*. Jerusalem: Ir Amim.
Ricca, S.
2007   *Reinventing Jerusalem: Israel's Reconstruction of the Jewish Quarter after 1967*. London: Taurus.
Scham, S. A.
2009   Diplomacy and Desired Pasts. *Journal of Social Archaeology* 9: 163–99.
Scham, S. A., and Yahya, A.
2003   Heritage and Reconciliation. *Journal of Social Archaeology* 3: 399–416.
Shankland, D.
2000   Villagers and the Distant Past: Three Seasons' Work at Küçükköy, Çatalhöyük. Pp. 167–76 in *Towards Reflexive Method in Archaeology: The Example of Çatalhöyük*, ed. I. Hodder. BIAA Monograph 28. Ankara: British Institute of Archaeology.
Shiloh, Y.
1984   *Excavations at the City of David I, 1978–1982, Interim Report of the First Five Seasons*. Qedem 19. Jerusalem: Institute of Archaeology, Hebrew University of Jerusalem.
Tarawneh, M.
2000   *House Form and Cultural Identity: The Case of Bedouin Housing in Southern Jordan*. MA thesis, McGill University.
UNOCHA (United Nations Office for the Coordination of Humanitarian Affairs)
2009   *The Planning Crisis in East Jerusalem: Understanding the Phenomenon of "Illegal" Construction*. East Jerusalem. On-line: http://www.ochaopt.org/documents/ocha_opt_planning_crisis_east_jerusalem_april_2009_english.pdf.
Vaughn, A. G.
2003   Is Biblical Archaeology Theologically Useful Today? Yes: A Programmatic Response. Pp. 407–30 in *Jerusalem in Bible and Archaeology: The First Temple Period*, ed. A. G. Vaughn and A. E. Killebrew. Atlanta: Society of Biblical Literature.
Ziadeh-Seely, G.
2007   An Archaeology of Palestine: Mourning a Dream. Pp. 326–45 in *Selective Remembrances: Archaeology in the Construction, Commemoration, and Consecration of National Pasts*, ed. P. L. Kohl, M. Kozelsky, and N. Ben-Yehuda. Chicago: University of Chicago Press.

Response to Bert de Vries, "Site Preservation in Jordan: The Case of Umm el-Jimal"

S. Thomas Parker

I should immediately confess that I have known Bert de Vries for more than three decades, ever since we worked together at Tell Hesban in 1976. I was privileged to work with him again at Umm el-Jimal in the late 1970s and early 1980s. In addition, he played a key role on my own Limes Arabicus Project throughout the 1980s. So I speak as someone who knows Umm el-Jimal quite well and, as director of my own archaeological projects in Jordan, I am all too familiar with the difficulties presented by issues of site preservation and presentation. Bert once told me, long ago, that he is sympathetic to the perspective of local people toward foreign archaeologists "who come here, dig holes in the ground, and then leave."

The approach of Bert de Vries to these issues at Umm el-Jimal is appealing in many ways. It is both ambitious and multi-facted, combining research, preservation, and presentation through a variety of media and reaching a wide diversity of audiences. Bert has forged critical partnerships both within and without Jordan, among several institutions, including Calvin College, Open Hand Studios[1] (founded by former Calvin College students), the American Center of Oriental Research in Amman, the Department of Antiquities of Jordan and other key government ministries, and, most significantly, the village of Umm el-Jimal.

Particularly appealing is the plan to integrate the site into the local educational curriculum, educating students about the importance and uniqueness of this extraordinary site. Many Westerners who work

Author's note: I wish to thank Eric and Carol Meyers for the invitation to participate in this important event, Erin Kuhns for all her efforts, and to Bert de Vries for providing his paper to me for comment well before the symposium.
Editors' note: Thomas Parker is responding to the paper delivered at the Duke conference and not to the retitled version, which was expanded to include a comparison of Silwan to the Umm el-Jimal example, in this volume.

1. See http://www.openhandstudios.org/.

in Jordan are amazed to learn how many Jordanians have never visited Jerash or even Petra, proclaimed one of the "new" Seven Wonders of the World in 2007. It is imperative that future generations of Jordanians become better acquainted with their cultural heritage right in their own backyard. This will develop a constituency for its future protection and development.

Because of the extraordinary degree of preservation of the site, only limited reconstruction is being undertaken and then largely for purposes of consolidation of a few structures in a precarious position. The walking tours with proper signage are a necessity, along with the on-site museum. The virtual tour, once completed, should help to bring the site to life for remote visitors.

I do offer one caveat. Open access to the entire project archive on the project Web site is promised. I found it difficult to access this portion of the project since the Web site is still in its infancy.[2] And then there is the issue of making raw data available to anyone, even while much of the evidence from Umm el-Jimal remains unpublished. This is a problem common to all such endeavors. Generally, one would expect that the initial publication of the evidence from any site would stem from the project itself and only then allow others to reassess the data. In the discussion following the delivery of his remarks, Bert assured us that this would in fact be the case.

This small caveat aside, Bert's approach to the long-term management of Umm el-Jimal looks to be an outstanding model for the management of cultural heritage in Jordan and elsewhere. His plan as outlined combines all the essential elements that will allow future generations to continue to explore this extraordinary site (the vast majority of which remains unexcavated) while protecting and explaining the site to visitors, both on-site and remotely. This is the wave of the future, built on close partnership with the local people.

---

2. See http://www.ummeljimal.org/.

Archaeology, Identity, and the Media in Cyprus

Thomas W. Davis

Archaeology and the results of archaeological research are not just of interest to the ivory tower; they also resonate very strongly in the 21st-century world. This adds a layer of responsibility for archaeological practitioners and interpreters that few of us archaeologists normally consider. Bruce Trigger's postmodern rationale for archaeology is especially relevant for Cyprus:

> In a world that, as a result of increasingly powerful technologies, has become too dangerous and is changing too quickly for humanity to rely to any considerable extent on trial and error, knowledge derived from archaeology may be important for human survival. If archaeology is to serve that purpose, archaeologists must strive against heavy odds to see the past and the human behaviour that produced it as each was, not as they or anyone else for their own reasons wish them to have been. (Trigger 2006: 548)

Too often, the media, having become the main purveyor of "archaeology" to the nonacademic community, trumpet our reasoned conclusions—guarded by caveats and hedging—beyond the halls of academia as "assured results." Shorn of their academic context, archaeological data then become props in modern political and social debates remaking the past as it is wished to be, not as it was.

The subtheme of the Duke conference of which this paper forms a part was "Re-visioning the Middle East," and archaeological data provide some of the foundation blocks for such a re-visioning. This leads to an obvious question: Why discuss Cyprus if we are "re-visioning the Middle East"? Politically, the Republic of Cyprus is a part of Europe, having joined the European Union in 2004 and having used the Euro as its legal currency since 2008.

A dose of geographic reality is needed. Cyprus is the third largest island in the Mediterranean Sea, measuring approximately 225 km east/west × 95 km north/south. It is located in the northeast corner of the

189

Mediterranean, approximately 70 km south of Turkey and 120 km west of Syria. Geographically, Cyprus is enveloped by Asia and is part and parcel of the Middle East. To the general public, the island is marketed primarily as a tourist destination with sandy beaches, a relaxed Mediterranean lifestyle, and a rich cultural heritage with archaeological sites, magnificent ecclesiastical monuments, and Crusader castles. Sadly, it is also dominated by "the Cyprus Problem," the ethnic conflict between the Greek Cypriot community and the Turkish Cypriot community that resulted in the de facto political division of the island in 1974.

Cyprus's rich architectural and archaeological heritage is the product of a violent history marked by a succession of disruptive incursions that saw the invaders and/or colonizers eventually amalgamated into the indigenous culture in a negotiated dialogue that continues today. It could be argued that indigenous Cypriots first had to deal with "invasions" as early as the ninth millennium B.C.E., when Neolithic settlers from the Levant introduced fully developed sedentary agricultural communities into a world of transient hunter/gatherers who had periodically used the island as a resource for at least the previous 1500 years (Simmons 2007). Major incursions from Anatolia occurred in the Cypriot Bronze Age (ca. 2000 B.C.E.); and colonizers from the west and the east arrived at the end of the Bronze Age, when a variety of peoples took advantage of the collapse of the eastern Mediterranean polities around 1200 B.C.E. to establish new settlements (Steel 2004). Prominent in the Cypriot story at this time were colonizers from the Aegean world and the Phoenicians from the Levant. Cypriot history records the presence of Assyrians, Egyptians, Persians, the successors of Alexander the Great (specifically the Ptolemies), the Romans, the Byzantines, the Umayyad Arabs, Richard the Lionheart and Latin Crusaders (including the Hospitalers and Templars), the Genoese, the Venetians, the Ottomans and finally the British, who granted independence to the Republic of Cyprus in 1960. In 1974, the invasion of elements of the Turkish army, entering Cyprus in response to a Greek-supported coup against President Makarios, resulted in the de facto split that characterizes the existing political landscape of Cyprus. The most recent incursion has been a ballooning of the expatriate community including Northern European retirees and East Asian domestic servants.

Fernand Braudel provides a way forward through this morass with his concept of *la longue durée*: "a history in slow motion from which permanent values can be detected," which underlies the development of Cyprus's cultural identity (Braudel 1973: 23). These "permanent values" are almost unobservable in the short term, particularly with the shortened attention span of the 21st century, but are critical to understanding the island's current cultural milieu. Such permanent values include *spatial* features and *temporal* features. Dominating Cyprus's spatial features are its island identity, its strategic location, and its abundant natural resources. Dominating Cyprus's temporal features are the twin pillars of language and religion.

Cyprus's island identity provided an almost insurmountable protective shell around Cyprus's cultural identity. As an island, Cyprus forced invasions and colonization attempts to be episodic in nature rather than massive population inundations that would have drowned the indigenous culture under a tsunami of new cultural elements. The several-millennium-long process of cultural negotiation between indigenous populations and newcomers produced acculturation rather than annihilation. Additionally, the local Cypriots had no choice about accommodation; they had no easy escape route before the advent of the Industrial Age, so they had to come to terms with the latest dominant elite. The fragmentary footprints of this process are found in linguistic and cultural shifts, which form signposts in the history of Cyprus.

Cyprus's physical location, as an island link between the Levant and the West, gained strategic value at certain critical moments when Cyprus found itself situated between competing empires who sought to dominate or deny domination to others. The island functioned as a bulwark for protection and as a base for expansion depending on the specific circumstances. The Venetians gained control over Cyprus as an offensive move toward the Turkish-dominated Levant, and the Ottomans conquered Cyprus and removed the Venetian enclave as a defensive measure. Even when Cyprus was entirely absorbed by imperial powers and lost its strategic status in military or political terms, it still maintained a strategic economic role, as in the Roman period when the Mediterranean was the *Mare Nostrum*. The abundant natural resources of lithics, copper, timber, and agricultural products had a strategic role as well, varying in value as technology changed and attracting groups who lacked these resources.

The fundamentals of self-identity and the consequential societal fault lines on Cyprus remain the temporal features (in Braudel's terminology) of language and religion. In the realm of language, Greek speakers first gained cultural ascendancy after the collapse of the Bronze Age world when the Iron Age city kingdoms were established by Greek-speaking elites. Other languages used by Cypriots included Phoenician and the as yet untranslated local Bronze Age language labeled Eteo-Cypriot by modern scholars. Against the linguistic rock of Cypriot Greek, other languages such as French, Arabic, and Italian would advance and recede.

Today, the two main linguistic challengers to the domination of Cypriot Greek are Turkish and English. These are both the bi-products and the tools of imperial domination. After the Ottoman conquest of 1571, Turkish became the official language of the island; and its usage gradually expanded in the general population, replacing Italian as the second tongue. Greek remained the primary language of the majority of the island's inhabitants; but the linguistic barriers were fluid, and many

Cypriots were bilingual to at least some degree. After the establishment of British control in 1878, the three languages of Greek, Turkish, and English were all given official standing. When Cyprus became independent in 1960, Greek and Turkish were decreed the two official languages of the Republic of Cyprus. Today, English is almost universally spoken in both linguistic communities as a second language.

The other main Cypriot *temporal* feature is religion. After the conversion of the island to Orthodox Christianity (evidenced by the building of churches and the lack of reconstruction of earthquake-damaged pagan temples in the late 4th century C.E.), the Cypriot Church became a major component of Cypriot identity in the 5th century C.E., when it gained autocephalous status. This link between Church and people was strengthened when the Orthodox Church became the guardian of indigenous culture after Latin Catholic Crusaders gained power at the end of the 12th century. After the Ottoman conquest, the Latin Catholic churches were turned into mosques because they represented the influence of the defeated political power, Venice. However, the Ottomans respected some of the Orthodox churches, allowing parish churches and monasteries to continue to function. The Ottoman governors made the Greek Orthodox archbishop the responsible authority for internal governance of the non-Muslim Cypriot community. The Church became the acknowledged guardian of "Greek-ness," both linguistically and culturally, by being the most visible element in the society that was not overtly Ottoman. It gained a great deal of its current wealth when landowners sold or gave property to the Church, thereby escaping taxation. Archbishop Makarios, the first president of independent Cyprus, exemplified the continuing political activism of the Cypriot Orthodox Church. Although today most Cypriots are very secular in their daily lives, religious identification remains a major element of communal self-definition. The normal Greek Cypriot, if asked "Are you a Christian?" will reply, "Yes, I am not a Turk"; the reverse is true in the Turkish Cypriot community.

Ironically, it is clear from the historic record that many self-defined Turkish Cypriots are of the same stock as Greek Cypriots. Many pre-1974 Turkish Cypriots are descended from Orthodox or Latin Catholic Cypriots who converted to Islam after the Ottoman conquest, generally for economic/political reasons, leaving only a minority of the Turkish Cypriot community who actually immigrated to Cyprus from Anatolia. What makes the communities "other" is their primary language and their religious identification.

The true core elements of Greek Cypriot identity were fashioned in Byzantine Cyprus rather than mainland Greece, and the Turkish Cypriot community's roots are in the Ottoman Empire, not the Turkish Republic. Both historic empires were multi-ethnic, multi-lingual imperial states that treated Cyprus as a relatively unimportant province. As a recent study of archaeology and ethnicity puts it, "created histories are often used to justify political or nationalistic claims" (Lucy 2005: 87). It is ironic that one of the visible manifestations of the linkage of religion and identity on Cyprus is the ubiquitous presence of the national flags of Greece and Turkey at the Orthodox churches and the mosques on the island. The off-island national flags are paired with the flag of the Republic of Cyprus at the churches and with the flag of the self-proclaimed "Turkish Republic of Northern Cyprus" at the mosques, as in Famagusta where the old Latin cathedral is now a mosque. The modern political entities overshadow their imperial forerunners and have absorbed their status as cultural forerunners.

The sense of identification with off-island entities was brutally strengthened when, after a Greek-mainland-sponsored coup against President Makarios, the Turkish Army invaded the north and took 38 percent of the island in 1974. This led to a population exchange that ended with 99.9 percent of the Turkish Cypriot community in the North under the protection of the Turkish Army and 99.9 percent of the Greek Cypriot community settled in the South under de facto control of the Republic of Cyprus. This emphasis on "Greekness" and "Turkishness" is underscored by the celebration of Greek and Turkish National Days as holidays within the separate communities.

This of course works strongly against the development of a distinctly Cypriot identity. Asking "What is a Cypriot?" is like asking "What is an American?" and the answer is equally elusive. The difference is that, for the United States, the melting pot has been boiling for only four centuries; this constrictive timeframe forced rapid acclimatization and led to the near annihilation of the indigenous cultures. In contrast, on Cyprus the pot has bubbled for millennia. With such a long time frame, it is no wonder that archaeology is one of the primary sources of data on Cypriot identity. As a result, archaeology functions in a highly charged political space, and the results of archaeological investigation send ripples across the entire Cypriot pond. "There is no way of choosing between alternative pasts except on political grounds," wrote Shanks and Tilley (1987: 195) in a spasm of postmodernist despair. On Cyprus, these words are embodied because the *preferred* way of choosing a past is through politics.

In a study on the archaeology of ethnicity, Sian Jones writes, "the critical role that the past plays in the assertion and legitimation of modern ethnic and national identities ensures that archaeological knowledge is frequently used in the construction of essentialist ethnic histories" (Jones 1997: 136). This has indeed been the case on Cyprus since before independence. Michael Given (1998) has highlighted the attempts in the 1930s of the British colonial authorities to support the idea of a non-Hellenic "eteo-Cypriot" cultural identity in the interpretation of Cypriot archaeology as a counterweight to the political *enosis* movement, which sought Cyprus's unification with Greece. Vassos Karageorghis, the dean of Greek Cypriot archaeologists, argued strongly for a fundamental Greek identity for Cyprus as a result of Mycenaean invasions at the end of the Bronze Age (Karageorghis 1982: 77–89). Yet, Karageorghis is too good a scholar not to have also a nuanced appreciation of the diverse cultural influences in Cyprus's history.

In a profound irony, Rauf Denktash, the fiery former leader of the Turkish Cypriot community and the vehemently anti-Greek founder of the so-called "Turkish Republic of Northern Cyprus" agrees with Karageorghis! "The inhabitants of Cyprus have no common language except English and no common religion; nor have they, except at the surface, any common culture" (Denktash 1988: 7). This attitude provides a justification for some Turkish nationalistic scholars to dismiss the common cultural value of pre-Ottoman monuments in the north of Cyprus. "There is not, and never has been, a 'Cypriot Nation,'" says Denktash (1988: 7). Trigger reminds us that "overtly competing groups may use material culture to emphasize their dissimilarities" (Trigger 2006: 453).

Archaeology on Cyprus was very negatively affected by the events of 1974. Widespread damage and looting occurred at many sites and monuments. An additional impact was that the division of the Republic led to an almost complete halt to international archaeological investigation in the areas of the island outside of the de facto control of the Republic of Cyprus. UNESCO resolutions and international academic bodies quickly condemned any archaeological investigations in the north because they would be "permitted" by a governmental authority lacking international recognition. Respecting the sovereignty of the Republic of Cyprus, all of the international archaeologists working in the areas outside of the de facto control of the Republic of Cyprus halted their fieldwork in 1974, and none of those original permit holders have resumed fieldwork. It became well known in the archaeological community that any violator would never be permitted to work in the Republic of Cyprus again, nor would their students or their university.

The Second Protocol of the 1954 Hague Convention provides a framework for salvage archaeology in occupied lands.[1] This has never been invoked on Cyprus, however, because the Turkish Cypriot community does not recognize their political status as "occupied." Ultimately, the absence of the original permit holders led to archaeological "claim jumping" at Salamis, when in the 1990s an archaeologist from Ankara University began working there. The only other non-Cypriot team working in the north is a German team at Galiporni. They have not claim jumped, nor have they followed the Second Protocol, and their work has been correctly condemned by the international archaeological community.

---

1. See http://portal.unesco.org/en/ev.php-URL_ID=15207&URL_DO=DO_TOPIC &URL_SECTION=201.html

Turkish Cypriot archaeologists are in the most difficult position. Perhaps the best excavation from a methodological standpoint has been at Akanthou, where Dr. Muge Sevketoglu, a Turkish Cypriot archaeologist, has undertaken a rescue operation at a Neolithic site on the northern coast. Since this excavation has taken place outside the de facto control of the Department of Antiquities of the Republic of Cyprus, the results have not been published internationally; this is a situation with no winners, only losers.

The political division on Cyprus has also affected archaeological interpretation. Data regarding settlement patterns and land use has become skewed towards the South. Conclusions drawn on an island-wide basis are of necessity more speculative than is normal in the discipline. The opening of the intercommunal boundary in 2003 has since improved this situation, now that all scholars may visit sites they were unable to see firsthand before.

The Cyprus American Archaeological Research Institute (CAARI), located in Nicosia, has had to steer a delicate political course, particularly since 2003. As the only international archaeological research institute on the island, CAARI is uniquely positioned to be an academic bridge linking the Cypriot communities. CAARI welcomes all Cypriots of any community who wish to use the library and benefit from the study collections. While I was CAARI Director (2003–2011), I often visited sites in the north to ensure that they were being protected and that no illicit digging was being undertaken. During my visits, I would informally meet with Turkish Cypriot Community authorities to discuss issues of concern to the antiquities authorities of both communities. This helped maintain communication and prevent politicization of heritage issues. Thanks to the generosity of P. E. MacAllister, the board chair of the American Schools of Oriental Research, the Director of the American Research Institute in Turkey (ARIT), and I as Director of CAARI gave exchange lectures in 2009. CAARI also hosted the Turkish excavator of the site of Tarsus. This ground-breaking bridge across a geopolitical divide was not universally welcomed by the local community. Like any bridge, difficulties sometimes arise when it gets "walked on."

Today, for the most part, the media in both communities report on archaeological discoveries with pride and a sense of ownership. The press of the Turkish Cypriot community has widely reported (and praised) the excavation of Neolithic Akanthou, demonstrating that Denktash's views dismissing all pre-Ottoman culture are not universally held. The press in both communities criticizes the officials responsible for heritage protection when they perceive a failure of stewardship. However, it is somewhat more difficult to do this in the Turkish Cypriot community, where actions of the Turkish army remain difficult to criticize openly. Each community naturally tends to highlight discovered links, such as Mycenaean pottery in the South or Anatolian obsidian in the North, to the "mother country."

The increasing sense of ownership of their entire heritage shown by the press in both communities is an optimistic sign for the future. Archaeology is one of the best tools available for restoring the shared Cypriot identity of the two communities, and a shared identity is the fundamental building block of a lasting political solution to the Cyprus Problem. Perhaps on Cyprus, the past can help point the way to the future.

References

Braudel, F.
    1973   *The Mediterranean and the Mediterranean World in the Age of Philip II.* 2nd ed. London: Fontana/Collins.
Denktash, R. R.
    1988   *The Cyprus Triangle.* 2nd ed. London: Rüstem.
Given, M.
    1998   Inventing Eteo-Cypriots: Imperial Archaeology and the Manipulation of Ethnic Identity. *Journal of Mediterranean Archaeology* 11: 3–29.
Jones, S.
    1997   *The Archaeology of Ethnicity: Constructing Identities in the Past and the Present.* London: Routledge.
Karageorghis, V.
    1982   *Cyprus from the Stone Age to the Romans.* London: Thames & Hudson.
Lucy, S.
    2005   Ethnic and Cultural Identities. Pp. 86–109 in *The Archaeology of Identity: Approaches to Gender, Age, Status, Ethnicity and Religion*, ed. M. Díaz-Andreau, S. Lucy, S. Babić, and D. Edwards. London: Routledge.
Shanks, M., and Tilley, C.
    1987   *Social Theory and Archaeology.* Cambridge: Polity.
Simmons, A.
    2007   *The Neolithic Revolution in the Near East.* Tucson: University of Arizona Press.
Steel, L.
    2004   *Cyprus before History.* London: Duckworth.
Trigger, B.
    2006   *A History of Archaeological Thought.* 2nd ed. New York: Cambridge University Press.

Response to Thomas W. Davis, "Archaeology, Identity, and the Media in Cyprus"

Donald C. Haggis

Cyprus invites, or perhaps instigates, multiple narratives of the past—a kind of constant inexorable construction and destruction of cultural identities. If identity is a kind of cultural distinctiveness, then Tom Davis has done an excellent job shaping a paraphrase of Cypriot insularity, liminality, and the complex cultural layering and mixing that seem to have shaped the fault-lines, as he puts it, and current and temporal values of language and religion.

If archaeology and indeed the media themselves are to be viable tools for restoring a shared Cypriot identity, as Davis suggests, there are two contingent problems. One is the implication that a shared identity actually exists in spite of centuries-old discourses and conflicting narratives—Eteo-Cypriot, Hellenic Cypriot, and Hellenic *enosis*, and so on, just to name a few. The second problem is what appears to me to be an apposition of narratives: that archaeology and the media can challenge the dominant ideological text of the state, and, more important, that this is perceived to be an effective, preferred, and positive process, regardless of the inherent political agenda of any narrative structure—whether it originates from the individual, the state, the local community, foreign or local archaeologists, or the international media. This cuts to the core of the concept of multivocality as it pertains to archaeological interpretation, as well as to issues of cultural heritage and concepts of ownership of the past. I will address this second problem, but I would say first that I think archaeology can help to establish or to encourage—rather than "restore" per se—a shared Cypriot identity. That identity, in my mind, is a construct, a kind of romantic past-still-present along the lines of transposed "little Indias" (Bayly 1997: 664); it is a virtual but no less dynamic world, not dissimilar in its idea or form or concept to the Eteo-Cypriot myth or perhaps the Turkish-Cypriot picture of a pre-Ottoman landscape. In my own experience conducting fieldwork in Greece for the past 27 years, this past-still-present continues to exist in the minds of most of my teachers (cf. Fotiades 1995).

As someone who is not familiar with Cyprus, I found Davis's conclusions remarkably positive. If I am following him correctly, he asserts that the media—a competent and critical press, with its pride of ownership—aims at the preservation and stewardship of the past. But I was left with the following persistent question: do the media really try, or are they even able, to nurture a conceptual Cypriotness or Cypriotism, that is, a Cypriot identity distinct from both the state-sponsored Mycenaean myth and the diverse but persistent claims of Eteo-Cypriot origins? Am I to believe that archaeologists and journalists can challenge and inflect, if not rewrite, the normative narratives? Perhaps so, but I still wonder what impact this can have on the formation and longevity of cultural identity. In this, I might depart from much of the current discourse, which views the structure of society as a form: a synchronic outcome of historical events and of the growth and change of dominant political parties, state-mandated educational and cultural policies, and nationalistic ideological frameworks.

To take a ground-up perspective, local identity—as distinct from a state's transparent manipulation of media and symbols—is shaped by an individual's interaction with a local environment, an imperceptibly changing and continuous cultural and physical landscape that becomes part of a larger community's narrative of place. It is remarkably resilient and born of local discourses and memories, across generations, within and throughout physical landscapes. In this, archaeology should logically play a significant role, as it actively engages and transforms these landscapes. Archaeology necessarily involves and negotiates with communities; it invades, borrows, or completely expropriates land and sometimes livelihoods; it transforms the landscape while unconsciously developing active conversations on multiple social and spatial scales; and it often becomes actively or passively part of the place, if not the community.

I do not doubt the effectiveness of a Mycenaean myth or Mycenaean pottery (that Davis mentions in his essay). However, the real connectedness to Hellenism as religion and language, on a local Greek level, is arguably through orthodox Christianity and also purely local settlement histories and kinship or community memory. These are rather disconnected from and irrelevant to the state myth, even if the latter forms a more compelling platform for tourism and a more tangible datum for the arguments of anthropologists and postprocessual archaeologists (cf. Stritch 2006).

My point is simply that, if competent media or academic archaeology challenges state mythologies, how precisely relevant are their narratives to a local cultural identity that is formed from a variety of very active and dynamic influences? I do not intend to debate or discuss this here, only to raise the question. Nationalist or even local archaeo-logical narratives are seen as reductive, uncomplicated, unilinear, his-torical condensations of material culture. Yet material culture in our consciousness as archaeologists consists of really complex and most of-ten disconnected but diachronic material patterns requiring a nuanced theoretical commentary on both recovery and interpretation. How do we bridge these two worlds? And how precisely different are the media and academic attempts at public programming from any other narrative structure that aims to communicate with an undifferentiated public au-dience? Is it a difference of method, motive, or perceived outcome? Or does the difference lie in the belief in our own academic mythologies?

All identity is local and shaped by personal experience, notwith-standing the importance that we attribute to the verbiage, symbols, and images that shape a national historical text. But I remain as skeptical of the longevity and coherency of purpose of such top-down structures, as much as I am of the narratives of journalists and academics in affect-ing processes that I see derived from a local discourse that has its own mythology, and therefore its own material reality.

So, not to be completely negative here, I do think that archaeological excavation—as a physical connection to a place, as an active transfor-mative process, and as a physical, even sometimes visceral, and visual symbol of itself—can create a distinctive narrative, and indeed one that can shape how people look at and form their own history and culture. Excavation as a combined research process and public discourse is po-tentially a viable player in a political discourse. It is a place to start—a synergistic collaboration derived from integration of research into and from within local communities and local living cultural landscapes. In many ways the excavation, even if it tries to be politically neutral, can-not avoid creating a political discourse or impact on some level, nor does it generate narratives that are any less alienating to local commu-nities. Not only can they be alienating, but also they can sometimes be socially or politically disruptive. If they are not, then they are probably politically correct, diplomatically expedient but no less superficial, or meant to be disingenuously reaffirming of both local and national my-thologies. In my view, this process of alienation is true education; it is the first real step in the right direction and the only way for archaeology or the media (should they choose to follow the academics) to reshape local and regional identities. If developed as part of a local exchange, an active ground-up conversation among archaeologists, communities, media, and state administrators, then real change could conceivably re-sult. Unfortunately, in my experience too few archaeologists actually participate in such an open-ended discourse because they lack the time, experience (and language experience and cultural literacy), ability, re-sources, or perhaps even interest in actually engaging intimately and in-tellectually with a community or with an uneducated and uninformed media. It takes time, patience, real commitment, and some (or a lot of) courage. This might also involve reshaping one's own role as archaeologist, for far too many of us are so used to multiple political narratives in our own teaching, writing, and pro forma outreach and fundraising. Moreover, I would have to say that reductive distortion and over-generalizing simplification by archaeologists in television and newspaper appearances have become as commonplace as the ideological histories constructed by state-sponsored tourism, education, and the media. (As the character George Costanza says on *Seinfeld*, "It's not a lie if you believe it.") And the media simply want to sell certain ideas and popular concepts to self-defined markets.

But Cyprus seems always to have been a mythic or perhaps mythopoeic cultural landscape formed of real and constructed memories. Kazantakis (1975) first came to Cyprus looking for a sense of Hellenic identity, which he ultimately found by deconstructing his own solipsistic poetic environment. While walking through a small village, he sought a romantic and, of course, erotic version of Aphrodite—and this long before the appropriation of the image, a piece of Hellenistic sculpture, was used as a visual symbol of Cypriot cultural heritage (Stritch 2006). On entering the village his myth quickly evaporated; he quickened his pace through town lest he be invited by the girl's mother to stay for dinner. His discovery of an ordinary Greek girl (instead of Aphrodite) was a mythopoeic reduction of innocence lost. In a similar tendency to extremes, Lawrence Durrell (1957) created his own Hellenic identity by inventing a mythic brother who had died fighting the Germans at Thermopylae—this was poetically expedient: he was a British national in a *cafeneion* fending off an angry gathering of Greek Cypriots on the eve of independence.

Cyprus invites or begs for these multiple narratives: and all narratives are local, individual, and intrinsically personal and political. As Tom Davis said so poignantly, on Cyprus, the preferred way of choosing a past is through politics. I agree completely, but I hardly think that either archaeologists or the media are really up to the task of rewriting the linear histories of community experience, personal tragedy, or cultural territoriality. Yet I suppose, or hope, that it is not entirely impossible.

References

Bayly, C. A.
  1997   Modern Indian Historiography. Pp. 663–77 in *Companion to Historiography*, ed. M. Bentley. London: Routledge.
Durrell, L.
  1957   *Bitter Lemons*. London: Faber & Faber.

Fotiades, M.

1995   Modernity and the Past-Still-Present: Politics of Time in the Birth of Regional Archaeological Projects in Greece. *American Journal of Archaeology* 99: 59–78.

Kazantzakis, N.

1975   *Journeying: Travels in Italy, Egypt, Sinai, Jerusalem and Cyprus.* Boston: Little Brown.

Stritch, D.

2006   Archaeological Tourism: A Signpost to National Identity. Pp. 43–60 in *Images, Representations and Heritage: Moving beyond Modern Approaches to Archeology,* ed. I. Russell. New York: Springer.

The Quest for the Temple Mount
The Settler Movement and National Parks in Israel

Eric M. Meyers

Archaeologists often say that digging is just the tip of the archaeological iceberg. What one does with the material remains one uncov-
ers—how one publishes them, how one interprets them, and how one
preserves them—is also part of the archaeological process. Some countries require monies to be earmarked for preservation and safekeeping
of the site and take such regulations very seriously. But how and when
one presents archaeological discoveries to the public is virtually un-
regulated. Who gets to tell the story about a site's importance is a critical step that often leaves out the excavators and the historians and
brings other individuals into the picture; and often those other individuals have a very different agenda altogether from that of the excavation
team and thus a very different story to tell. Indeed, that story sometimes comes as a complete surprise to the excavators. How projects are
funded—that is, where the funding comes from—often has a profound
impact on how the story is told.

For example, at Khirbet Qumran near the Dead Sea, the importance
of the Dead Sea Scrolls found in the caves adjacent to the site surely
attracted the École Biblique, the Jordanians, and then the Israelis to provide great care and abundant resources to investigate the very modest
archaeological remains alongside the caves (Brooke and Schiffman 1999:
9–20). Hordes of tourists visit the site today, where the Israel Nature
and Parks Authority (INPA), an arm of the Israel Antiquities Authority
(IAA), controls the visitor's center and site maintenance. At Seppho-
ris in the Lower Galilee near Nazareth, the historic role of the city in
early Judaism and Christianity led the Israeli government and funders
of the excavations there to develop the site into a national park; with
its beautiful mosaics, elaborate water tunnel, and monumental buildings as well as its impeccable Jewish pedigree, it became one of most
visited sites in the country.[1] And at Masada, it was Josephus's memo-

---

1. For a rich account of the development of the national park there, see Bauman
2004: 205–28.

rable narrative of heroic resistance to Rome and mass suicide that led the Israel Defense Forces (IDF) and government to make the site not only a national park but also a symbol of courage and fierce resistance to the hostile neighbors all around, with the saying "Masada shall not fall again" inscribed on the Masada medal given to each volunteer who participated in the excavations.[2] That Yigael Yadin's excavations brought together volunteers from all over the world to participate in the "big dig," Israel's first major volunteer operation, did not hurt either.

Clearly, these sites transcend individual historic interests and have a more universal appeal. But for no site is this wide appeal more prominent than Jerusalem, where, unfortunately, its universal message has been blurred because of the politicization of the visitor's center in the City of David.[3] This center, which is being run by the settler movement and their NGO, the Ir David Foundation, is also known as El'ad, an acronym for "to the City of David." Its presentation of the archaeological discoveries at the site gives the false impression to visitors that it represents the views of the many distinguished archaeologists, past and present, working at the site (Millstein 2010).[4]

The situation in Jordan is somewhat different.[5] Cultural resource management, which involves much advance planning and cooperation between government agencies such as the national antiquities authority and funding sources such as USAID, has been extensive in developing sites such as Jerash, Petra, Umm el-Jimal in the Golan[6] and the Amman Citadel (de Vries 1997). The success of many Jordanian reconstruction or development projects is often the result of cooperation with the excavation team. Examples include Jerash—with the restoration the Temple of Zeus and South Gate by a French team and the hippodrome by a Polish team—and Petra—with the restoration of the Byzantine Church and Roman-period temple by American excavators.[7] The sheer splendor of these sites led to major funding and Jordan's decision to build touristic

---

2. As Silberman (1989: 100) first noted, the international press labeled this attitude "the Masada Complex," an expression coined by Stewart Alsop of the International Herald Tribune. The subject of Masada and national myth-making became a hot topic in Israeli archaeology after the publication of Ben-Yehudah's book *The Masada Myth: Collective Memory and Mythmaking in Israel* (1995); see also Ben-Yehudah 2007: 76.

3. See the City of David official Web site homepage: http://www.cityofdavid .org.il/hp_eng.asp.

4. An important essay by Michael Feige (2007) discusses how the settler movement influences Israeli archaeology but does not deal with more recent developments in the City of David, a situation that belongs to his "second stage."

5. For an introduction to some of the later materials in Jordan see Addison 2004.

6. See the contribution by de Vries to this volume: "Community and Antiquities at Umm el-Jimal and Silwan: A Comparison," pp. 161–186.

7. Similar cooperation occurs elsewhere; consider, e.g., the current work of the Italian excavators in the Celsus Library at Ephesus.

centers or national parks at a given site. A combination of factors led to site development at Umm el-Jimal in Jordan, where the local population has benefitted greatly from the site development, which was the plan of the excavator, Bert de Vries of Calvin College, from the outset.

The impact of site development on the local population is radically different at the City of David in Jerusalem, which today draws some 400,000 visitors annually. The local Arab population, which claims to have lived there for thousands of years, does not benefit from visitor traffic but instead has become the object of a plan meant to dispossess them and replace them with Jewish settlers. In the words of the City of David's Web site: "Today, the Ir David Foundation is actively involved in redeeming land bought by Baron Rothschild and in repurchasing much of the additional surrounding area. Land and buildings acquired in the area are used primarily for the building of a residential neighborhood, archaeological salvage operations, and capital projects geared towards tourism of the site."[8]

This statement raises the question of cultural patrimony—not so much in a legal sense but in the general sense of whose culture can lay claim to archaeological sites. UNESCO (the United Nations Educational, Scientific, and Cultural Organization) asserts that a particular culture owns its own cultural patrimony; that is, the country of residence owns whatever is discovered in its territory.[9] Amman and Jerusalem, among many other places, are complicated examples with respect to UNESCO's view. What does it mean for cultural property to belong to the Hashemite Kingdom of Jordan or the State of Israel when neither existed in the periods to which their many artifacts and sites are dated? The contested nature of the city of Jerusalem makes this question even more fraught.

Others have a view antithetical to that of UNESCO; they argue for an inclusive or universal understanding of patrimony, asserting that archaeological sites belong to all humanity. James Cuno, president and director of the Art Institute in Chicago, claims in his recent book *Who Owns Antiquity* (2008) that museums are the best repositories for the world's artifacts since they are the most responsible locations for preserving and explaining the cultural history of the past. Similarly, Anthony Appiah of Princeton, frequent commentator on African artifacts

8. See the "Baron de Rothchild" page of the City of David official Web site: http://www.cityofdavid.org.il/Baron_eng.asp. For a full and critical statement on the City of David situation by Emek Shaveh (an organization of archaeologists and community activists concerned with the role of archaeology in Israeli society and politics), see Mizrachi 2010.

9. The statement that "World Heritage sites belong to all the peoples of the world, irrespective of the territory on which they are located" is found on UNESCO's official Web site: http://whc.unesco.org/en/about/. For further discussion of the UNESCO position, see Magness-Gardiner 2004: 27–40 and Atwood 2008.

(Ghanaian artifacts in particular), argues for understanding artifacts and cultural patrimony in universal, nonnational terms and has criticized UNESCO and the 13 bilateral treaties that the U.S. has with individual nations endorsing UNESCO (Appiah 2006). Appiah would have agreed with Cuno, who writes that UNESCO and the nations that made bilateral treaties with the U.S. represent "nationalist retentionist cultural property laws" (Cuno 2008: 2). Appiah (2006: 41) proposes that objects central to the cultural or religious life of a community should be returned to that community, assuming that the community can act as a responsible trustee. He argues that most governments, national museums, and antiquities authorities are not responsible enough to be guardians of such treasures and therefore the country's treasures would be better off in New York or London.[10] Predictably, Appiah and Cuno have defended the Metropolitan Museum of Art (MMA) in New York and its collecting practices, even though the Metropolitan Museum, like the Getty Museum in Malibu, has recently had to return a significant number of key artifacts to their countries of origin after highly publicized trials. In fact, the MMA has taken a more proactive position in respect to its considerable holdings of Egyptian antiquities, agreeing recently to return some 19 important items.[11]

Both Appiah and Cuno are concerned primarily with museums and the pipeline, usually from private collectors, supplying them with artifacts. Their claim that local governments should not be trusted with the care and presentation of local artifacts is surely relevant to the case of Elad's control of the City of David's visitor's center, although taking their logic and applying it to national monuments and historic sites is more problematic. They would probably argue that the Dome of the Rock and the rest of the Temple Mount compound (Haram esh-Sharif; see fig. 1) should be the inheritance not just of Israel or of Islam but of the world. I would agree that humanity has a stake in seeing these wonders carefully preserved and presented. But at present, the Supreme Muslim Authority in Jerusalem (the Waqf) has sole and absolute authority over the Temple Mount area, and in recent years has often closed the Dome of the Rock to non-Muslims—while the municipality of Jerusalem and the IDF control access to this space and argue with the Waqf over what it controls.

Jerusalem's Church of the Holy Sepulcher, which arguably belongs to all humanity, involves another kind of contested space. The Israelis control its external space; and its sacred, internal space is divided among six orthodox Christian groups. In the words of Jerome Murphy-O'Connor:

---

10. Appiah is dependent for his views on Merryman 1986.
11. A recent *New York Times* editorial praised these efforts; see "Repatriating Tut," November 28, 2010. On-line: http://www.nytimes.com/2010/11/29/opinion/29mon4.html?_r=1&ref=opinion.

Figure 1. Aerial view of the Temple Mount from the southeast with City of David before excavation in foreground. Stones at right are in the Jewish cemetery on the Mount of Olives. Courtesy of Todd Bolen.

> One expects the central shrine of Christendom to stand out in majestic isolation, but anonymous buildings cling to it like barnacles. One looks for numinous light, but it is dark and cramped. One hopes for peace, but the the ear is assailed by a cacophony of warring chants. One desires holiness, only to encounter a jealous possessiveness: the six groups of occupants—Latin Catholics, Greek Orthodox, Armenians, Syrians, Copts, Ethiopians—watch over one another suspiciously for any infringement of rights. The frailty of humanity is nowhere more apparent that here; it epitomizes the human condition. The empty who come to be filled will leave desolate; those who permit the church to question them may begin to understand why hundreds of thousands thought it worthwhile to risk death or slavery in order to pray here (1998:45).

The World Monuments Fund (WMF)—the leading private organization dedicated to saving the historic sites around the world—and UNESCO can both be praised for helping to preserve some of the most endangered and important ancient and monumental treasures, but clearly there remains much more to do. Perhaps the WMF or UNESCO could be involved in Jerusalem. In any case, using the City of David as a case study, I hope to demonstrate that when a particular site with a universal message is taken over by a group with narrow interests and a political agenda, the world suffers a real loss. Because the site involves sacred space venerated by the three religions of the book—Judaism, Christianity, and Islam—the situation is especially problematic. Would Israel qualify today as a responsible trustee? Would the Hashemite kingdom qualify? It is hardly clear whether Israel or Jordan might qualify as a disinterested guarantor of the universal legacy of Jerusalem sites as a group, let alone individually.

Those responsible for telling the story of a particular place and presenting the finds and artifacts to the public within the framework of a coherent and compelling story or history at a visitors center or in a national park have the power to shape and mold a narrative in a very distinct way that may not truly reflect the reality of what has been uncovered there through the years. The challenges and complexity of presenting in a fair and unbiased way archaeological sites and their associated material remains are especially enormous in a place like Jerusalem, where the lineage of its sites is so multicultural and multireligious and where the archaeological and monumental remains are of such great interest to visitors of so many different religious backgrounds and from so many countries. Also, Jerusalem's archaeological remains and monuments span many different chronological periods—some from the early Canaanite to the Greco-Roman era, others from the First Temple period to the Crusades, still others from the Second Temple period to the medieval and early modern Islamic periods—and represent for the Jewish, Christian, and Muslim visitor different legacies and narratives. Thus, the fact that Jerusalem's story may be shaped to defend a certain ideological bias that reflects only aspects of the cumulative history of the place is part of the problem we must face in relation to the city. Cultural heritage is a commodity that requires marketing and management, and proper marketing can take even the most unique of cultural artifacts and universalize it (Baram and Rowan 2004). In the case of Jerusalem, however, despite the enormous effort to market the City of David as a tourist site, its universal message has been muted by the particularistic way it has been presented to the public by Elʿad.

Similar muting of the past appears in Jordan. The Jordanian antiquities authority decided, after the 1994 peace treaty with Israel was signed, to bury the Byzantine-period (6th century C.E.) synagogue at Jerash with its beautiful mosaics, including a scene depicting the biblical story of Noah. The synagogue lies covered in sand, its signage removed, to this day. This decision was meant to discourage Israeli tourism to the site, which they feared might ignite on-site tensions, and also to cover up the evidence of ancient Jewish settlement in Transjordan. In contrast, the Jordanians did not efface the Jewish presence at Iraq el-ʿEmir, where the Tobiad family of the late Hellenistic period built a large and spectacular trading emporium, probably because this site is not regularly visited by tourists. Another example is Gaza, where the archaeological museum provides little evidence for the presence of Jews on the Coastal Plain and where hardly a trace of the ancient Gaza synagogue is visible, although its famous mosaic featuring David as Orpheus was transferred to the Israel Museum (but not before it had been defaced to obscure the identity of the biblical figure; see Meyers 2003: 73–4).

Clearly, the expectation for a fair and multicultural legacy of a historic region has not been met in Jordan and Gaza, just as it has not in the City of David and in Jerusalem's "Historic Basin"—the Old City and its environs (see fig. 2).[12] That it has not happened in Gaza is unfortunate but not surprising in light of the profound political divisions between Hamas and Israel. Political tensions also underlie the situation in Jordan, although there are hints that Jordan is now more interested in its biblical past, for it is willing to lend some of the Dead Sea Scrolls in its possession for exhibitions around the world and has also recently endeavored to teach its citizens about the contents of the scrolls.[13] These are signs that the climate there in respect to its biblical and Jewish past may be changing. These examples provide dramatic illustrations of the problematic nature of presenting the story of the past, especially when aspects of that past have already become part of the collective memory of a group that has been excluded.

The situation in the City of David is perhaps the most blatant, current example of archaeology being misused. Archaeology at that site, as Israeli archaeologist Yonathan Mizrachi has said, has become "a weapon of dispossession."[14] This phrase highlights that aspect of archaeology whereby the actual excavation results in the displacement of people living on the site, Silwan Village (see fig. 3), where Palestinian residents claim their families have lived for thousands of years. But the larger problem—the telling of the exclusionary narrative of who lived there in times past and what those claims mean—occurs in the Elʿad visitor's center and in the stream of publications and videos produced by the Ir David Foundation. One would assume that the IAA and its affiliated organization, the INPA, would be in charge here; but that simply is not the case. Apparently, the IAA has given that authority to Elad, which has managed the visitor's center since 1992 (Greenberg 2007). Moreover, Elʿad's other activities are extensive. Elʿad operates an elabo-

---

12. For a discussion of the Historic Basin and the sites included, see Lapidoth and Ramon 2006: 20–23.

13. As reported by Weston Fields to the Board of Advisors of the Dead Sea Scrolls Foundation on November 22, 2010 in Atlanta, Georgia.

14. Quoted by Y. Bronner and N. Gordon in "Beneath the Surface," *The Chronicle Review*, April 25, 2008; see http://chronicle.com/article/Beneath-the -Surface/15094/.

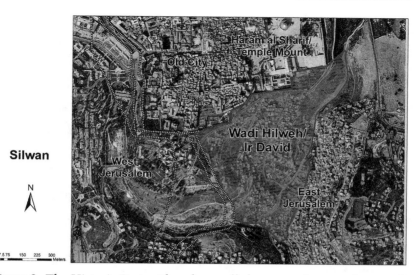

Figure 2. The Historic Basin. Plan shows all the areas of contention south of the Temple Mount. "Ir David" is also known as the City of David. Photo with captions courtesy of Danny Seidemann.

rate Web site.[15] It has funded numerous excavations over the Green Line (marking the border between Israel and the "occupied territories"), paying a significant amount of money to the IAA for that privilege. Elʿad is also the umbrella organization for approximately 12 excavations in the Old City of Jerusalem, mostly in the Palestinian neighborhood of Silwan and the Historic Basin including the Wadi Hilweh just north of Silwan, in the oldest part of the city. The intent of these excavations—to evict Palestinians from their homes and to replace them with Jewish settlers—seems clear. An attempt to expand the Jewish occupation in Silwan in 2005 involved a plan to evict from their homes Palestinian families who were supposedly living in "King David's Garden" in the al-Bustan neighborhood. Although opposition caused it to be shelved in 2005, it was revived in 2009 (Greenberg 2009).

But this is not all. One of Elad's most recent plans is a project to tunnel from the Shiloach Pool, hundreds of meters below and to the south of the Dung Gate, all the way to the Western Wall (Wailing Wall) of the Temple Mount and even to build an underground synagogue beneath or adjacent to the Haram or Temple Mount and contiguous with the Hasmonean tunnels that were uncovered in 1996 when Netanyahu was Prime Minister.[16] A stop order fortunately was issued by the high

15. See http://www.cityofdavid.org.il/index.html.
16. Personal communication from Danny Seidemann.

Figure 3. View of Silwan and Area G of Shiloh's 1980s City of David excavations, looking south. At right is the stepped-stone structure. Courtesy of Danny Seidemann.

court in Israel in March of 2008 and the future of this particular project is now in doubt thanks to the intervention of a group of dedicated Israelis in an organization known as "Ir Ammim" (literally, "City of the People").[17] One of its members, a prominent lawyer named Danny Seidemann claims that Elʿad has ambitions far beyond Silwan, according to a *Time* magazine article (McGirk 2010). Moreover, Seidemann says that since mid-2008 the Israeli government has accelerated a policy "of aggressively and covertly expanding and consolidating control over Silwan and the Historic Basin surrounding the Old City." He goes on to say that the plan involves "the takeover of the public domain and Palestinian private property . . . accelerated planning and approval of projects, and the establishment of a network of a series of parks and sites steeped in and serving up exclusionary, fundamentalist settler ideology." The *Time* reporter, Tim McGirk, puts it this way: "In its essence the plan places a large area of Arab Jerusalem under Jewish control." And Se-

---

17. See the "Mission and Strategy" page on the Ir Ammim official Web site: http://www.ir-amim.org.il/eng/?CategoryID=151. Another activist group opposing Elʿad is Emek Shaveh, "an organization of archaeologists and community activists focusing on the role of archaeology in Israeli society and in the Israeli-Palestinian conflict"; see the "About Us" page on the Emek Shaveh official Web site: http://www.alt-arch.org/aboutus.php.

idemann warns: "It risks transforming a manageable, soluble political conflict into an intractable religious war."

The sensitive nature of this contested sacred space is clear from a series of inflammatory incidents at the Temple Mount.[18] In 1996, then Prime Minister Netanyahu ordered the tunnels that skirt the Haram compound and run alongside the Western Wall to be opened for Israelis; this led to the first major outbreak of violence between the IDF and the security forces of the Palestinian Authority, leaving a total of 80 dead, mostly Palestinians. In the summer of 2000 a major renovation undertaken by the Waqf under the El Aqsa Mosque, in the area known as "Solomon's Stables," removed the earthen fills there without any archaeological oversight. This caused an uproar in Israel, and Israeli archaeologists have since been sifting the earthen fills that were removed and in which significant artifacts and remains of the First and Second Temple periods have been identified. In September 2000, a visit to the Temple Mount by Ariel Sharon, a Member of Knesset at the time, was one of the factors leading to the Second Intifada. More recently, in 2007 and continuing into 2008, a repair at the Mugrabi Gate, just above the women's section of the Western Wall, turned into a major excavation and repair that remains contested and controversial to this day. It is not an overstatement to suggest that the archaeology of the Temple Mount area is a powder keg that can be ignited at any moment. Yet, for a variety of reasons, the public at large has been very quiet on the matter and seems resigned to the status quo.

In the Silwan area, efforts in 1998 by a number of Israeli archaeologists from Hebrew University, who filed suit against El'ad's monopoly on digging in the Silwan part of the Historic Basin, failed. The High Court ruled that the authorities needed to hand over the management of the archaeological park to a disinterested party. Nonetheless, 12 years later the situation of Elad control remains the same; approximately 90 settler families have moved into Silwan and many more purchases of Arab properties are in the works. What is the present arrangement with the IAA that allows the current situation to continue? Current information provided by Ir Ammim and Emek Shaveh indicates that the IAA has ceded to Elad the right to oversee the excavations in the areas under the umbrella and legal term "salvage operations" (Mizrachi 2010: 23–4). This rubric requires no regular archaeological license or permit; thus, it bypasses the normal procedure of oversight by the IAA or its academic advisory board, which normally screens all applications for licensing. This means that the archaeologists working on the Elad projects report to the Elad management and publish within their mechanisms or

---

18. A summary of these incidents appears on the "Archaeological Excavation Controversy" page of the Sacred Destinations Travel Guide official Web site: http://www.sacred-destinations.com/israel/temple-mount-excavation.htm.

outlets (Greenberg 2009: 42), although some also publish in more accepted scholarly outlets. To be sure, many if not most of the archaeologists working on these excavations—including Eilat Mazar, Ronny Reich, Eli Shukron, and others—are qualified or even distinguished archaeologists; yet their excavating and publishing under the auspices of an outside, private organization, with a known political agenda, is most irregular, if not unprecedented.

In short, El'ad and the City of David visitor's center, which claims on its Web site to have accommodated 400,000 visitors in 2009, is the main source of information to the lay public about the excavations. In addition, Elad's electronic and print forms of communication provide information, as do the publications of individual scholars in other, more traditional outlets. The question of who pays for all this activity is appropriate to consider in this connection (Greenberg 2009: 41). The Israeli government, especially the Jerusalem municipality, is part of a much larger group, including private sponsors, that underwrites the work. The private sponsors include donors who regularly support the settler movement in the United States. In this group are several prominent Israeli billionaires and various evangelical Christian groups, especially those with dispensationalist views of the end of time, when Jesus will return to earth and all peoples will convert. As I understand it from Ir Ammim, the archaeologists working in these areas, even though some hold positions elsewhere in the country, are paid by those sources through El'ad—or, at least, the money originates with them. As already noted, the visitor's center and the Web site are administered by El'ad and not by the IAA or its affiliate the INPA, with the IAA having received a lump sum payment for agreeing to these conditions. Rafi Greenberg has recently described El'ad and its outreach activities in the City of David this way: "Their incorporation of the site into the Jewish settler narrative is multi-faceted, mixing religious nationalism with theme-park tourism. The past is, of course, a palpable present, used both to shore up the new Jewish settlers' claim from primacy and to attract Bible-oriented tourism. As a result, conflict with local Palestinians occurs at the very basic level of existence, where the past is used to disenfranchise and displace people in the present" (Greenberg 2009: 35).

The Web site presentation of the City of David is worth noting for its tone as well as for the one-sided perspective of its narrative. Accessible in both Hebrew and English, it opens with a emotive song in English and Hebrew that sets one up for the rather emotional treatment of the excavations, which one soon learns have brought to light, after thousands of years, the city where King David unified the Israelite nation and King Solomon built the temple next to the City of David on top of Mount Moriah, where the binding of Isaac took place (Genesis 22) and where that "hilltop became one of the most important sites in the world. A tour through the City of David brings visitors face to face with the personalities and places of the Bible. As such, this is the only place on earth where the only guidebook needed is the Bible itself."[19] In a recent documentary, an El'ad spokesman, Doron Spilman, says that 60 percent of the Bible was written "on this little hill" (at 4:50) and that the energy emanating from this very place enables the visitor to get closer to the heroes of the Bible—David, Bathsheba, Jeremiah, Isaiah, and all the prophets (at 8:30)—and all the archaeology of the place speaks with this voice: "This is not just a stone; this wall is not just a wall; I'm not touching just a stone here. . . . I feel King David's hand as I put my hand on this stone" (at 10:00).[20] The invocation to the numinous and the mystical in this context offers the visitor an opportunity to relive the past in a unique fashion and provides the tourist with a religious sense of authority of what they conceive to be the past. This kind of archaeological or "pilgrim" tourism is not only selective and non-inclusive but also is designed to strengthen all sorts of contested national and religious claims.

Archaeology, when properly practiced, is all about documenting the complexities and richness of the past's diversity, especially at one of the most special places on earth, Jerusalem. Archaeologists must strive to find a way to let all the voices of its past be heard. Archaeology can do this but must first remove those forces—those who control the visitor's center and other City of David outlets—who would control Jerusalem's narrative and stifle the voices of the past that do not accord with their exclusivist, nationalist agenda.

Thus, it is fair to demand answers to these questions: Whose memories of the past are encoded in the materials uncovered? Whose narrative of the present is embedded in the publications of the visitor's center in the City of David? Who is being displaced by these activities? And who stands to lose by virtue of these continued activities? (If the truth is not being communicated, or if only one version of the perceived truth is being put forward, we all stand to lose.) Whose collective memories can be culled from excavations of this sort? Whose cultural patrimony do these remains and artifacts represent? And how can we, as humanistic scholars and interested individuals, allow such important aspects of our biblical heritage to be commandeered by so extreme a group as El'ad? Asking these questions and demanding answers and changes present a challenge to all fair-minded people who value the universal heritage of Jerusalem as well as its particular Jewish, Christian, and Muslim

19. Quoting http://www.cityofdavid.org.il/about_eng.asp [accessed in April 2009]. The quoted material has since been removed from the Web site, but the tone remains.
20. N. Dudinski, *Digging for Trouble—Israel/Palestine*, Journeyman Pictures. On-line: http://www.youtube.com/watch?v=aRNAJCHxa7w.

components. If peace will ever come to the holy city, all the voices of its past must be heard, especially on the holiest of mounts: Mount Moriah, the Temple Mount, the Haram esh-Sherif.

References

Addison, E.
  2004   The Roads to Ruins: Accessing Islamic Heritage in Jordan. Pp. 229–48 in Rowan and Baran 2004.
Appiah, K. A.
  2006   Whose Culture Is It? *New York Review of Books* 53: 38–41. On-line: http://www.nybooks.com/articles/archives/2006/feb/09/whose-culture-is-it/.
Atwood, R.
  2008   Guardians of Antiquity? *Archaeology* 18: 66, 68, 70.
Baram, U., and Rowan, Y.
  2004   Archaeology after Nationalism: Globalization and the Consumption of the Past. Pp. 3–26 in Rowan and Baram 2004.
Bauman, J.
  2004   Tourism, the Ideology of Design, and the Nationalized Past in Zippori/Sepphoris Israeli National Park. Pp. 205–28 in Rowan and Baran 2004.
Ben-Yehudah, N.
  1995   *The Masada Myth: Collective Memory and Mythmaking in Israel.* Madison: University of Wisconsin Press.
  2007   Excavating Masada: The Politics-Archaeology Connection. Pp. 247–76 in Kohl, Kozelsky, and Ben-Yehuda 2007.
Brooke, G. J., and Schiffman, L. H.
  1999   The Past: On the History of Dead Sea Scrolls Research. Pp. 9–20 in *The Dead Sea Scrolls at Fifty: Proceedings of the 1997 Society of Biblical Literature,* ed. R. A. Kugler and E. Schuler. Early Judaism and Its Literature 15. Atlanta: Scholars Press.
Cuno. J.
  2008   *Who Owns Antiquity?* Princeton: Princeton University Press.
de Vries, B.
  1997   Conservation Archaeology. P. 60 in vol. 5 of *The Oxford Encyclopedia of Archaeology in the Near East,* ed. E. M. Meyers. 5 vols. New York: Oxford University Press.
Feige, M.
  2007   West-Bank Settlers and the Second Stage of National Archaeology. Pp. 277–98 in Kohl, Kozelsky, and Ben-Yehuda 2007.
Greenberg, R.
  2007   Contested Sites: Archaeology and the Battle for Jerusalem. *Jewish Quarterly* 208: 20–26.
  2009   Toward an Inclusive Archaeology in Jerusalem: The Case of Silwan/The City of David. *Public Archaeology* 8:35–44.
Kohl, P. L.; Kozelsky, M.; and Ben-Yehuda, N., eds.
  2007   *Selective Remembrances: Archaeology in the Construction, Commemoration, and Consecration of National Parks.* Chicago: University of Chicago Press.

Lapidoth, R., and Ramon A.
2006   *The Historical Basin of Jerusalem: The Status Quo and Alternatives for Agreement.* JIIS Studies Series. Jerusalem: Jerusalem Institute for Israel Studies. Available on-line at: http://www.jiis.org/.upload/publications/Historical_Basin.pdf.
Magness-Gardiner, B.
2004   International Conventions and Cultural Heritage Protection. Pp. 27–40 in Rowan and Baram 2004.
McGirk, T.
2010   Archaeology in Jerusalem: Digging Up Trouble. *Time,* February 8. On-line: http://www.time.com/time/magazine/article/0,9171,1957350,00.html.
Merryman, J. H.
1986   Two Ways of Thinking about Cultural Property. *American Journal of International Law* 80: 831–53.
Meyers, E. M.
2003   Archaeology and Nationalism in Israel: Making the Past Part of the Present. Pp. 64–77 in *Zeichen aus Text und Stein: Studien auf dem Weg zu einer Archäologiedes Neuen Testaments,* ed. S. Alkier and J. Zangenberg. Tübingen: Francke Verlag.
Millstein, M.
2010   No Saints in Jerusalem: How Religion, Politics, and Archaeology Clash On—and Under—the Streets of Jerusalem. *Archaeology* 63: 18, 60–61, 65–66.
Mizrachi, Y.
2010   Archaeology in the Shadow of Conflict: The Mound of Ancient Jerusalem (City of David) in Silwan. Jerusalem: Emek Shaveh. Available on-line at: http://www.alt-arch.org/docs/booklet_english.pdf.
Murphy-O'Connor, J.
1998   *The Holy Land: An Oxford Archaeological Guide from Earliest Times to 1700.* 4th ed. Oxford: Oxford University Press.
Rowan, Y., and Baram, U.
2004   *Marketing Heritage: Archaeology and the Consumption of the Past.* Walnut Creek, CA: AltaMira.
Silberman, N.
1989   *Past and Present: Archaeology, Ideology, and Nationalism in the Modern Middle East.* New York: Doubleday Anchor.

On Tourism and Politics in Israel
A Response to Eric Meyers

REBECCA L. STEIN

Let me begin my comments by flagging what I took to be Eric Meyers's most provocative suggestion in his paper—namely, that the ongoing archaeological project in the Palestinian neighborhood of Silwan is itself an act of military occupation—a means of "evict[ing] Palestinians from their homes and replac[ing] them with Jewish settlers." He is arguing that archaeology, in this particular context, constitutes yet another "weapon of dispossession" within the Israeli arsenal. But what, precisely, is the nature of this weapon? As Meyers has suggested, the archaeological project in Silwan is also a tourist project; indeed, tourism is a critical arena in which El'ad's broader political efforts to expand the Jewish settler infrastructure in the Jerusalem area are being advanced. My own research has focused on the relationship between tourism and politics in the Israeli context (Stein 2008a), and my comments will briefly explore this relationship as an attempt to historicize the phenomenon that we are witnessing today in Silwan. This brief paper is also an attempt to explore the ways that tourism might be considered a companion "weapon of dispossession" in the Israeli case, albeit of a different kind.

Consider, for example, the onset of the Israeli occupation of the West Bank and Gaza Strip, following Israel's victory during the course of the 1967 war.[1] While Israel's military occupation of the Palestinian territories is not traditionally viewed through the lens of the tourist culture it spawned, this culture is an indisputable part of its legacy. Indeed, any Israeli Jew or Palestinian who lived through the 1967 war can attest to the massive Israeli tourist crowds that the war and subsequent occupation unleashed—the surging tourist crowds in Jerusalem's Old City, and the stream of Jewish-Israeli travelers, hikers, and sight-seers into the remainder of the Palestinian West Bank. These tourist forms did not take long to coalesce. Rather, Israeli visits to the newly occupied

---

1. For an elaborated version of this argument and research, see Stein 2008b.

216

Palestinian territories began in large numbers immediately after the cessation of war-time violence. Newspapers from June 11, the first day after the war's conclusion, reported that "curio shops [in the Old City were already] doing a roaring trade" and that soldiers were "wander[ing] around [the city] with a gun in one hand and a camera in the other" (Bat Haim 1967). By June 17, some 350,000 persons had reportedly "walked to the wall" (Gillion 1967a). Private tourist companies were operating in Jerusalem on both sides of the Green Line by this time and advertising their tours in the press (noting that "owners of accordions, who are prepared to play Hebrew songs, will travel for free"; Anonymous 1967). Israeli tourists continued to "swarm" the streets of Jerusalem through the end of the month, and newspapers from this period were flush with scenes and photographs of the surging crowds. Here is one example:

> Everyone who can has taken a holiday and come to Jerusalem, and spends it packed in a solid . . . mass of people who cannot see anything except the upper parts of the houses. Soldiers on leave carry their Uzis over their heads so that nobody will set them off by accident (Gillion 1967b).

Both state and popular responses to the new tourist cartography were rapid. In the week after the cessation of violence, the Israeli Tourism Ministry began a "refresher course" for licensed tour guides in the "new territory" and announced plans to revise its promotional material (Gillion 1967b). In tandem, the mainstream press offered tips to prospective tourists, outlining the proper etiquette to employ when visiting Arabs in their homes; what to wear on such visits (avoid the miniskirt, they warned); how to consume the honorific coffee (advising that "one should drink drop by drop"); and how to greet one's host in appropriate Arabic (Lavie 1967). Travel to these newly available sites was like walking "through the looking glass," one Israeli editorial remarked. This was an uncanny kind of leisure landscape, both familiar from days of the prestate *tiyul* [hike or walk] and strange in this new geopolitical formation. Israeli tourists continued to "swarm" the streets of East Jerusalem through the end of the month, and newspapers from this period were flush with scenes and photographs of the surging crowds.

The motivations for travel into the newly occupied territories were multiple. Many Jewish Israelis went as secular pilgrims to sites of biblical importance. Others sought pleasure in the natural landscape, returning to routes enjoyed prior to 1948 (Stein 2009). Large numbers were also motivated by consumptive desires. Despite bans on consumption, and the punitive actions faced by violators, the press of the period reported shelves stripped clean of souvenirs and "cola and chocolate sold in large quantities" (Gillion 1967a). Consumption took two forms, primarily. The early days of the tourist frenzy saw a run on souvenirs, culinary delights, and luxury goods. Next came the demand for the household goods and appliances that could be purchased at a fraction of their Israeli prices. Although prices rose rapidly, and despite the Israeli taxes levied on goods purchased in the territories, the rush to consume was not tempered. In mid-July, the "scope of Israeli shopping in the West Bank" was valued at 25 million liras per month (Meron 1967). Jewish merchants and sellers complained that the magnitude of Israeli purchases in the territories was devastating their profits. When Gaza City opened to Israeli visitors on July 21, headlines announced that "Thirty-Five Thousand Israelis Spent a 'Shopping Shabbat' in Gaza" (Appel 1967).

What I propose in the longer version of this analysis is that post-war Israeli tourism into the Palestinian territories was a primary means by which Israeli civilians experienced the occupation and came to terms with their newfound status as occupiers. As a body of both spatial and discursive practices, tourism was a primary register by which Israeli civilians experienced the occupation—its territories, people, vistas, and markets. This mass tourist phenomenon was thus crucial in laying the groundwork for popular Israeli investment, in both economic and psychological terms, in the Palestinian territories themselves.

The Israeli media played an active role in cementing this investment in the occupation through the avenue of tourism. In and through stories about tourism, the mainstream Israeli media was able to narrate the effects of the war on everyday Israelis. Indeed, the proliferation of media stories about the surging Israeli crowds of this period helped to fuel Israeli interest in the territories as a leisure landscape, thereby helping to perpetuate the occupation, which made this landscape possible. Media stories about tourism tended to eschew the political rhetoric of the day, speaking about leisure, pleasure, and consumption in the territories rather than about Israeli ideological platforms or security concerns—a shift in idiom that positioned tourism as something of an alibi for the occupation itself. I want to argue that these stories functioned as what postcolonial theorists have called "anti-conquest narratives"—narratives that participated in the work of conquest through a rejection of the rhetoric of subjugation in favor of accounts of consumption, pleasure, and benign exploration (Pratt 1992).

Why, in the context of a conference focused primarily on the political effects and contexts of archaeology, dwell on this case study? Because I think that the lessons learned from this study of post-war tourism are echoed in Meyers's study of the situation in Silwan. As I have already suggested, the Silwan case has much to tell us about the often intimate relationship between archaeological and national ideological projects in the Israeli context. But the case also does more, helping us to complicate the ways that academics and journalists tend to conceptualize the Israeli military occupation. The case of Silwan, like the tourism history I have outlined, encourages us to think beyond the merely repressive mechanisms of the military occupation—the incursions, checkpoints,

the wall—to consider the wider range of Israeli institutions and knowledge practices through which the occupation is ratified and perpetuated.

References

Anonymous
  1967   Tour of Liberated Jerusalem. *Maʿariv*, June 21. [Hebrew]
Appel, D.
  1967   Some 35 Thousand Israelis Spent a "Shopping Shabbat" in Gaza. *Yediot Aharonot*, July 23: 19. [Hebrew]
Bat Haim, H.
  1967   Lost in the Old City. *Jerusalem Post*, June 11.
Gillion, P.
  1967a   Fraternization Banned Except with Old Friends. *Jerusalem Post*, June 11.
  1967b   Big Tourism Publicity Push. *Jerusalem Post Economic Reporter*, June 20: 6.
  1967c   200,000 at Western Wall in First Pilgrimage Since Dispersion. *Jerusalem Post Economic Reporter*, June 15.
  1967d   350,000 Have Walked to the Western Wall. *Jerusalem Post Economic Reporter*, June 18: 4
Lavie, S.
  1967   "The Israelis Are Coming. The Israelis Are Coming . . ." *Maʿariv*, June 25. [Hebrew]
Meron, H.
  1967   The West Bank Economy in Disorder and Ruin. *Yediot Aharonot*, July 14: 7. [Hebrew]
Pratt, M. L.
  1992   *Imperial Eyes: Travel Writing and Transculturation*. London: Routledge.
Stein, R. L.
  2008a   Souvenirs of Conquest: Israeli Occupations as Tourist Events. *International Journal of Middle East Studies* 40: 647–69.
  2008b   *Itineraries in Conflict: Israelis, Palestinians, and the Political Lives of Tourism*. Durham, NC: Duke University Press.
  2009   Traveling Zion: Hiking and Settler-Nationalism in Pre-1948 Palestine. *Interventions: International Journal of Postcolonial Studies* 11: 334–51.

PART 4

Voices of the Media

Responses from a Television Producer

RAY BRUCE

I am very much the outsider at this conference, coming as I do from London; but like many present I have a passion for archaeology and its presentation in the media. As a television producer, I believe it is crucial that the relationship between the archaeological community and the media be both positive and creative. It serves all our interests to ensure that archaeologists and media professionals feel comfortable together. Thus, I offer some observations and suggestions as we look to the future.

Let me begin by establishing a light-hearted context with due respect to Holy Scripture:

> In the beginning when the archaeologist created the dig, the earth was a formless void and darkness covered the face of the Sony 42-inch High Definition Plasma Screen Television with surround sound audio and subwoofers. As work progressed, the archaeologist said, "Let there be light"; and there was light. And the archaeologist saw the light was good, rewarding him with wondrous finds and information. And the archaeologist separated the light from the darkness. The light he called integrity; and the darkness he called Sony 42-inch High Definition Plasma Screen Television with surround sound audio and subwoofers, now showing a spurious film about a tomb discovery in Jerusalem lacking any intellectual rigor, misrepresenting leading world experts and, what's more, threatening to shake the foundations of western civilization. And there was evening and there was morning of repeats.

For some 20 years, I have had the privilege and honor of making documentaries for all the major United Kingdom and international broadcasters, including National Geographic and the Discovery Channel in the United States, working with some of the finest archaeologists. I know that a great number of archaeologists have enjoyed and do enjoy working in television, whether in my productions or those of colleagues. However, alarm bells have been ringing of late. Certain high profile programs focusing on archaeological endeavor have raised real concern and

223

anxiety on the part of contributors to such programs and within the
wider academic community. Some members of the archaeological community maintain that you should not play with the television, boys and
girls, as it will always end in tears and your integrity will be jeopardized.
For me, this is a sad state of affairs. So, what if you do want to engage
with the media–in my case, television? What are the rules? What should
the landscape of archaeology and the media look like? What are the
politics involved? This is what I would like to explore.

Much of the academic community's concern, anxiety and anger
about archaeology and its representation on television derive from particular high profile productions such as Simcha Jacobovici's controversial *The Lost Tomb of Jesus* shown on the Discovery Channel in 2007.
Let me declare at the outset that I have produced a Jesus Family Tomb
documentary that I hope is more judicious in its approach and conclusions. I also have to confess that I must take some responsibility for the
Jesus Family Tomb media circus. I want to reflect briefly on that experience without engaging with Simcha's film overmuch. Jodi Magness and
others in this volume have charted the lessons learned from what Jodi
has called the "Talpiyot Tomb Fiasco."

In 1996, I was producing a documentary about the Easter story and
wanted the presenter to engage with the world of Jerusalem some 2,000
years ago. I thought that looking at ancient ossuaries would help in this
endeavor. I identified a "Yeshua" ossuary. Then, with the help of Joe
Zias, who was working for the Israel Antiquities Authority (IAA) at the
time, I went in search of that particular ossuary in the IAA warehouse.

To our amazement, along with our Yeshua ossuary we discovered
five others from the same Talpiyot Tomb in the suburbs of Jerusalem.
Inscriptions on the other ossuaries had familiar-sounding names associated with the Jesus story. Our discovery sent shock waves around the
world, including a piece on the front page of the *Sunday Times*,[1] but,
in our defense, we made no claims beyond the Talpiyot ossuaries suggesting an "interesting" set of names. We felt the discovery was worthy
of further investigation, but we bowed out. However, Jodi Magness and
others should perhaps feel free to throw cabbages in my direction.

What I learned from that experience has left an indelible mark on
my work as a television producer. My job is to manage expectations:
the expectations of broadcasters, production teams, and, not least, archaeologists and scholars. Such management on the part of responsible
TV producers is crucial and can determine the success or failure of a
production.

It is heartening to learn that many in the archaeological community itself believe that they should engage creatively and responsibly

---

1. Joan Bakewell, "The Tomb That Dare Not Speak Its Name," *Sunday Times*
(London), March 31, 1996.

in the enterprise of working with media. However, this is not without difficulties. Chris Rollston admits that members of the academy "are sometimes the problem and not the solution."[2] Byron McCane talks about "scholars behaving badly."[3] Is this due to ignorance concerning the politics and language of television? Do academics have unrealistic expectations?

With respect to managing expectations, let's start with the broadcasters. I see little difference in ambition and aspiration between broadcasters in the United States and in the United Kingdom. It is crucial to understand the seminal role of the broadcasters. And it is particularly important to understand the constraints within which responsible producers have to operate in the media food chain. It is the broadcaster that commissions and funds the program. In spite of declining production budgets, it is somewhat easier to obtain program funding in the United Kingdom than it is for my television colleagues in the United States. If I pitch an idea directly to the BBC and they like it, they give me the budget, whereas producers in the United States have to look for funding from a variety of sources. Doing so is time-consuming and often very frustrating. Perhaps co-production with a number of broadcasters in play may be the way forward in the contemporary broadcast market.

So what are the broadcasters looking for? What are their expectations? What is the program's USP, its "Unique Selling Point"? What will keep an audience glued to their TV sets to ensure it will not slip away? Let us not forget, we inhabit a multichannel universe with the ability of the viewer to channel-hop at the press of a button.

Let me share with you what commissioning editors have told me they want from their programs.

Broadcasters want *"noise"* surrounding their programs. They want "previews, reviews," and as many awards as can be mustered. They want programs that "break through the schedule," "stand-out programs," "programs with a trouble-making spirit," and "risky and surprising programs." And broadcasters hanker after superlatives. This program looks at something "as never before." Or it reveals the "oldest, biggest, and rarest." And of course, this program "shakes the foundation of Western civilization" and—the classic—"forces us to rewrite biblical history."

It is little wonder that archaeologists are nervous about playing with the television boys and girls. Nevertheless, this competitive, wow-seeking, audience-hooking broadcast universe has to be understood by all; and it is my role to do the explaining in an honest, open manner to help archaeologists manage expectations.

---

2. See Rollston's essay in this volume: "An Ancient Medium in the Modern Media: Sagas of Semitic Inscriptions," pp. 123–136.

3. See McCane's essay in this volume: "Scholars Behaving Badly: Sensationalism and Archaeology in the Media," pp. 101–108.

We producers have a responsibility and a duty of care to explain the politics and language of television. I repeat, on the basis of appropriate information: archaeologists can choose to play in television or not. The decision is ultimately theirs.

Let us look at one facet of the production process that directly affects participant engagement. The question always arises: how much screen time will my contribution take up? This raises the issue of editorial control, which is a significant area of expectation management. Ultimately, editorial control rests with the broadcaster; and however much I might admire a particular contribution, it may not be a view shared by the commissioning editor. It is difficult to say to someone that he or she did not make the final cut after spending hours in the grueling sun riding a donkey. As a responsible producer, I have a duty to explain what has happened, but potential contributors should be apprised of the editorial situation.

Milton Moreland touched on the documentary form with his poignant remark concerning the "high level of audience trust."[4] This trust can only be maintained if the relationship between the television producer and program contributors delivering content is responsible and rigorous. And what are the demands of the television audience and their expectations? The problem here is one of making archaeology easy and accessible to a wide public. Some archaeologists are better suited to this task than others. Some argue it is not possible to tailor complex and nuanced theories and data to fit a popular documentary form.

Broadcasters know their audience—at least, they think they do. Let me cite an actual case, albeit a contentious one. Channel Five is a terrestrial broadcaster in the United Kingdom with a specific target audience of males aged 18 to 36. For this reason, they are always bemoaning the fact that archaeology programmes are short of young, female presenters to appeal to this target audience.

Once we have lured the audience to our television screens, what are their expectations? Jesus on the cover of books or in the titles of documentaries does lift sales and increase audiences. Jesus is a powerful brand. We do have opportunities as never before to produce documentaries that can garner an audience and make an impact.

Here, I salute Dan Brown and others who are opening up matters of history and archaeology as never before. This may raise some eyebrows in the academic community. It is not that I uncritically buy into all that Dan Brown and others like him present in their novels. Far from it. But what they have done is to introduce a mass audience to Jesus and Mary Magdalene, the emperor Constantine, even the Council of Nicaea. In other words there exists an appetite for programs in this area. In many

4. See Moreland's essay in this volume: "Forged by a Genius: Scholarly Responses to 'History Channel Meets *CSI*,'" pp. 109–122.

respects, documentary programs can set the record straight with regard to some of the fanciful stories narrated by Dan Brown and company.

At the conference, Jonathan Reed talked about the tantalizing "lure of proof" that can excite and engage an audience. Here lies a difficulty for archaeologists. While we can discuss ifs, buts, and maybes, the audience wants proof. They want to know: is it true? "*X* marks the spot" can make for great television, but archaeology is more sophisticated than that. It is as much about process as it is about finding the Holy Grail. The demands of television will not always fit the aspiration of the archaeologist. Whether we find the Holy Grail or not, the key to a good documentary is a thumping good story.

So my colleagues in the archaeological community must make an effort to understand the television industry if they feel its allure. They must not be afraid to ask searching questions about the proposed documentary. What is the production company? Does the producer have experience in archaeological programming? Who are the broadcasters? They must be bold and imaginative in their questions. And if they are not happy with the answers, they should walk away.

Archaeologists and scholars are woefully unfamiliar with the language, politics, and competing expectations of the television world. This breeds a great deal of suspicion, frustration, and disappointment. They can feel compromised by the whole experience, their integrity far from intact, vowing never to work in television ever again. I can now say, publicly, that it was a task of titanic proportions to win the confidence of contributors and have them work on my Jesus Family Tomb film because of their bitter experiences in that other, more lavish production, even though I had known many of these contributors for a number of years both personally and professionally. All I would say is that not all TV producers are tarred with the same brush!

This brings me to a concern accompanied by one or two more alarm bells. In the opinion of some archaeologists at this conference, when it comes to archaeologists and the media, the former should "control the agenda" by "retaking the field" and "policing the subject." There has even been talk of blacklisting certain producers. This makes me nervous. Draconian techniques will not work. It fast produces an us-versus-them mentality and is not conducive to harmonious working possibilities. By all means, archaeologists should become TV-literate and discuss ways of improving the image of archaeology in the media. Chris Rollston is right to suggest that media, television included, do not know the archaeological world, with its possible players. And media, for our part, have a responsibility to understand the archaeological world before entering it. At the very least, producers should do some homework before approaching archaeologists for a possible contribution. If this is patently not the case, archaeologists should walk away; they could be in for a rough ride if they do not.

My final point is a bit of flag-waving for the United Kingdom. This volume has concerned itself with archaeology, politics and the media. However, when I look around at colleges in the United States, I do not see a graduate course in Archaeology and the Media. I apologize if such a course does exist, but it just happens not to have crossed my radar.

In the United Kingdom, we have a very successful, long-running archaeology series called *Time Team*. Archaeologists have three days at a particular site to discover something about the history of a particular place—it is well worth a watch. As a result of the subsequent public interest in archaeology on television, the University of Bristol now runs an interdisciplinary Masters degree program in Archaeology for Screen Media—it is well worth a search.[5] As you can imagine, I receive a number of resumes from graduates of this course.

I sincerely hope that gatherings such as this one at Duke will bring the worlds of archaeology and the media together. I, along with other television professionals, simply want to make engaging and informative programs—with the help of archaeologists, of course.

---

5. See the "MA in Archaeology for Screen Media" page on the University of Bristol official Web site: http://www.bristol.ac.uk/archanth/postgrad/screema .html.

Areas of Concern as We Go Forward

MOIRA BUCCIARELLI

I want to sum up the areas of concern that I heard expressed at this conference and pose some solutions to these concerns in an open-ended way, for new ideas are welcome and I certainly do not have all the answers.

Concern 1: *Scholars feel they are being passed by, their views distorted or exploited by the media for material gain.*

In other words, "the media" quite often have a monetary incentive to fudge the academic subtleties and accentuate dramatic or sensational claims that play on people's interest in physical evidence of biblical texts and persons. One possible practical solution might be improved media relations. For example, the American Academy of Religion (AAR) has "Religionsource," a database for journalists that includes names of academics in religion, Bible, and archaeology and their areas of research; the people in the database all have academic posts. How can it be improved? It does offer a screening function. The problem is that we do not know if TV documentary producers are using it or if they rely on Google searches, which do not necessarily provide context about credibility or a sense of "who's who in the field."

Scholars also need better skills for talking to media and for translating their work into lay terms. I think Jodi Magness's comment about knowing your elevator pitch—how to describe your work in a few clear simple sentences—is well taken. To that end, the Society of Biblical Literature (SBL) organized a session, which I chaired, on "Talking with the Media" at its annual meeting in November, 2009; two scholars (Jodi Magness of the University of North Carolina at Chapel Hill and Robert Cargill of the University of California-Los Angeles) and two journalists (Jennifer Howard of the *Chronicle of Higher Education* and Marcia Nelson of *Publishers' Weekly*) formed a panel to discuss many of the same issues that this conference has addressed. Since then, we have turned that session into an attractive PDF accessible at the SBL Web site.[1] Scholars also need to learn how not to leave the interviewer or the audience empty-handed. Academics have a tendency to be absolutist,

---

1. See http://www.sbl-site.org/assets/pdfs/SBLMediaGuide_lowres.pdf.

or, on the other end of the spectrum, relativizing. Either way, the audience is left hanging, wondering, "What am I supposed to believe?" If someone asks "Did Moses write the Pentateuch?" one doesn't answer by saying "Hell no!" or "Gosh, we really don't know." Rather, the scholar should take the audience into the world of scholarship and show them some of the landmarks. That is the kind of nuance we have been talking about at this conference.

Concern 2: *People are getting their information about the Bible and archaeology from TV and the Internet.*

Obviously, scholars need to have an internet presence, as many of the participants in this conference already do. But how could scholars be more proactive in sharing their work? Eric Clines has mentioned the many ways to be involved: articles, books, blogs, consulting roles on documentary films, Web sites, institutional collaboration, etc. I will suggest another way: SBL received a National Endowment for the Humanities (NEH) planning grant to develop a Web site for the general public, called *Bible Odyssey: Exploring Places, People, and Passages*, that will translate scholarly research into lay terms in a fully multimedia way. It will not be just an on-line encyclopedia. Rather, it will be a place for media to come to fact check and get updates on the latest research. It will also be a resource for educators by offering educational components for both high school and college settings. We are excited about it and will hear in April 2011 whether we get funds to build the site. I should mention that three of the advisors to the project are participants in this conference: Carol Meyers, Jonathan Reed, and Mark Goodacre. This project will provide a great venue for scholars to share their research in language that is accessible to the public.

An open question is whether SBL should introduce a blog on its Web site. People at this conference have been talking about the need to update a blog daily. This seems like a lot of work, and I do not know how this is handled. Should one person be assigned to maintain the blog, or should it rotate among staff? Ideas about how to manage the blogs of professional societies need to be shared.

Another area in which SBL is working is Bible electives in public schools—providing quality information and training about the biblical corpus, both of which are in short supply, for teachers at the high school level. To that end, SBL has created a monthly e-publication for teachers (*Teaching the Bible*) that gives concrete, credible information, written by scholars, that teachers can use in the classroom. Teachers are an audience that we at SBL are eager to reach, and preparing materials for teachers is another way for scholars to get involved.

Concern 3: *How best to respond to "media circuses"?*

Jodi Magness has told us how she wished that in the past there had been swift, collaborative reactions from SBL and ASOR (the American Schools of Oriental Research) in response to significant discoveries or archaeological controversies.[2] Perhaps that is something we can be prepared to do in the future; the SBL staff should be in regular contact with the ASOR staff in order to formulate a swift response when the next sensational news story crops up. I also wonder if we need a "fact or fiction" page on the SBL Web site, something like a *Snopes.com*, where readers can find out the true story behind a current debate or find. I'm even thinking about Steven Colbert's "Yahweh or No Way" segments;[3] there are creative, clever ways to deal with this issue.

Still, would it not be better for scholars to stop being in the position of *reacting* to sensational stories? In other words, how can we "play the game" and respond to public interest, and do so responsibly? I think this relates to Jonathan Reed's comment at the conference that we need to decouple—or maybe even work with the association—of artifacts as prooftexts of the Bible. Maybe we should call this "nuancing the stone." There is a need for general explanatory pieces that illuminate the broader contexts of the Bible and the ancient Near East; these pieces can also articulate the goals of scholarship and indicate what can and cannot be said about the Bible.

As many have noted, explaining complicated issues in a sound bite to a media professional is difficult. The Talpiyot Tomb controversy is a prime example. How can journalists understand that the tomb may not be what some have claimed it to be if they do not know a thing about Judean burial customs in the first place? Judean burial customs are a fascinating topic. If we take the time to educate people and put out the contextual information that scholars take for granted, maybe we begin to build a more educated audience.

I encourage scholars and organizations such as ASOR and SBL to be more proactive content producers rather than just reactors. Academics should tell the public what they do, why they find it interesting, why they find it compelling. Provide answers to the classic "so what?" question, or the question "why should we care?" Some people are already doing that. Christopher Heard at Pepperdine is doing short video interviews with scholars for the general public. Mark Goodacre of Duke University maintains the highly successful *New Testament Gateway* Web site. SBL makes available "SBL Interviews," which are 20-minute podcasts with some SBL members.[4] And the proposed Web site, *Bible Odyssey*, offers a potential popular venue for crossover content.

---

2. See Magness's essay "Confessions of an Archaeologist: Lessons I Learned from the Talpiyot Tomb Fiasco and Other Media Encounters," pp. 89–95 in this volume.

3. See, for example, the "Yahweh or No Way" segment from the January 8, 2009 broadcast of *The Colbert Report*, found on-line at the *Colbert Nation* official Web site: http://www.colbertnation.com/the-colbert-report-videos/215452/january-08–2009/yahweh-or-no-way—-roland-burris.

4. See the "SBL Interviews" page on the SBL official Web site: http://www.sbl-site.org/membership/SBLinterviews.aspx.

In conclusion, while I am doubtful that we can move the public to a place where the reliquary impulse is tamed, where we no longer need shrouds, or arks, or proof of a great flood to affirm our religious beliefs or even our interest in the biblical world or text, I think there is much more to share. It should be both challenging and exciting to translate the amazing discoveries of archaeology into forms and formats that are educational, ethical, and, just maybe, entertaining.

Scholars at the Limits of Science and the Borders of Belief: Finding Proof for Faith

A Journalist's Perspective on the Oded Golan Case

NINA BURLEIGH

I first read about the curious case of the forged biblical artifacts in the *New York Times* around Christmas 2004. A story buried in the international section reported that Israeli police had indicted four men, accused of enhancing existing ancient artifacts, or fabricating entirely new ones, to make them appear to prove Bible stories. As I read the article about the forgery scheme, I wondered what manner of men would deviously prepare objects to feed the desire for proof among people of faith, and why would faithful people—who by definition seek to transcend materiality—want such proof in the first place? Eventually, my curiosity led me into a thriving, if murky subculture—that of the antiquities dealers who specialize in ancient Holy Land artifacts, the scholars who verify them, and the millionaires who collect expensive bits of cracked clay, stone, and bronze with the avidity and obsessiveness of boys collecting baseball cards.

When I embarked on this project, I thought of it as an exotic crime story, *The Maltese Falcon* meets *Raiders of the Lost Ark* with a little bit of *The DaVinci Code* thrown in. I did not at the time understand that it would eventually lead me to contemplate the motives and personalities of scholars involved in verifying them. Below are my firsthand impressions from interviews with three of the main scholars involved in the Oded Golan forgery case.

Author's note: This essay is comprised of excerpts from my monograph *Unholy Business: A True Tale of Faith, Greed, and Forgery in the Holy Land* (New York: HarperCollins, 2008).

233

Ada Yardeni

When I arrived to talk about how she became a witness in an archaeological forgery trial that Israeli police had called "the fraud of the century," Ada Yardeni was well prepared. Ada is the sort of woman who keeps detailed records of her days in small annual diaries. At the end of each year, she tucks them—filled with her tiny Hebrew script, tied with a white ribbon—into a cardboard box, and these boxes are now the piled-up story of her years. Opening a box, she easily found the diaries she needed, because they bristled with yellow Post-it Notes, marking the pages she had referred to during interviews with the police and then in court. She proceeded to leaf through each page, reading from right to left, entries highlighted in pink.

Her annual diaries always start in October, the beginning of the Jewish year. The series of events she needed to remember began in October 2001. That's when she got the first call from a Tel Aviv collector named Oded Golan, a wealthy aficionado of Bible-era archaeology whom she'd heard of but never met. Because of her reputation and experience, it was not unusual for Ada to receive calls from people she didn't know, offering to pay for her opinion, and she was always meticulous about recording her business affairs.

Thumbing through her book, she turned to the first Post-it. "Exactly the 24th of October, 2001. You see? I wrote it down. Afterwards I made it red because they asked me about it all the time, so I marked it. He phoned me and asked me to decipher some ostraca. On the 1st of November, he came here and brought pictures of 12 Idumean ostraca. One with a strange Jewish script. And an inscription on an ossuary in a cursive Jewish script, difficult to read. And he showed me a bowl and I couldn't identify the script. Perhaps Arabic or Idumean. I didn't know. He promised to let me draw the ostraca from the original."

Just two weeks after his first phone call, Ada received a call from a second stranger, a deliberately mysterious man who identified himself as a member of the Israeli Secret Service, the Shin Bet. It was early November 2001, and the man told her he had a very important object in his possession—very old, inscribed in ancient Hebrew—and would she be willing to have a look at it?

"He wanted me to write an official opinion," she recalled. "And he had already been to [Joseph] Naveh." In her diary, she wrote, "Maybe it is a forgery." She hadn't seen it yet, but the fact that the man was seeking an official opinion from her after having shown it to Naveh, the master, made her suspicious. Still, she agreed to have a look. "The situation was suspicious to me," she recalled. "I don't know why . . . a Shin Bet will show me an inscription? That was somehow suspicious."

Like any Bible-era epigrapher, Ada was no stranger to fakes. Inscribed objects from the ancient Hebrew and Phoenician people are much less common than the prolific hieroglyphs left by the Egyptians or the cuneiform of the Babylonians. Whenever an inscription appears in Syro-Palestinian archaeology, it is by definition an important piece, not least because of its scarcity. Experts—from archaeologists to epigraphers—know to be on their guard for forgeries, especially when the object is not from an official excavation. Ada's mentor, Naveh, had published warnings about forged inscriptions.

A week later, according to her diary, she spoke with Naveh, and her suspicion was confirmed. The old professor told her that the same Shin Bet agent had shown him the tablet inscription and that he thought it was fake. And the circumstances had been equally mysterious. Naveh had been summoned to a Jerusalem hotel room to see the tablet. There, he met two people, a man who introduced himself as Tzur and "an Arab youth who never opened his mouth the entire time, so I don't know his name," Naveh later recalled. Tzur told him the tablet was found in a Muslim cemetery outside the Old City in Jerusalem and speculated that it had actually come from the inner sections of the Temple Mount, a politically charged and religiously important location for Israelis and Palestinians. Tzur, Naveh said, "made me promise not to mention [the tablet] or talk about it with anyone, because the life of the Palestinian who found and sold it would be endangered." According to Ada's diary, on the same day Naveh told her the tablet was forged, the mysterious man phoned her again, and offered to send her photographs. She told him she wanted to see the original object, not a picture.

As she related this, she squinted at her diary. "And I called Oded Golan that same day. For what, why did I call him? For the pictures he had promised to let me make, of the ostraca." Eventually, he did bring them to her house. He was in a terrible hurry. She promised to finish copying them quickly.

On the 20th of November 2001, the mysterious agent finally came to her door with photos of the inscribed tablet. He introduced himself as Tzuriel, an ancient Hebrew name that means rock of God. Ada remembered the inscription, but the man's face left almost no impression. "That was very strange, because they asked me later, 'What does he look like?' I remember he had a long face. I couldn't say more than that. Usually I have a good eye for faces. But I can't remember his face! And later they showed me a picture, and asked, 'Is this the man you saw?' I didn't know. It's interesting that there are faces that you can't remember. They are very . . . regular." The mystery man with the forgettable face gave her the photograph of the inscribed stone, asked her to analyze the writing, and went away. The photograph showed a rectangular black stone tablet, with 16 lines of perfectly legible ancient Hebrew. The inscription she does recall. "I thought that the letters were a little similar to the Tel Dan inscription." The Tel Dan inscription is a basalt rock "stele" discovered in 1993 in northern Israel, in the region known as the Upper Galilee. It is theologically and historically significant as the first archaeological object ever found—dated before 500 B.C.E.—confirming the existence of a monarchy claiming David as an ancestor. Ada thought the writing on the tablet looked like ancient Hebrew, but her gut told her something was not right. She could read the inscription, which seemed to refer to repairs to a building, but something about the style of the language itself struck her as wrong, and some individual letters seemed anachronistic. Still, she couldn't say for sure.

"Here," Ada pointed at her handwritten notes from that day's meeting, "here, I wrote that 'I feel that this is a forgery, but I can't prove it.'" The very next day, Ada received a phone call from yet another man she didn't know, Shimon Ilani from a government agency called the Geological Survey of Israel. A geologist, Ilani too had been visited by the mysterious Tzuriel. "And he said he got my phone numbers from Oded Golan. He wanted to know what I thought. And I told him I had a feeling, but I didn't know, because the circumstances were very suspicious. The script was not bad. I could somehow put it between Phoenician and Hebrew and very early times."

Ada's date book indicates that from the 26th to the 29th of November, the mystery man phoned her three more times. He seemed to be in a great hurry and yet was unwilling to cooperate with her request to see the actual tablet. Finally, he relented. He carried into her kitchen a package containing a black stone tablet that looked old but was surprisingly clean and shiny. It was, in fact, a lovely piece. The man let her look at the tablet, but he refused to leave it with her. Ada took more notes and pointed out some suspicious letters she had already noticed in a photograph, in particular a Hebrew letter *he* that looked suspiciously modern in style.

The next day, Shimon Ilani from the Geological Survey of Israel called Ada again. "He was very concerned because I had told the man about the problems with the letter *he*. Shimon Ilani tried to convince me that it was ancient. He said that he would come talk to me, but he didn't." Ada felt that the government geologist was trying to convince her, and she didn't like the pressure. "The mystery I didn't like! The whole circumstances were suspicious somehow. The phone calls, the 'I bring you. I won't bring you.' 'I come to you. I show you.' . . . 'I take it with me. I can't leave it.' I didn't like the mystery." But she needed the money, so she set to writing a report. After conferring with Naveh, she decided she couldn't verify the inscription as genuine. But she made a comparative chart of the individual letters, and in her report Ada stated that she simply wasn't sure what to make of it. The man paid her 1,400 shekels (about $500) for her report. She never saw him again. She took the fee and went on about her life, which at the time was heavy with imminent loss. Her beloved 90-year-old mother was fast deteriorating, and while new grandchildren were being born, they were far away in Australia, and she could not afford to visit them. Naveh, her emotional pillar and mentor, was also getting old and sick. For diversion, she had piles of ancient letters to trace and more and more strays on the door-step to care for.

Ada would see Oded Golan again. (He brought her some inscribed seal impressions to trace in spring 2002, and he was again in a great hurry.) But she didn't connect the impatient Tel Aviv collector and his artifacts and the Shin Bet man with the forgettable face and his inscribed tablet, not at all, until three years later, when a policeman arrived among the myriad cats at her doormat. He carried photo-graphs of men, not ancient letters, for her to compare and identify, and he leaned hard on her rusty, recalcitrant doorbell.

André Lemaire

French scholar André Lemaire is an expert in ancient epigraphy at the Sorbonne. A tall, sallow, almost spectral presence, in his native French he might be described as *sec*—utterly dry and deeply restrained. One of eight sons of a provincial French Catholic farmer, born during World War II, he originally studied for the priesthood and succumbed to the lure of Jerusalem and its antiquities after a youthful summer drive from France to Israel with a pair of seminarians. It was the late 1960s, and he decided to stay in Jerusalem for a while, signing on to do research at the École Biblique. After a year there, Lemaire returned to France, dropped out of the seminary to get married, and entered the Sorbonne to study and eventually teach ancient Semitic epigraphy. In 30 years at that post, he has published hundreds of papers and dozens of books on obscure, rare inscriptions in ancient Hebrew and Aramaic. Lemaire lives mod-estly in suburban Paris, but since the late 1970s, he has been a familiar figure among the antiquaries of Jerusalem and Old Jaffa.

Lemaire is personally inclined to believe in the possibility of unex-pectedly finding something of great significance because of an incident in his own life. "We are completely sure that they [ancient Hebrews] kept precious or semiprecious objects in temple treasuries for centu-ries, for centuries," he told me during an interview at his Paris home. "And myself, I am perhaps more inclined to accept that, because I had an experience when I was young. I was maybe, I don't remember, 16 or 17, and I visited the granary of my grandmother, near the farm where I lived with my parents. And in my grandmother's granary, I found among debris and so on, big sheets of paper. I took them outside, and finally, reading them a little bit, I realized that it was a French Bible from the end of the 16th century." The antique Bible contained a list of names of people from the nearby town who had owned it over the centuries. Lemaire never learned how or why the artifact found its way into the family silo, but he never forgot the fortuitous accident that recovered a piece of history.

In Jerusalem over the years, he combed the shops, hoping to discover rare pieces and occasionally authenticating inscribed objects for owners and interested buyers. Lemaire's willingness to examine and write about objects in private collections had not endeared him to the archaeological academy, however. Lemaire was one scholar who wasn't above publishing objects whose origins were unknown.

In spring 2002, Lemaire was in Israel on one of his regular forays to the Holy Land to seek out newly discovered objects and strengthen his ties with local collectors, scholars, and antiquities dealers. Although Lemaire knew of Oded Golan and his large collection by name, and Golan knew Lemaire's scholarly reputation, the two men had never met, they claim, until that spring evening at collector Shlomo Moussaieff's house.

As Moussaieff bargained with individual visitors over bits of archaeology for sale, Lemaire and Golan talked. Golan told the French professor that he possessed an ossuary with an ancient Hebrew inscription in cursive that he couldn't read. Golan, like any collector in Jerusalem interested in Bible-era objects, had collected a sizeable number of inscribed ossuaries over the years. He asked if Lemaire would like to have a look at one with an inscription he couldn't read. The Frenchman said he would be happy to see it. Lemaire was, he now admits, a bit flattered by the man. "Oded more or less, maybe not using the words, but the meaning was clear, told me he knew my name," Lemaire recalled in an interview in Paris in 2007. "I didn't know him, but he told me he had a collection and he had some inscription he should like to show me. And I told him, I am always interested to see new inscriptions. That's my job, my professional job!" Two weeks later, Lemaire had the opportunity to follow up with Golan as the collector's Tel Aviv apartment. "The vitrines, oh, he showed me very quickly the vitrines," Lemaire recalled. "I looked at a few things. And then he showed me pictures, mainly of his collection of ossuaries. He wanted to show me an inscription. It was in cursive and very difficult for him to read."

Golan laid out a series of photographs of ossuary inscriptions and pointed out the one in cursive ancient Hebrew that he couldn't decipher. While looking at that inscription, Lemaire spied another picture laid out on the table next to it. It was of another inscribed ossuary, and this particular inscription, Lemaire says, caught his eye instantly. In sloppily scrawled but easily decipherable Aramaic, it read, "Ya'akov bar Yosef achui Yeshua," translated as "James, son of Joseph, brother of Jesus." When Lemaire asked Golan about the inscription, the collector casually replied that he had never thought much of it—although he could read it. Lemaire was immediately intrigued because he was something of an expert on the biblical James, having written a book about the early Christian figure described in the Bible as Christ's brother. Golan maintained that he wasn't all that interested in it. For Lemaire, though, this other ossuary, the one that Golan had accidentally shown him, seemed by far the most interesting thing he'd seen in a long time. "Now it is considered the main point, but at this time for Oded, it was not the main point," Lemaire recalled. "That wasn't the ossuary he wanted to show me. That is very key. That is very key."

Lemaire had already made one historic discovery in the Jerusalem antiquities market some two decades before, one that had had profound significance for biblical archaeology, while also making a great deal of money for an anonymous owner. The discovery was so important that his name would have been well known to Oded Golan for that reason alone. In 1981, Lemaire noticed a tiny inscribed ivory pomegranate in a dealer's shop in Jerusalem. It read, "Holy to the priests, belonging to the "T [illegible] h." Lemaire decided that the scratched-away letters between the Hebrew *T* and *h* were, translated, "Temple of Yahweh," and that the tiny hole through its base meant that the pomegranate was likely once an ornament for a small priest's scepter, used in Solomon's Temple.

As Lemaire well knew, any discoveries relating to the First Temple are enormously important, not only for historians but also for religious Christians and Jews who seek verification of biblical history. Lemaire's pomegranate interpretation was thus both politically and archaeologically groundbreaking—and instantly increased the market value of the pomegranate, which was initially offered for sale for $3,000. An anonymous donor for the Israel Museum ultimately paid $550,000 to acquire the piece. By 2002, it had been on display at the museum for nearly 20 years, with a placard in both English and Hebrew explaining its significance. (In the wake of the Golan case, it was reexamined and removed from display as a forgery.)

After finding the pomegranate, Lemaire continued prowling the antiquities shops and collections of Israel, hoping against hope to stumble on another rare piece. A man of science, he knew that the likelihood of finding another object of such great importance was slim. Most biblical scholars work all their lives and never unearth a single sherd (the archaeological term for a bit of broken pottery) or decipher a single phrase that interests the world beyond the academy. But Lemaire was deeply ambitious. Having tasted the fruits of spectacular discovery once, he longed to experience it again. When he spotted the picture of Golan's "James" ossuary, it is unlikely that his heart actually skipped a beat because Lemaire is a rather cool man, but he certainly felt an unusual amount of excitement. To find an ossuary with the names Jesus, Joseph, and James on it was almost too good to be true. Almost. But quite possibly, it was both good and true. Lemaire asked to see the ossuary itself, and Golan took him to another location in Tel Aviv, a warehouse where he stored antiquities that he didn't display in his Tel Aviv apartment. There, Lemaire examined the small, simple limestone box—20 inches long, 12 inches high, and 10 inches wide, decorated on one side with a small rosette and on the other with a scratched inscription—and found it much like the thousands of other such boxes around Jerusalem dating from the 1st century C.E.

Back in France, armed with pictures of the box, the French scholar set to work researching the probability that the James on the box could be the New Testament James who was the leader of the Jerusalem branch of the early Christian church. He based his interpretation that it was this James on statistical calculations, which were in turn based on assumptions about the number of adult males living in Jerusalem during the 90 years when ossilegium was common. He determined that only 20 men in that time period who also had a father named Joseph and a brother named Jesus could have been named James. The clincher was that on only one other ossuary ever studied was a brother mentioned—indicating to Lemaire that the James whose bones had lain in this ossuary had had a very important brother indeed. Lemaire decided to date the box itself to 62 C.E., the year the biblical James died.

When Lemaire told Golan that he wanted to publish a paper on the ossuary in French, Golan urged him to publish in English, "because," Lemaire recalled, "he doesn't read French." Lemaire chose to publish his first article about the ossuary in the popular English-language magazine *Biblical Archaeology Review* (*BAR*)—the same magazine that had published his interpretation of the ivory pomegranate 20 years prior.

When Lemaire told him about the James Ossuary, Shanks was so excited that he personally arranged for two researchers at the Geological Survey of Israel to authenticate the ossuary's inscription as well. The main business of the Geological Survey, or GSI, is mapping Israeli mineral and water resources. But certain scientists employed by the GSI were known to have an interest in private collections, and Shanks knew they would be happy to examine an important but unprovenanced find. The geologists examined the James Ossuary's patina—the natural coating that builds up on objects over time. After a single day of tests, the geologists said it was consistent with 2,000-year-old stone and didn't appear to contain any modern materials.

Shanks then turned to the task of getting backup for Lemaire's epigraphic conclusion, and first on his list was Ada Yardeni. According to Ada's datebook, on September 15, 2002, Susan Singer, an associate of Hershel Shanks, called to invite her to a dinner with Hershel in Jerusalem in two weeks. Ada knew Shanks "superficially," she says, and had written occasionally for *BAR*. The invitation flattered her, and she accepted. They met at a Jerusalem restaurant, joined by a classics professor from Hebrew University.

"Hershel saw me before we went inside and he said, 'You know, Ada, we have something very important to talk about.' I thought he meant the stone tablet. I said, 'Well yes, I think I know what you mean.' And then he said, 'Ya'akov.' And I said, 'Why Ya'akov?'" She didn't think of the ossuary, because, she says, she didn't know Jesus had a brother named James. Then Shanks told her about the ossuary, and insisted it was very important. "He tried to pressure me to go to Oded and draw the original. I said, 'I can't leave my mother. My mother is 95, and I cannot leave her alone to go to Tel Aviv.' And he said, 'Look, it is important.' " Shanks offered to pay her cab fare to Tel Aviv and back.

Ada reluctantly agreed, but went home after the dinner feeling troubled. "I couldn't sleep. Somehow it bothered me. I had a bad feeling about the whole thing—I don't know why. My intuition is very, very strong. And I had a really bad feeling about the whole thing. I phoned Oded Golan Sunday morning and ask him if I can come to see this ossuary. And he said I should come the same day, in the afternoon, because he was going to put the ossuary in Shanks's magazine, soon."

Ada left her aged mother at home, and took a taxi for the one- hour trip from Jerusalem to Tel Aviv. Shanks and Golan were waiting for her at Golan's apartment when she arrived about three in the afternoon on Sunday, September 29.

"I saw three ossuaries. He put them in the kitchen, where I could really see them under the window where the best light is, because his apartment was very dark. I don't know why, but it was dark and gray. Not nice! Beautiful piano. But I didn't like his apartment."

Oded and Shanks watched as Ada took tracings onto her paper from the ossuary. As soon as she'd finished, Shanks hurried her out the door. "I drew all this, and then Shanks immediately took me to a Xerox machine. We took a taxi to the shop. And in the taxi he asked me, 'Ada do you like adventures?' I said, 'No, I'm not particularly fond of adventures.' " She laughed at the memory. "This was strange you know? Strange."

Months later, when Lemaire's article was finally published by Hershel Shanks, in *BAR*, news of the box was touted in the world media as the first material proof of the existence of Jesus Christ—a man with a brother. The box was shipped to Canada and exhibited at a major museum with great fanfare. The faithful lined up by the tens of thousands to stand before it in silent prayer. A book was written. A documentary was filmed. By then, the saga that the Israeli police described three years later as "the fraud of the century," involving a series of increasingly brazen archaeological forgeries designed to fool scholars and religious believers, was well underway.

Chaim Cohen and the Tablet

Israeli Air Force jets thundered overhead as I approached philologist Chaim Cohen's suburban Beer Sheva house on an otherwise quiet street. When they passed, the distant sound of a muezzin's call echoed over the barren hills from somewhere beyond a guarded checkpoint. While most street signs in Israel are in Hebrew and English letters, in the enclave called Omer where Chaim Cohen resides, not a single street or commercial building sign is in anything but Hebrew script, and it was a challenge to find his house, because he is also a classic absent-minded professor, incapable of giving directions by phone. Beer Sheva is a true desert outpost. To drive to it from the east, one passes for hours through the great yellow void of the Negev, an inhuman, waterless landscape of sand and towering rock. Like the U.S.'s Phoenix, nothing green grows in Beer Sheva naturally, but is the product of man's best efforts to exist in an inhospitable habitat. Somehow, Bedouin live outdoors in the stark beyond, and a few minarets in the distance attest to the presence of settled Palestinian villages nearby.

Like Ada Yardeni, the philologist has a soft heart when it comes to homeless cats, and his front yard was inhabited by many happy felines. A fluffy dog named Doofus had pride of place on a couch indoors. Cohen, 60, is a Brooklyn native who made aliyah to Israel in 1973 ("on the second day of the war," he tells me) and raised two children there. His daughter has a natural talent for micrography—infinitesimal writing. Among her framed projects, she wrote the entire book of Esther on a single piece of paper, in letters smaller than grains of couscous.

Cohen agreed to talk to me on a Sunday afternoon about why he thinks the scholars are all wrong about the Jehoash Tablet. He believes it is a groundbreaking inscription, with never-before-seen grammatical constructions that will change some of the basic assumptions philologists have about ancient Hebrew. He was about to publish a 65-page defense of the tablet in a scholarly journal, which he'd worked on for a year. Cohen studied Assyriology at Columbia, and learned biblical Hebrew and Akkadian, and he became an expert in comparing the two ancient languages. He teaches philology at Ben Gurion University and is every inch a professor. A balding, expansive fellow who recently underwent bariatric surgery to drop some of the 400 pounds he'd been carrying most of his adult life, he was wearing black pants and Crocs, had four different-colored pens tucked into in his left breast pocket, and wore a kippa. He is observant and Orthodox.

Cohen has only seen the Jehoash Tablet in pictures and videos, and he will only speak to the philology—the language—not to its physical or geological properties. He works in the same university as Avigdor Hurowitz, one of the members of the IAA committee that examined the tablet's writing and found it historically unsound. Cohen says that he was "excited" when he first heard about the tablet, but didn't express himself on it until after Oded Golan—whom he'd never met—asked for his opinion in 2004, after Golan had been indicted for forgery. He went on to say:

> The reason why he called me the first time was that an amateur who knew Golan had visited me and showed me a copy of the tablet inscription and said he had some ideas. I told him he was wrong. Then I got a call from Golan. He said, "What do you think?" And I said, "With all due respect, I don't know you, and I'm not willing to talk to you

until I'm convinced you're not a forger." I said, "I am not willing to tell you things that you may use in your defense." So, I asked him about the forgery tools and he convinced me he was not the forger. I don't think he has the knowledge. I don't know if he's honest or dishonest. I don't have an opinion about what's going on. But I do want people to know there have been many cases in the past of good inscriptions that have been dealt with in an illegal manner, and the fact that they have been dealt with illegally does not mean they are forgeries.

Cohen looked at the tablet, and, based on his knowledge of comparative ancient languages, he found the word usages perfectly consistent with 7th-century B.C.E. grammar. Cohen claims that the term *batqu*, cognate with Hebrew *bedeq* in the tablet, is used in Akkadian texts to refer to making renovations:

> Now, my claim is that the word in this inscription means "to renovate." Okay? I have some evidence in biblical Hebrew for it. But my main evidence is Akkadian. Okay, it's a totally different word in Akkadian. But it's a very clear link to this word in biblical Hebrew, semantically. . . . Semantics also includes the comparison between similar genres and again there are no other building inscriptions as such in biblical Hebrew, so we have to go outside biblical Hebrew to find the same genre. When we do that, the greatest number of building inscriptions, royal building inscriptions in the ancient Near East come from Mesopotamia and are written specially in the Semitic language. They're also written in Sumerian, but the main ones for us in discussing the Jehoash inscription are in Akkadian. And once you do that, you see the main term for renovation is in fact the same word.

Cohen worked out a complex analysis of the inscription of the Jehoash Tablet, and his 65-page critique was published by Sheffield Press, in England, the same press that routinely publishes works by so-called minimalists who debunk the entire Bible as fiction.

> I have never said it is definitely not a forgery, but if it's a forgery it's brilliant. He chose to work in a genre that didn't exist in biblical Hebrew! He also chose to write 16 lines of text! Why in heaven's name 16 lines? The ossuary was one line. The pomegranate was half a line! Now the scholars I debate about this say he did that because he wanted me to think it's authentic.

Cohen admitted he was "excited" when he first heard about the tablet, because of its implications about the First Temple. I asked Cohen whether he was letting his religious beliefs color his scholarship in this regard. He denied it.

> I would tell you this. This goes to my own persona here. I am a religious Jew. I certainly do not hide that by any means. And I'm Orthodox in my practice. I completely separate my religious faith from my

scholarship. The scholarship in Israel is basically conservative—and not accepting, for the most part, postmodern ideas. That's what [conservative] has come to mean these days. There's a lot of postmodern research going on outside of Israel. And Israeli scholars—not all, but most—find themselves resisting postmodern trends, mainly on the basis of language. In other words, what we have learned is to be very appreciative from the scholarly point of view of the biblical consonantal text. Not the vowels. The vowels are late. But the consonants.

Later, he gave me a tour of his basement library, where he has 20,000 volumes, among them his most prized possession, a rare 19th-century volume of early Assyriology. His store of knowledge is clearly immense. He has no axe to grind. He's a mild-mannered professor, with a point of view that his colleagues simply can't understand. He says it comes down to the fact that it is extremely hard for him to turn away from a 16-line inscription in ancient Hebrew, provenanced or not.

"I have seen and I know all the inscriptions from Israeli excavations," he says.

Almost all are provenanced, but I use them all. I use the Moussaieff inscriptions in my classes. I have grave doubts that they are forgeries. Philologically, in some ways they are more beautiful than most. From the point of view of biblical Hebrew, the Moussaieff ostracon—the widow's plea and the three-shekel contribution—are two of the most beautiful inscriptions in the language.

Cohen eventually testified for the defense.

Cohen's 65-page essay in defense of the Jehoash Tablet formed the basis of some of the defense questioning at Golan's trial, according to other linguists who were prosecution witnesses. Did Oded Golan really come across him, as Cohen believes, by pure coincidence? Or did the collector do his homework and decide that, of all the respected philologists in Israel, the Orthodox, kindly, and deeply learned gentleman from Brooklyn, who gave up New York and made aliyah to dwell in the remote desert town of Beer Sheva, who has trucked 20,000 books, many quite rare, into the basement of his humble suburban house, like a real-life Fitzcarraldo, would be perhaps a good prospect for a sympathetic interpretation of his tablet?

That is what Tel Aviv University's Israel Finkelstein and Detective Amir Ganor would propose. For them, the carefully thought-out selection of scholars was part of the forger's genius. "I'm telling you, they are the cleverest people, the most sophisticated people, because they knew how to exploit people like this." Finkelstein said. "I think that all of them were puppets played by those people. They wouldn't come to me to authenticate something. They went to the people who they knew in advance would be willing to do this because of their convictions. That's the trick there, you see? It's a highly sophisticated game. I would be extremely surprised if there was more than that here."

Not Another Roadside Attraction
The Holy Land Experience in America

MARK I. PINSKY

For some evangelical Christians, faith is the belief in things *seen* as well as unseen. The Holy Land Experience, a Bible-based theme park in Orlando, Florida, serves as just such a concrete illustration of Jesus' experience of 1st-century Jerusalem Herod's Temple (see fig. 1). It is, in a sense, the word made flesh—or at least weathered stucco. The creators of this polished, vest-pocket attraction, located not far from Universal Studios Florida, Sea World, and Disney World, designed it in part for those without the means to travel to the Middle East or those who had security concerns. As an American Protestant pilgrimage site, the Holy Land Experience is not unique; it is deeply ingrained in a phenomenon chronicled by many, including Timothy Beal in *Roadside Religion: In Search of the Sacred, the Strange, and the Substance of Faith* (2005).

Central Florida is a place where men and women dream big dreams, including grandiose visions about religion and faith. Some of these materialize: glass-walled megachurches, a Catholic shrine, and worldwide ministries. But many more dreams do not succeed, such as a live, year-round, nine-million-dollar musical production of *Ben-Hur* at the Orange County Convention Center that flopped. Others seem to succeed at first, only to crash and burn—or run their course and fizzle, like the New Testament–based musical *The Rock and the Rabbi*. A few dreamers are cast out of their own creations by the donors and supporters who helped build them. Marvin Rosenthal, who was born Jewish in Philadelphia and later converted to Christianity, had two big dreams. For most of his adult life, he has worked to lead other Jews in the United States and Israel to Jesus, while at the same time educating Christians about the Jewish roots of their faith. And in late middle age, in order to help accomplish both dreams, he moved his ministry to central Florida to build the Holy Land Experience.

Author's note: This essay is adapted from Pinsky 2006. Used by permission of Westminster John Knox Press.

Figure 1. Façade of Herodian Temple, with Qumran caves at right. Photo by Sarah M. Brown.

Rosenthal converted to Christianity as a teenager in the late 1940s, together with his brothers and mother, after their father and husband left their home, and missionaries prayed with them. Marvin led a color-ful early life, including a stint in the U.S. Marines and some time as a professional dancer. Ultimately, he married a Christian, was ordained a Baptist minister, and spent much of his early career as a pulpit minister and church speaker, ultimately joining the Friends of Israel Missionary and Relief Society in New Jersey, an old-line organization devoted to converting the Jews. (These groups, like the "Hebrew Christians," some with roots in the 19th century, were largely eclipsed by higher-profile efforts in the 1970s and 1980s such as "Jews for Jesus" and "Messianic Jews," both of which tried to integrate Jewish ritual practice and He-brew prayer with Christian theology; Rosenthal steadfastly opposed all of them.) After a doctrinal dispute with Friends of Israel over the timing of the world-ending Rapture, Rosenthal left to found his own ministry to the Jews, Zion's Hope, and moved to Orlando in 1989. His dream was to build a "living museum" of 1st-century Jerusalem. Within five years, his dream was a reality.

When guests enter Holy Land, Rosenthal promised in 1996, "They will leave the 21st century behind and embark on a journey that is un-equalled anywhere in the world. It will be an experience that is edu-cational, historical, theatrical, inspirational, and evangelical" (cited in

Figure 2. Tourists entering theme-park gate. Photo by Sarah M. Brown.

Pinsky 2001a). Rosenthal turned to a professional theme-park design firm, ITEC Entertainment Corp., which has worked for major attractions such as Universal Studios Florida, as well as for the Kennedy Space Center.

For a Saturday morning, the small, sunny market square in the Old City of "Jerusalem" is often quiet—almost too quiet. Nearby, the Temple Mount area is equally deserted: no Arabs, no Jews, no Israeli soldiers. The only noise, before 10 a.m., comes from above: cars and trucks hurtling down Interstate 4 toward Orlando's world-famous tourist corridor linking Disney World, Universal Studios, and Sea World. But even here, in one of central Florida's newer theme parks, thousands of miles from the embattled region it tries to re-create, the Sabbath peace is short-lived. Soon, tourists and curiosity seekers swarm through a massive entryway, modeled after Jerusalem's Lion's and Damascus gates (see fig. 2), as they have in large numbers since the park's February 5, 2001 opening. They pay for tickets fed into high-tech, electronic turnstiles, like those at the other theme parks. Guides, dressed as 1st-century residents of the Old City, greet them with a hearty "shalom." The scenes elsewhere in the park look innocent enough. A bearded man sounds a shofar—the ram's horn—in front of a six-story, scale model representation of Herod's Temple.

At the Holy Land Experience, the already-pervasive Christian culture of America's traditional Bible belt and the more aggressively evangelical forces of the modern Sunbelt collide—with a force that made not just

Jews but even some Christians uneasy. The week the $16 million, 15-acre attraction opened, there was barely-controlled chaos. Paying customers had to be turned away as the park filled each day before noon. Under a winter sun, journalists and camera crews from around the world swirled through the crowds, searching for yahoos—anything that would make Americans look like morons and cement Orlando's image as the capital of kitsch—with considerable success. Even the Israeli daily *Ma'ariv* and Israeli television showed up. Central Florida's talk radio was dominated by the park's opening. In addition to widespread coverage in print and broadcast media at the time, Holy Land has attracted academic interest in the years since its opening (e.g., Branham's "The Temple That Won't Quit" [2008] and Long's "The Holy Land and Its Bible in Orlando" [2009]).

Outside the park's front gate, the Jewish Defense League's Irv Rubin shouted insults about "soul-snatchers" through a bullhorn—a reference to charges that the park's primary goal was to lure unsuspecting Jews in hopes of converting them—making all the network newscasts. And, not surprisingly, jokes about Holy Land soon began to pop up on late-night TV, mocking the latest offering from the state that, in 2000, was unable to run a proper presidential election. Why the furor? How was this theme park different from all other theme parks? The bizarre combination of religion and entertainment spectacle—the sacred and the trivial—accounted for much of the hubbub. The weather was nice, there were dramatic visuals, and no big national or international stories were competing for the headlines.

Jewish symbols, texts, and prayers abounded at the park, beginning with its gift store, just inside the gate. The Old Scroll Shop was filled with skullcaps, prayer shawls, shofars, mezuzahs, menorahs, braided Havdalah candles,[1] and Passover plates—all imported from Israel—along with official Israeli maps and archaeological guides to historic sites. The park's décor included a display of what appeared to be a lacquered section of Hebrew Scripture parchment. Among the books on display were some serious titles, such as the Penguin Classics edition of Josephus' *The Jewish War*, Paul Johnson's *A History of the Jews*, and Thomas Cahill's *The Gifts of the Jews*, alongside missionary titles such as *Christ in the Passover*. *The Diary of Anne Frank* was next to a biography of the Apostle Paul, and Chaim Potok's popular novel *The Chosen* was opposite evangelical materials such as *What Every Jewish Person Should Ask*, promoting conversion to Christianity. Not so much an eclectic religious display, it seemed to be one lacing evangelical hooks with Jewish bait. Also crowding the shelves were music CDs in Hebrew and books produced by Messianic leaders such as Mitch Glaser, of Chosen People Ministries. The hottest-selling piece of jewelry in Methuselah's

---

1. Special multiwick candles are used for the Jewish ceremony of Havdalah, which marks the end of the Sabbath.

Mosaics gallery was a silver Star of David with a cross in the center, to Jews an egregious example of religious syncretism. At the nearby Oasis Café, the menu on the wall—which included Goliath burgers and Hebrew National hot dogs—was posted on what looked like a stylized open Torah scroll.

Dramatic presentations at the park touched a nerve with central Florida rabbis. One, "The Wilderness Tabernacle," was a sound-and-light show that mixed laser and special-effect fireworks to create a fiery pillar of light, along with taped narration, slides, and live actors in a faithful re-creation of the desert worship experience of the children of Israel following the exodus from Egyptian bondage. Much was taken directly from the book of Exodus, with prayers such as the Yom Kippur candle blessing, chanted correctly and, though no acknowledgment was provided, hinting at the participation of someone knowledgeable about Judaism. But at the very end of the presentation came the hook: The narrator, speaking as an aged Levite priest, wondered if this sacred worship experience had merely been a "rehearsal" or a "shadow" of what was to come for the Jewish people. Then a slide of the nativity was spotlighted and a singer intoned, "Behold the lamb of God, who taketh away the sins of the world." Then the lights came up.

No rabbis were among the 150 clergy and others who previewed the park prior to its official opening. Whether this was just an oversight, as park officials insist, or something more calculated, was never clear. Rosenthal says the invitations were not sent but rather were printed in his ministry's magazine, *Zion's Fire* (to which few if any rabbis subscribed).[2] After the opening, the rabbis balked at paying their way in, reluctant to have their entry money used to evangelize Jews. Rabbi Daniel Wolpe, then spiritual leader of the Southwest Orlando Jewish Congregation and at the time president of the Greater Orlando Board of Rabbis, was appalled when he learned of the use of Hebrew prayers. "That's disgusting," he said. "It's quite a different thing to create a monument that celebrates your tradition than it is to create a monument that is to be used to proselytize people outside of your tradition."[3] But he and other rabbis were in a bind when journalists began calling, not having visited the park themselves.

Most of the media questions about the park were not about proselytizing. And Rosenthal, a man who had devoted his entire adult life to bringing Jews to Jesus, dodged and downplayed that goal. Rosenthal's purpose—to share the Gospel with the Jews—was clear and unambiguous. He had repeated it in several interviews from 1997–2001—stressing it in his ministry's magazine and literature and, more critically, in fund-raising materials aimed at the Christian evangelical community.

2. A preview of the current issue can be seen at http://www.zionshope.org/link_ZF_preview_3col.aspx.
3. See Pinsky 2001b.

The money raised to build the park came from a donor base cultivated for that purpose over more than a decade. One of the first guests through the turnstiles on opening day was Lloyd Locklier, a Bradenton, Florida, retiree and longtime financial supporter of Zion's Hope, who told me he saw the park's sponsoring ministry as "a mission to the Jews—to win them to Christ."

However, the image of a Christian theme park whose ultimate purpose is to draw Jews from their faith was not the one Rosenthal wanted to convey to the national and international media. So when reporters asked him if conversion of the Jews was his goal, he replied with studied sophistry. There would be no buttonholing or tract distribution on the grounds, he said firmly. "Visitors have every right to be left alone." The purpose of The Holy Land Experience was to be "a living Bible museum" and to share the good news of Christianity, "to sow the seed of the word of God," he said, adding that he was including—but not targeting—Jews. It was true, in a way. The park's promotional literature promised "a wholesome, family-oriented, educational and entertainment facility, where people can come and be encouraged, instructed and reinforced in their faith."

The reality was that, far more than Jews, Rosenthal needed Christian residents of central Florida and some fraction of the 43 million tourists drawn to Orlando each year by the major theme parks to make his park financially viable. In the Sunbelt, many evangelicals prefer something more tangible and life-like to reinforce their faith. A month after the park opened, Rosenthal insisted that Jews from around the world were visiting, despite the negative comments from Jewish and some mainline Christian leaders. Those who attacked Holy Land as a lure to gull unsuspecting Jewish visitors into converting missed the point: the park, he said, was designed to be a fund-raising vehicle, almost entirely dependent on Christian patronage, in order to bankroll Zion's Hope. That organization's sole, direct, and historic purpose was to "present Christian truth to the Jewish people and the Jewishness of the Bible to Christian people," in the words of its magazine, *Zion's Fire*.[4] A Zion's Hope video sold in the gift shop put it this way: "As a missionary agency, Zion's Hope places personnel in strategic places throughout the world with the supreme task of reaching Jewish people in the world God so loves with the message of Christ's saving grace."[5]

Indeed, after a while, Rosenthal's dissembling on this point became too much, even for some area Christian leaders, who complained that Rosenthal—under pressure, to be sure—was denying his life's purpose

---

4. See the "History and Legacy" section of the Zion's Hope official Web site: http://www.zionshope.org/history/.

5. For more about Zion's Hope and its mission, see the "Missions" section of the Zion's Hope official Web site: http://www.zionshope.org/ZH_missions.aspx.

with the same vigor that the Apostle Peter denied Jesus on the eve of the crucifixion. A local Southern Baptist evangelist, who asked not to be quoted by name, said that Rosenthal's comments created a "credibility problem" in the Christian community. Within weeks of Holy Land's opening, its hiring practices also opened an additional rift among Christian groups. Word spread that Pentecostals and charismatics (who believe in ecstatic forms of worship like "speaking in tongues" and faith healing by "laying on of hands") need not apply for jobs at the park, not even to sell hot dogs. Such worship practices are anathema to fundamentalist Baptists like Rosenthal, though as many as half of evangelicals consider themselves Pentecostals or charismatic, especially in the South. "We are not charismatics," he said. "We love them. We appreciate them. But we would not offer them a job."

As might be expected, the whole idea of melding entertainment and evangelism also provoked criticism, some of it derisive, in the local press. When plans for Holy Land were first announced, one *Orlando Sentinel* columnist suggested a ride called a Holy Roller Coaster. Another thought a better name for Holy Land might be Cross Country, or perhaps Six Flags Over Israel, jibes Rosenthal shrugged off. "Our purpose was to spread the word of God," he said years later, "but of course we needed to make it pay." More serious criticisms, some from other evangelical Christians, hit a nerve, especially from those concerned about Holy Land's potential to trivialize faith. Quentin Schultze, professor of communication at Calvin College and author of *Communicating for Life: Christian Stewardship in Community and Media* (Schultze 2000), said in an interview with the author that an attraction like Holy Land "makes religion more superficial and transitory," and contributes to a "consumerization" of faith. When people visit a tourist attraction, he said, they bring with them "a tourist mindset, which is: spend money and have a good time" (cited in Pinsky 2001a: 4).

John Dominic Crossan, a historian of 1st-century Christianity and co-founder of the controversial Jesus Seminar, moved to the small central Florida town of Clermont after his retirement from the faculty of DePaul University in Chicago. The author of more than 20 books (for example, Crossan 1994, 1995), Crossan voiced concern about the park before its opening. Any depiction of Jesus' life and death that used the New Testament as its sole source, rather than presenting a fuller context of available sources, ran the risk of appearing anti-Semitic, he said. The evangelical view of Jesus' crucifixion, he said in an interview with the author, "is that the bad Jews convinced the good Romans to do their dirty work for them" (cited in Pinsky 2001c: 61).

Several weeks later, as he toured the park with me, Crossan's fears were more than justified. He expressed that he was impressed by some of the park's physical attractions and exhibits, including the six-story façade of Herod's Temple (fig. 1), calling it "a pretty good reproduction":

and he termed the 45-by-25-foot scale model of ancient Jerusalem (fig. 3) "first class." But a talk given at the model by a guide was more amusing than scholarly, he said, closer to a sermon than a lecture. Crossan, an Irish-born former Catholic priest, called it "a commercial for Christianity over Judaism and also for Protestantism over Catholicism," in particular with respect to the location of Jesus' tomb. And as his visit wore on, Crossan became increasingly distressed by the content of the presentations. The Wilderness Tabernacle would have been more honest, he said, if it stated that the Levitical, sacrificial traditions observed in the desert gave rise to two legitimate traditions in the years following destruction of the Second Temple—rabbinic Judaism and Christianity—rather than implying that one was superior to the other. Most disturbing were images in a movie, *The Seed of Promise*, shot in Israel in high-definition video. Images of a crucifixion are intercut with scenes of the Romans sacking the temple in 70 C.E. "It's a most ghastly justification for the destruction of Jerusalem," he said. The movie also depicts Roman soldiers appearing to spare from Jewish sacrifice a lamb—obviously Jesus. "A lamb saved by the Romans from being slaughtered? What's the message? The destruction of Jerusalem was God's vengeance, justice or retribution for the Jews' crucifixion of Jesus, the lamb. What the hell kind of God is that?" That interpretation came straight from the Book of Matthew, Crossan said. "The Jews killed God, so the destruction of the temple is God's judgment against them." In an interview with me, Rosenthal reacted sharply to Crossan's interpretation: "That was not in our mind," he insisted. "That was not what we're presenting in our film. . . . The Romans were responsible for Jesus' death" (cited in Pinsky 2001c: 61).

In the years that followed the park's opening, there were ups and downs in the relationship between Holy Land and the Jews. There were signs of deference to Jewish sensitivities, although they may be coincidental. An announced plan to add a live drama of Jesus' driving the moneychangers from the temple, one of the more inflammatory and arguably anti-Semitic episodes in the New Testament, never materialized. And the annual Easter season reenactment of Jesus' crucifixion (fig. 4) was constructed to begin with the Via Dolorosa, eliminating the equally controversial scenes with the high priest and of crowds of Jews calling on Pilate to execute Jesus.

But in 2002, Holy Land expanded, opening an additional attraction, a $9.5 million scriptorium (fig. 5) to hold part of the biblical antiquities collection, valued at $20–$100 million, of the late Chicago financier Robert D. Van Kampen. In addition to paying for the domed, copper-sided structure built to resemble a miniature Byzantine basilica, the Van Kampen Foundation agreed to lend the Scriptorium its 12,000 artifacts and manuscripts. These included Babylonian cuneiform tablets from 2200 B.C.E., a Coptic Bible from 4th-century C.E. Egypt, a 1611

Figure 3. Scale model of 1st-century Jerusalem. Photo by Sarah M. Brown.

King James Bible, and a Bible from one of Gutenberg's presses. What troubled Jews in central Florida and further afield was the announcement that the Van Kampen collection also included 10–20 complete Torah scrolls—containing the Five Books of Moses—and fragments of others, including one from the historic Jewish community of Kaifeng, China.

Over the centuries, many Torah scrolls had been stolen and looted; and during World War II, the Nazis seized hundreds, if not thousands of sacred scrolls from European synagogues and communities. Naturally, the foundation's officials and curators were asked about the provenance of the Jewish artifacts. They said there was none, raising serious questions about the manner in which they were acquired. This brought up a larger issue. "A Torah should not be a display item," said Rabbi Wolpe, in an interview with the author, regardless of how it is acquired. "It is a holy item, and it should be used in this way. If a synagogue took a holy item of another faith and displayed it like it was a museum piece, the other faith would be justifiably upset. We would be justifiably upset to see something holy to us used as a museum piece."[6] Rosenthal's response was that he had seen plenty of Jewish ritual art on display in museums in Israel, including the Dead Sea Scrolls.

---

6. See Pinsky 2001b.

Figure 4. Actor playing Jesus carrying the cross. Photo by Sarah M. Brown.

There were other controversies involving the Holy Land Experience, some not involving the Jews. Orange County Tax Assessor Bill Donegan ruled that the property was a tourist attraction and theme park, rather than a non-profit educational and cultural facility. This forced Rosenthal to file suit, which was ultimately successful, the court ruling that Holy Land had been denied due process. Donegan vowed to appeal the decision, he said, in order to avoid setting a precedent for other religious organizations who might want to start their own attractions. Ultimately, the Florida legislature passed (and then Governor Jeb Bush signed) a special law exempting Holy Land from any future taxation—a testament to the political influence of its supporters.[7]

But the park's biggest problem, one that wouldn't go away, was the brutal and unrelenting competition for the tourist dollar in Orlando. Holy Land's big crowds following the opening—308,000 in the first 11

---

7. See "Holy Land Tax Effort Dropped," *Orlando Sentinel*, June 14, 2006. Online: http://articles.orlandosentinel.com/2006-06-14/news/STBRIEFS14_4_1_holy -land-bill-donegan-property.

Figure 5. The Scriptorium, a Byzantine-looking building, overlooking a lake. Photo by Sarah M. Brown.

months, according to Rosenthal—melted over time, especially during the unbearably hot and humid summer months. When the attraction opened, Rosenthal said it would need between 180,000–200,000 visitors per year to break even. For four and a half years, except for a severe drop following the terrorist attacks of September 11, 2001, Rosenthal said that Holy Land averaged 220,000 visitors a year. The three hurricanes that struck central Florida in 2004, while doing relatively little physical damage to Holy Land, devastated ticket sales.

Despite such a promising start, things did not end well for Marvin Rosenthal and The Holy Land Experience. He parted ways with the park on July 20, 2005. The dreamer was expelled, albeit with a separation agreement; asked to clean out his desk, he left Holy Land for the last time as its chief operating officer. Also departing were his wife, Marbeth, his son David, and his brother Stanley. "We just had a difference of opinion, the board and I," Rosenthal said, in an interview with me. Holy Land was taken over by Scott Pierre, head of the Van Kampen foundation and also chair of the theme park's board. Pierre said the vote to dismiss the Rosenthals was unanimous. "Marv's strength really was in the ministerial arena," said Pierre, Van Kampen's son-in-law.[8]

In the end, what happened to Marvin Rosenthal is that his second dream, The Holy Land Experience, eclipsed his first dream, converting

8. See Jackson 2005b.

the Jews. One newspaper article compared Rosenthal to a circus ring-
master, suggesting the only thing the showman lacked was a top hat.[9]
He liked the image so much he said that he thought about going out and
buying one. "I believe I was an able administrator and a good CEO," he
said, while refusing to criticize Pierre or the board.

If he made a serious mistake, Rosenthal said, it was treating the expanded park staff as his mission family, which made him reluctant to
make cutbacks when attendance declined. He still wished local rabbis
had come to Holy Land to see The Wilderness Experience. With great
feeling, he said he would have opened the park at night for them without charge to avoid controversy about contributing to evangelism; and
he wouldn't have minded if they left before the final minutes of the
Christian message. The park could still succeed, he said. If it expanded,
and operators could figure out more activities for children, it could ultimately draw 600,000–800,000 visitors a year. Perhaps. But on October
12, 2005, Holy Land's new executive director, Dan Hayden, announced
that the park would be closed on Sundays, "to give the staff of 225 time
to spend that day in worship with their families."[10] Not coincidentally,
the action would also reduce operating expenses.

In 2007, Trinity Broadcasting Network—the world's largest religious television system—bought a Christian television station in Orlando and, several months later, purchased the Holy Land Experience
in a complex, $37 million deal.[11] The change in ownership, all parties
agreed, was more a handover than a takeover. It erased the park's debt
and at the same time provided a nationwide (and worldwide) promotional platform to remedy sagging attendance. "We want to take this
ministry to a worldwide market," said Paul Crouch Jr., Trinity's executive vice president, and the oldest son of its founders, Paul and Jan
Crouch. "We want to build studios on the site, upgrade the shows and
program, and use the park as a 'back lot' for production."[12] The arrangement also represented a theological turnaround for Holy Land. Founder
Rosenthal was a Baptist. Trinity and its founders were avowedly Pentecostals, believers in faith healing, speaking in tongues, and what has
become known as the "prosperity gospel." Jewish products and artifacts
quickly vanished from the gift store.

The network's founders, Paul and Jan Crouch offered public and
private reassurance to longtime park employees; but the couple, their
extended family, and assorted cronies streamed through the park's replica of Jerusalem's gates like an invading horde, lopping dozens off the

---

9. See Pinsky 2002.
10. See Jackson 2005a.
11. See the current Web site of The Holy Land Experience: http://www
.holylandexperience.com/.
12. See Pinsky 2007a.

payroll and pillaging the park.[13] On their first live broadcast from the park, Jan mentioned that Jesus had once healed her pet chicken. The Crouches were, one laid-off staffer said, "A cross between *The Sopranos* and *The Beverly Hillbillies*."[14]

Neither historical recreation nor theme parks is terra incognito to Trinity. The network's headquarters in Costa Mesa, California, include a replica of the Via Dolorosa, a street in old Jerusalem believed to be the path Jesus walked to his crucifixion.[15] In 1995, the network purchased the estate of the late country music artist Conway Twitty outside of Nashville. Trinity paid $2.75 million for Twitty City and spent an additional $10 million turning the spread into a Christian-music entertainment park called Trinity MusicCity USA.[16]

---

13. Pinsky 2007b.
14. Pinsky 2007b.
15. A photo appears on the Trinity Broadcasting Network Web site: http://www.tbn.org/about-us/southern-california.
16. See http://www.tbn.org/about-us/tennessee.

References

Beal, T.
2005   *Roadside Religion: In Search of the Sacred, the Strange, and the Substance of Faith*. Boston: Beacon.
Branham, J. R.
2008   The Temple That Won't Quit: Constructing Sacred Space in Orlando's Holy Land Experience Theme Park. *Harvard Divinity Bulletin* 36: 18–31.
Crossan, J. D.
1994   *Jesus—A Revolutionary Biography*. San Francisco: HarperSanFrancisco.
1995   *Who Killed Jesus? Exposing the Roots of Anti-Semitism in the Gospel Story of the Death of Jesus*. San Francisco: HarperSanFrancisco.
Jackson, J. W.
2005a   Holy Land Attraction Will Close on Sundays. *Daily Press*, October 13. On-line: http://www.dailypress.com/go2-ver3-tourismnews-holylandsunday,0,7946378.story.
2005b   Holy Land Founder Resigns. *Orlando Sentinel*, July 21. On-line: http://articles.orlandosentinel.com/2005-07-21/news/HOLYLAND21_1_david-rosenthal-holy-land-experience-new-ministry.
Long, B. O.
2009   The Holy Land and Its Bible in Orlando. Pp. 257–81 in *Performing Memory in Biblical Narrative and Beyond*, ed. A.Brenner and F. H. Polak. Sheffield: Phoenix.
Pinsky, M. I.
2001a   The CT Review: "Six Flags Over Israel": An Evangelical Alternative to Disney World Makes a Stormy Debut in Central Florida. *Christianity*

Today 45. On-line: http://www.christianitytoday.com/ct/2001/march5
/34.101.html.

2001b Holy Land Theme Park Concerns Jewish Leaders. *Sun Sentinel*, January 12. On-line: http://articles.sun-sentinel.com/2001-01-12/news/
0101111207_1_bible-based-theme-park-holy-land-experience-rabbi-
daniel-wolpe.

2001c Soul-Snatchers in the Sun Belt. *Moment* 26: 38–43, 58–63.

2002   Holy Land Set to Open $12 Million Attraction. *Orlando Sentinel*,
August 16. On-line: http://articles.orlandosentinel.com/2002-08-16/
travel/0208160407_1_holy-land-experience-optics-curtain.

2006   *A Jew among the Evangelicals: A Guide for the Perplexed*. Louisville:
Westminster John Knox.

2007a Holy Land's Debts Erased in Christian Network Deal. *Orlando Sentinel*,
June 6. On-line: http://articles.orlandosentinel.com/2007-06-06/news/
TRINITY06_1_holy-land-trinity-broadcasting-network-paul-crouch.

2007b Scores Lose Jobs as Holy Land Undergoes Extreme Makeover. *Orlando Sentinel*, October 21. On-line: http://articles.orlandosentinel
.com/2007-10-21/news/holyland21_1_trinity-broadcasting-holy-land
-prosperity-gospel.

Schultze, Q.

2000   *Communicating for Life: Christian Stewardship in Community and
Media*. Grand Rapids: Baker.

PART 5

The Media:
A View from Jerusalem

How It Looks from the Other Side

Ethan Bronner

Last summer, a friend in Jerusalem introduced me to a colleague of his, a biblical scholar named Israel Knohl. My friend said that Knohl was working on an interesting project and there might be a little story in it for me.

My main job, of course, is political coverage for the *New York Times*, but one of the great pleasures of being a foreign correspondent is the broad menu of stories I am both permitted and expected to write—culture, sociology, science, even sports. And in Jerusalem, one of the great sources of stories is archaeology and religion. So I was game.

Knohl and I arranged to have coffee. The story, it turned out, was about a three-foot high stone tablet with 87 lines of Hebrew on it that he was interpreting. The writing dates from the decades before the birth of Jesus. The tablet is broken and the ink is unclear and faded in key spots. But two other scholars had rendered a reading of it with a few lines still to be interpreted. It is mostly a vision of the apocalypse transmitted by the angel Gabriel—and therefore they gave it the name in Hebrew of *Hazon Gavriel*, Gabriel's vision or revelation. It draws heavily from the prophets Daniel, Haggai, and Zechariah.

But the news, at least to Knohl, is that a couple of lines seem to speak of a suffering messiah who will rise after three days. Since this is an issue on which he had worked in the past—he had posited in a book in 2000 the idea of a suffering messiah before Jesus—he saw in *Hazon Gavriel* a key piece of evidence for his thesis.

I agreed that it seemed interesting and began to work. When I sent the story to New York, the editors shared my enthusiasm and put it on the front page one Sunday in early July.[1] That is what we in my business call success.

But it turned out to be only the beginning. I started getting e-mails from people all over the American Bible belt whom I never imagined to be *New York Times* readers. The *Times* Web site has a list of stories that are heavily e-mailed, and this one rose to the very top of the list

---

1. Bronner 2008a.

within 24 hours. Generally, that slot is reserved for stories purporting to tell you how to lose weight, extend the life of your brain through cross-word puzzles, or reduce the stress of travel through melatonin pills and carrot juice. My story stayed at the very top of the list for days. In fact over the following five days, the article on Knohl's stone tablet with the purported suffering messiah was the most e-mailed story in the entire *New York Times* stable, the most trafficked piece of *Times* copy for the better part of a week. Never before or since has a story with my byline had that distinction—although I may have an exclusive on a cure for baldness, so there is still hope.

What was most interesting for me about the publicity is that it seemed to strike a chord with so many that was simply inaccurate. Knohl's point was that, according to scholarly conventional wisdom, in the centuries before Jesus, the idea of a suffering messiah dying for the people's sins and rising from the dead had lost currency. So the story itself, it was widely posited by scholars, had been invented by his followers and cast backwards. Obviously, this was a question of a scholarly dispute rather than a popular or religious one.

But the bulk of e-mail and Web discussion of the story missed the distinction between the scholarly dispute and what was seen as an effort by Jewish scholars to besmirch the uniqueness and sacredness of Jesus Christ. For example: "Here we go again. Another relic pops up of questionable authenticity that one or two experts is saying casts doubts on the unique claims of Christian orthodoxy," Ken Shepherd wrote on a Web site called *News Busters*.

> What's more, it's laughable on its face that one obscure, questionably-interpreted transcript of an alleged angelic annunciation has anything on the public witness of the early church, which based its arguments for the resurrection of Christ from first-hand eyewitness accounts of some 500 people of the risen Jesus and Hebrew scriptures on the person and work of the Messiah.[2]

There were others that took the opposite view, arguing that this was a revelation of the presaging of Jesus that fit perfectly with Christian doctrine. From a blog called *Charismatica*:

> Can it be just a case of random luck that the greatest archeological discoveries supporting the Bible have all been found in the last sixty years? No, I don't believe so! I actually believe that God protected many of these artifacts, especially the Dead Sea Scrolls. It is a matter of God's own timing. Not only that, I do believe that there is even more to be come [*sic*]. (Davis 2008)

And from a blog called *My Latreia*:

2. Shepherd 2008.

The findings and reports as well as the arguments for and against are being made by Jewish and secular scholars . . . not Christian. In any case, I'm sure God has a plan too for this. Despite the efforts by non-believers to use the find to disprove Christianity or explain away Jesus as a commonplace or an invented phenomenon, I hold on to the possibly naive view that perhaps our Lord intends to use this find to point more Jewish people to the Rock of our lives, Jesus Christ our Lord, that He might become their Messiah and Saviour. ("Adriane T" 2008)

This was from another blog:

Now there are two ways of looking at this. One would argue that the ideas contained here constitute evidence that the supposedly unique views about Jesus' death and resurrection were really not so unique after all—and in the eyes of some this means that we need to reassess the entire understanding of Jesus and the early Christian community. On the other hand, it could be just as easily argued that the Gabriel Revelation is yet one more foreshadowing—this one extra-biblical— that the death and resurrection of the Messiah was something foretold and expected by Jews of the period around the time of Jesus, and that said expectation was fulfilled by Jesus. ("Greg" 2008)

The atheists and cynics also weighed in. Knohl was quoted in my story as saying this should shake our basic view of Christianity. Knohl was of course asking whether the find challenged not Christianity but traditional Christological scholarship, which is quite distinct from traditional Christian beliefs. Among the hundreds of Christians who e-mailed me, most said, "What is your problem? Everyone knows that Christ's suffering and resurrection were predicted in Isaiah and other early sources. It makes perfect sense that in the decades before Jesus such a theory would have been current." But traditional scholarship of Christianity argues that it had been hundreds of years since suffering and resurrection had been current and, in fact, that the posthumous followers of Jesus are the ones who invented the suffering/resurrection story and thereby entered it into mainstream Christian thinking. Knohl had been pushing for some years the point that this was likely not true, that a suffering/resurrection story had been part of traditional Jewish messianic thinking, alongside, parallel to, the heroic Davidic messianic tradition.

But millions of readers had their own gloss on what they read. Stories about religion, archaeology, and the Bible out of Jerusalem are like Rorschach tests.

I found the same sort of reaction to the story concerning the fortified city being unearthed above the Valley of Elah, some 15 miles south of Jerusalem, by Yossi Garfinkel of Hebrew University. Again, no matter what you'd like, a cigar, Dr. Freud, is never just a cigar.

The story of Khirbet Qeiyafa is of a 3,000-year-old, five-acre fortified city. Because it seems to have been used for a mere 10–20 years and

burnt olive pits found there have permitted relatively specific carbon
dating to ca. 1000 B.C.E., this site is going to play a role in reevaluating
the kingdom of David, especially whether he and his capital, Jerusalem,
were an important kingdom or a minor tribe. This issue divides not only
scholars but those seeking to support or delegitimize Zionism.[3]

The 10th century B.C.E. is probably the most controversial period in
biblical archaeology because it is then, according to the Hebrew Bible,
that David united the kingdoms of Judah and Israel, setting the stage for
his son Solomon to build his great temple and rule over a vast area from
the Nile to the Euphrates rivers. For many Jews and Christians, even
those who do not take Scripture literally, the Bible is a vital historical
source. And for the state of Israel, which considers itself to be a recla-
mation of the state begun by David, evidence of the biblical account
has huge symbolic value. The Foreign Ministry's Web site, for example,
presents the kingdom of David and Solomon along with a map of it as
a matter of fact.

But the archaeological record of that kingdom is exceedingly sparse—
in fact almost nonexistent—and a number of scholars today argue that
the kingdom was largely a myth created some centuries later. A great
power, they note, would have left traces of cities and activity, and been
mentioned by those around it. Yet in this area, almost nothing like that
has turned up. There is one stele found 15 years ago that speaks of Beit
David ("House of David") and thereby suggests there was such a kingdom and king as its ruler.[4] But little else.

Garfinkel said he had something here that generations had been
seeking. One of the most exciting parts of the find was a piece of pottery with writing on it.[5] The writing appears to be in so-called proto-
Canaanite script. Words such as *ebed* ("slave"), *melek* ("king"), and *al
ta⁀as* ("don't do") seem to have been deciphered although the work on
the inscription continues. This writing in a sealed site like Khirbet Qeiyafa would suggest that literacy may have been more widespread at the
time than is generally accepted. And if that is true, then the spreading of
the Bible could have taken place via this writing—more evidence, if you
like, that the Bible may not have been invented centuries later.

Because the site was apparently destroyed shortly after it was used
and was never used again, it could prove very useful. This contrasts
with the findings of Eilat Mazar at the so-called City of David just outside the Old City that Eric Meyers has talked about[6] and that I will

3. For a list of publications about and reactions to the discovery, see the
Web site (*Qeiyafa Ostracon Chronicle*) of Garfinkel's excavations: http://qeiyafa
.huji.ac.il/ostracon2.asp.

4. See Wilford 1993.

5. For information on this find, see the first page of Garfinkel's Web site cited in
n. 6 above: http://qeiyafa.huji.ac.il/ostracon.asp.

6. See Eric Meyers's essay, "The Quest for the Temple Mount: The Settler Movement and National Parks in Israel," in this volume, pp. 202–215.

discuss a bit more in a more specifically political context. The contrast is that it is very difficult to know when the building she has uncovered is from because the pottery found there is in a fill and it is hard to know how to relate it to the structure.

Still, how this new site relates to King David and the Israelites is far from clear. Garfinkel suggests that the Hebrew writing and location—a fortified settlement a two-day walk from Jerusalem—add weight to the idea that his capital was sufficiently important to require such a forward position, especially because it was between the huge Philistine city of Gath and Jerusalem. "The fortification required 200,000 tons of stone and probably 10 years to build," he said. "There were 500 people inside. This was the main road to Jerusalem, the key strategic site to protect the kingdom of Jerusalem. If they built a fortification here, it was a real kingdom, pointing to urban cities and a centralized authority in Judah in the 10th century b.c.e." (cited in Bronner 2008b).

Others say it is too early to draw such conclusions. "This is an important site, one of the very few cases from the 10th century where you can see a settlement fortified in a style that is typical of later Israelite and Judean cities," said Amihai Mazar, a professor of archaeology at Hebrew University. "The question is who fortified it, who lived in it, why it was abandoned and how it all relates to the reign of David and Solomon" (cited in Bronner 2008b).

The Philistines had a huge city, Gath, some seven miles away, but pottery found there looks distinct from what Garfinkel has found here. He says the David and Goliath story could be an allegory about a battle between the two. Seymour Gitin, an archaeologist and a director of the Albright Institute in Jerusalem, a private American institution, told me: "The real value is that there was an urban center in the 10th century. You can extrapolate and say this helps support a kingdom, a united monarchy under David and Solomon. People will rightly use this material to support that" (cited in Bronner 2008b).

And so that is exactly what is happening. Financing for the dig is now being raised by an organization called Foundation Stone, run by a Los Angeles–born Israeli named David Willner, who lives in the West Bank settlement of Efrat and told me that the point of his group was "to strengthen the tie of the Jewish people to the land." The group's Web site says that it is "redrawing the map in Jewish education."[7] The activities of Foundation Stone are anchoring traditional texts to the artifacts, maps, and locations that form the context for Jewish identity.

This is an approach to unearthing the land's past that disturbs Israel Finkelstein, an archaeologist at Tel Aviv University and a prominent skeptic of a Bible-based historical chronology. "Some of us look at things in a very ethnocentric way—everything is Israelite or Judahite," he said. "History is not like that. There were other entities playing a

---

7. See http://www.foundationstone.org/.

big role in the southern part of the country. And even if it belongs to
Jerusalem, fine. So there is a late 10th-century fortified structure there.
I don't believe that any archaeologist can revolutionize our entire understanding of Judah and Jerusalem by a single site. It doesn't work that
way. This is a cumulative discipline" (cited in Bronner 2008b).

It is also a divided discipline. Finkelstein is among the most prominent advocates of what is called the "low chronology," meaning those
who date David and Solomon's rule to closer to 900 B.C.E. than 1000
B.C.E. They argue that the kingdom was a minor affair that a later generation of Israelites in the 7th century B.C.E. mythologized for its own
nationalistic purposes.

Ilan Sharon, a radiocarbon expert at Hebrew University, said another
problem was that "we are working very close to the limits of measurement accuracy" when dealing with 3,000-year-old objects such as olive
pits. He added: "A measurement is expected to be within about 50 years
of the correct date two-thirds of the time and within a century 95 percent of the time." Given how hard it is to be sure that objects found near
the tested items were from the same time, "you can see that this is a
statistician's nightmare" (cited in Bronner 2008b).

So this brings us to the City of David and the Holy Basin of Jerusalem. Just as Foundation Stone is raising money for Yossi Garfinkel in the
hope that archaeology will deepen Jewish claims and links to the land
of Israel, so the City of David (Ir David) is being dug under the sponsorship of Elʿad, a settler group. Elʿad was started by David Beeri, whom the
Ir David Web site describes as "an undercover commander of an elite
military unit."[8] Beeri founded Elʿad in 1986. Elʿad's Web site, which, using Beeri's nickname, explains that "When David Beʾeri (David'le) first
visited the City of David . . . [it] was in such a state of disrepair and
neglect that the former excavations that had once been conducted were
once again concealed beneath garbage and waste. . . . Inspired by the
historical record of archeological discoveries made in the City of David
in prior years, and by the longing of the Jewish People to return to Zion,
David'le left the army to establish [Elʿad]" (cited in Bronner 2008b).

If you visit Ir David today, you get to sit through a 3-D film in which
an Israeli in a safari hat and vest tells you that he is going to show you
"where it all began." He then talks about the First Temple and the Second Temple and, after its destruction, moves to the 19th century and
the arrival of some Yemenite Jews to Jerusalem. Other traditions—Canaanite, Persian, Hellenistic, Roman, Byzantine, Islamic, Crusader, or
Ottoman—are not mentioned. The truth is that the dig at Ir David is
finding very important Jewish stuff. That's great. But serious archeolo-
gists are concerned that this is all at the expense of the other layers and
that this is a politicized agenda. In fact, the entire holy basin—the area

8. Ir David Foundation official Web site: http://www.cityofdavid.org.il/
IrDavidFoundation_Eng.asp.

around the Old City including the Mt. of Olives and the Armon Hanatziv promenade—is being developed by El'ad in exactly the same way.

Before we go any further, one point that needs to be made right away is that the Palestinians have been almost unbearably insular and hostile in their entire view of Jerusalem. Yasir Arafat consistently refused to acknowledge any Jewish history in Jerusalem, especially the existence of the ancient temple on the Temple Mount. He was hardly alone in this delusion. Quite recently, Saeb Erekat, the Palestinian chief negotiator, told Al Jazeera TV:

> On July 23, 2000, at his meeting with President Arafat in Camp David, President Clinton said: "You will be the first president of a Palestinian state, within the 1967 borders—give or take, considering the land swap—and East Jerusalem will be the capital of the Palestinian state, but we want you, as a religious man, to acknowledge that the Temple of Solomon is located underneath the Haram Al-Sharif." Yasser Arafat said to Clinton defiantly: "I will not be a traitor. Someone will come to liberate it after 10, 50, or 100 years. Jerusalem will be nothing but the capital of the Palestinian state, and there is nothing underneath or above the Haram Al-Sharif except for Allah." That is why Yasser Arafat was besieged, and that is why he was killed unjustly.[9]

Here, we see one of the more modern and reasonable Palestinian officials saying two very shocking things. One, that Arafat was in essence murdered by some unnamed but clearly Israeli group because he refused to lie about the Temple Mount. And he agrees with Arafat that there was no temple underneath. He also goes on to say that nothing short of every inch and stone taken in 1967 would be acceptable to the Palestinians. This means that not only do they expect 300,000 settlers in the West Bank to be removed but also 250,000 Israeli Jews living in East Jerusalem neighborhoods like Ramot and Gilo and Pisgat Zeev.

It is important to remember that in 1967, when Israel took East Jerusalem, it left control of the Temple Mount in the hands of the Muslim Waqf, a concession that has rarely been acknowledged.

So while the Israeli effort through El'ad to use archaeology for its own nationalist purposes, digging below the levels of Muslim, Roman, and Crusader remains, is something that is being rightly condemned, it must also be acknowledged fully and up front that if the digging were left in the hands of the Palestinians, it is most unlikely that any Jewish history would be dug up or highlighted. Fifty synagogues in Jerusalem were destroyed during the Jordanian hold on the city from 1948 to 1967. And many Jewish graves on the Mount of Olives were desecrated.

---

9. See the excerpted transcript of this interview on the official Web site of the Middle East Media Research Institute: "Chief Palestinian Negotiator Saeb Erekat: Abu Mazen Rejected the Israeli Proposal in Annapolis Like Arafat Rejected the Camp David 2000 Proposal," March 27, 2009. On-line: http://www.memritv .org/clip_transcript/en/2074.htm.

Israelis and many other Jews were denied access to their holy places
such as the Western Wall. Synagogues in Gaza have also been destroyed
in the past. Indeed I would argue that the Palestinians' refusal to acknowledge publicly Jewish history in Jerusalem and the Holy Land has
helped fuel the takeover of this project by those with a nationalist Jewish agenda. And because the power is so deeply in the hands of Israel,
this is a point that is often overlooked but should not be.

Now back to the problems of El'ad and the Ir David. If you drive up
what is called Route 1 in Jerusalem, the main road with East Jerusalem
on one side and West Jerusalem on the other, you can feel what could
be a border if a two-state solution with a shared Jerusalem were ever to
evolve. It is a road that offers a kind of glass wall of a boundary. If you
were to put GPS devices on Israelis and Palestinians, you would find
that some 90 to 95 percent of them never passed that glass wall (leaving
aside trips to the Western Wall). In that sense, there is a clear and natural boundary. But El'ad settler moves into East Jerusalem are changing
that. Hundreds have moved into the Old City area.

In the Sheikh Jarrah neighborhood not far from the American Colony
Hotel, you see a large plot of land fenced off with the names of Cana-
dian Jewish donors. Nearby, there is the Shimon Hatzadik tomb, a site
visited by religious Jews. There too, Palestinians are being pressured out
of their houses. As Hillary Clinton asserted on a recent trip, this is not
a municipal problem, but a political one.

If you keep going up toward the Mount of Olives, you see an Israeli
government plan, already in effect, to turn the green areas into a kind
of biblical theme park that is being billed as "The Jerusalem Trail."
It is the story of the pilgrimages to Jerusalem. You can walk, as they
say, in the footsteps of leading figures over the centuries. Some major
buildings are now used by settlers and religious study groups, including Ateret Hacohanim. Beit Orot yeshiva, since the late 80s / early 90s,
was located on a site that was designated for a girls' junior high school
for Silwan and At-tur neighborhoods. There are plans for a visitor center, hotel, and restaurant and underground reservoir. Just below what
is now called the Tzurim Valley National Park is the so-called sifting
center where El'ad permits visitors to sift through what is dug from
around the Old City to look for finds of Jewish history. Trails from here
lead across the Mount of Olives, with a large budget of 10–20 million
shekels to make a promenade.

As Danny Seidemann, a Jerusalem two-state activist, told me, "Preservation, instead of being pluralistic, humanistic, multicultural has
morphed into domination." And Rafi Greenberg of Tel Aviv University
put it this way: "While professing neutrality . . . archaeology has in fact
been implicated in the greater political project of unifying Jerusalem"
(Greenberg 2009: 36). He, like other left-leaning scholars, argues that
the sanctity of the City of David site has been largely manufactured
for political ends, a crude amalgam of history, nationalism, and quasi-

religious pilgrimage. But really, he argues, Jerusalem is not exclusively about Jewish history. Visiting Jerusalem should be experienced as a series of encounters with different pasts.

And who could disagree? One problem, as I pointed out earlier, is that the other side has never seen it that way. Given the chance, it did nothing to illuminate or expose the Jewish roots in Jerusalem. As an Israeli friend of mine, a woman of the left who cares about the Palestinians but who is frustrated, put it to me: "It's a fair fight. Each side is doing what it can to solidify ownership and roots here."

I'm not sure the phrase "it's a fair fight" is a just one now, given the distribution of power and resources. But I do have to acknowledge that it is a fight. It is not a story of an occupying power imposing its will on a population that would otherwise be sharing and decent about it all. It is a story about which side is dominant and therefore in a position to impose its view of history on the place. And one problem with all the criticism of Israel's position—from archaeologists, from the European Union—is that it fails to acknowledge how the Palestinians have acted over the decades and how that has affected the Israeli authorities. To be told that the Jews have no roots at all in Jerusalem—Arafat used to say there might have been a Jewish temple at one time but it was in Iraq or perhaps in Nablus—is galling and only makes the Israelis dig in their heels as well as their shovels. In truth, and as problematic as much of the digging around Silwan has been, it is unearthing a clear Jewish past there.

The Palestinian building around Silwan, the City of David, has been all illegal. In a normal city, taking down illegal building seems appropriate. But the Palestinians say they cannot get permits to build legally. Is that true? Partly. It is something I want to investigate further. As the mayor of Jerusalem, Nir Barkat, has put it, "I would like to see what [New York Mayor Michael] Bloomberg would say about illegal building in Central Park. Would he give up Central Park because there is illegal building there?" (cited in Lefkovits 2009). The problem, of course, is that Silwan is not Central Park. Nothing about Jerusalem is like other cities. Every breath drawn there has a political nature to it. People have developed a deeply unnatural attachment to the place. As Yehuda Amichai, the Israeli poet, once told me, "Jerusalem is like a fire hydrant on which every group seeks to urinate and claim as its own."

There is a story told of George Adam Smith, a Scottish historian and Bible scholar, who was said to have had a phenomenal knowledge of every detail of life in ancient Jerusalem (reported in Elon 1989: 56). Shortly before he died in 1942, he gave a lecture on Jerusalem topography at Aberdeen University. Every nook and cranny of the city was in his command. When the lecture was over, a young relative came to take him by the hand and lead him home because he didn't know the way. George Adam Smith knew every corner of Jerusalem but didn't know his way around his own town.

I just quoted a conversation I was privileged to have with Amichai some years ago before his death. But his poetry also speaks brilliantly of the conundrum of Jerusalem. In the 1970s, this is what he wrote:

The air over Jerusalem is saturated with prayers and dreams
Like the air over industrial cities.
It's hard to breathe. (Amichai 1996: 136)

References

"Adriane T"
2008   Ancient Tablet Ignites Debate and Messiah and Resurrection. *My Latreia*, July 8. On-line: http://blog.mylatreia.net/2008/07/08/ancient-tablet-find/.

Amihai, Y.
1996   *The Selected Poetry of Yehuda Amichai*, trans. C. Bloch and S. Mitchell. Berkeley: University of California Press.

Bronner, E.
2008a   Ancient Tablet Ignites Debate on Messiah and Resurrection. *New York Times*, July 6. On-line: http://www.nytimes.com/2008/07/06/world/middleeast/06stone.htm?_r=1.
2008b   Find of Ancient City Could Alter Notions of Biblical David. *New York Times*, October 29. On-line: http://www.nytimes.com/2008/10/30/world/middleeast/30david.html?pagewanted=1.

Davis, M.
2008   1st Century BC: A Dead Sea Stone Tablet about a Messiah Who Dies and Is Resurrected? *Charismatica*, July 6. On-line: http://www.charismatica.com/2008/07/06/dead-sea-stone-tablet-about-a-messiah-who-dies-and-is-resurrected/.

Elon, A.
1989   *Jerusalem: City of Mirrors*. Boston: Little, Brown.

"Greg"
2008   Gabriel's Revelation. *Rhymes with Right*, July 6. On-line: http://rhymeswithright.mu.nu/archives/267975.php.

Greenberg, R.
2009   Towards an Inclusive Archaeology in Jerusalem: The Case of Silwan/The City of David. *Public Archaeology* 8: 35–50.

Lefkovits, E.
2009   Barkat May Relocate Silwan Residents. *Jerusalem Post*, March 19. On-line: http://www.jpost.com/Israel/Article.aspx?id=136549.

Shepherd, K.
2008   Time Mag Latches Onto "Controversial Relic" to Question Christian Orthodoxy. *News Busters*, July 6, On-line: http://newsbusters.org/blogs/ken-shepherd/2008/07/07/time-mag-latches-controversial-relic-question-christian-orthodoxy.

Wilford, J. N.
1993   From Israeli Site, News of House of David. *New York Times*, August 6. On-line: http://www.nytimes.com/1993/08/06/world/from-israeli-site-news-of-house-of-david.html?scp=1&sq=Tel+Dan+Stele&st=nyt.

Index of Personal Names

271